WEIR'S WAY

BY THE SAME AUTHOR

Highland Days	Cassel	(1948)
The Ultimate Mountains	Cassel	(1953)
Camps and Climbs in Arctic Norway	Cassel	(1954)
East of Katmandu	Oliver & Boyd	(1955)
The Scottish Lochs Vol 1.	Constable	(1970)
The Scottish Lochs Vol 2.	Constable	(1972)
Western Highlands	Batsford	(1973)
Batsford Colour Book of the Highlands	Batsford	(1975)
The Scottish Islands	David & Charles	(1976)
The Scottish Lochs (Abridged into one volume)	Constable	(1980)
Tom Weir's Scotland	Gordon Wright Publishing	(1980)
East of Katmandu	Gordon Wright Publishing	(1981)

PART AUTHORSHIP

Wild Life in Britain	Automobile Association	(1976)
Wildlife in Scotland	Macmillan	(1979)
In the Country	Macmillan	(1980)

WEIR'S WAY
Tom Weir

GORDON WRIGHT PUBLISHING
55 MARCHMONT ROAD, EDINBURGH, EH9 1HT
SCOTLAND

ISBN 903065 34 7

Photography by Tom Weir

Typesetting by Image Services (Edinburgh) Ltd.
Printed and bound by Clark Constable Ltd., Edinburgh.

INTRODUCTION

I suppose you could call this a companion volume to *Tom Weir's Scotland,* with the difference that this one is more closely linked to the television series *Weir's Way* which began modestly in the mid-1970's and continues rather more ambitiously at the time of writing in 1981.

The Genesis of the programme arose out of a conversation with Russell Galbraith of Scottish Television. "Everybody knows you as an outdoor man. Suppose we gave you a camera team and you went out into the countryside and brought back a story or two for us. Go to some of your favourite spots, talk about them, introduce us to some of the people you meet. We are looking for short films of about eight minutes each to show as tail-pieces on our main news and current affairs programme *Scotland Today.* With all this bad news about give them something to cheer them up."

Apprehensive as I was, I liked the challenge and the prospect of tackling something different, even with the risk of being a flop. I had nothing to lose and I was not totally inexperienced. As a free-lance 16mm cameraman I had shot some films for the small screen, newsy things about Scotland, and longer pieces on Greenland and the Faroe Islands, but my main connection with broadcasting was in radio.

That day we reached agreement in principle, and the matter was left hanging in the air. Then one Autumn day I had a telephone call from the cheerful Russell, telling me that the camera crew could be mine, tomorrow or the next day if I was available. When I said it would be O.K. I had only the vaguest idea of what I should do. The difficulty was resolved when I had a phone call from the brusque Director appointed to work with me. "We'll begin with you working at your typewriter, show your house and where you live, then you'll tell us what these programmes are going to be about. We only have a few hours to shoot each story, so we've got to work fast."

It was all very good fun, slap-happy stuff. There was no forward planning. A telephone call one day would tell me the camera team was available the next, so I always had to have a story up my sleeve, and would read it to the Director as we motored to the location. Over a few months we shot about a dozen films, much of it in the cold grey of a normal Scottish winter. Uncomfortable, yes, but it didn't worry me unduly, the truth being that I didn't think the film would ever be shown. I regarded the experience as an apprenticeship, which might be useful to this old dog if I could learn a few new tricks.

Then, came a telephone call telling me transmission of the series was due to begin as a regular weekly feature, and I felt like going into hiding. Home-spun as they were, I was overwhelmed by the kindly response of the public as letters came pouring in and people stopped me in the street.

Each of the films has been made to stand on its own. With the end of the first showing, Russell Galbraith had another idea. Why not compile them and group them to make a series of half-hour programmes. We could have a studio set, with me in an Orkney chair, talking to camera and linking them together, easier said than done. But it worked.

The public were still asking for more. Brian Mahoney who had been working with me on the compilation was eager for something more ambitious, half-hour films which had their own continuity, made on the very best filmstock. I came up with stories that took us from Rannoch Moor to Glencoe and Fort William, basing them on stirring historical events and the opening of the West Highland Way, Scotland's first long distance pathway stretching ninety-five miles northward from Milngavie.

Heroic work was demanded of the camera team on the series, especially crossing the Devil's Staircase on foot and traversing the Glen Nevis gorge in heatwave conditions with the blood-sucking clegs feasting all the way.

Brian Mahoney was with me again the following summer, with a volunteer camera crew of experienced sailing enthusiasts for a trip to the remoter Hebrides to shoot the *Weir's Aweigh* series. This required the hiring of a racing yacht for a fortnight, beginning at Tayvallich on Loch Sween as gateway to the Sound of Jura, then west for Barrahead, Mingulay, Eriskay, Vatersay and back east by the Garvellach Isles and the whirlpool of Corryvreckan.

With Brian I went north again in 1980 to follow the footsteps of Bonnie Prince Charlie from the battlefield of Culloden to the wilds of Knoydart, and on to Glen Shiel and Rory's Cave deep in the high hills between Glen Moriston and Glen Affric. Our finish was at Cluny's Cage on Ben Alder.

We had still to deal with Charlie's Hebridean adventures, accomplished this year, with Les Wilson as Director, tracing a complicated route through the Outer Hebrides until his escape from Benbecula with Flora Macdonald, dressed as her maid Betty Burke.

This book is not about every *Weir's Way* programme that has been screened. It is a broader vision of Scotland using the medium of written words which demands a different technique from voice and moving pictures.

I have pulled together a lot of strands to try and provide a really "good read" to provide the maximum coverage and variety. I hope it is the book that you, the viewers, have been asking for.

Tom Weir

CONTENTS

"ALWAYS A LITTLE FURTHER"

This should have been about the Isle of Rum, but instead I am going to tell you about a book which I took there. Read it if you want a good chuckle and to share the fun of being a Glasgow laddie discovering a new horizon on the hills. The book *Always a Little Further* was written thirty years ago— so you could call it a period piece. But the fact that any copy coming on the market was fetching £5 shows how good it is. A new edition was published in 1969.

Since he wrote that book Alastair Borthwick has become a highly successful journalist and television personality. Nobody was more surprised than himself when, by popular demand, the book was reprinted without a word being altered.

It certainly took the drizzle out of the weather for me, by its blitheness and innocence. Alastair Borthwick once described it to me apologetically, as "a very young book"— meaning that the writing betrayed inexperience, that some of the jokes wore a bit thin, that some passages were overdone. This is true enough. But you cannot have the freshness of youth plus the experience of age. Reading this book you share with the author his discovery of the Scottish hills and of the gangrels who were out on them every week-end.

The people in the book, are of course, about as unsophisticated as the weapons with which we fought the last war now appear. Unemployed men could make their Buroo money last from Thursday afternoon until Tuesday on the hills, and save something for their holidays at the same time. Not for them the Youth Hostels, charging a shilling a night. They lived in "dosses"— which could be anything from the loft of an empty cottage, a barn, cave or caravan.

"Hard men" of these times carried no blanket or Primus stove. Newspapers did them. The bag on the back was light, because they preferred to get right up amongst the hills and live in caves for climbing. Some could boast that they hadn't spent a week-end at home for years. John Nimlin was one of these— the Joe Brown of the thirties. Before going on to Alastair Borthwick's book I would like to quote something from John.

"On the New Year of 1936, when I had cut down load-carrying to the exclusion of sleeping bag, five of us slept at the Shelter Stone of Loch Avon in the sub-zero temperature. With two men on either side encased in eiderdown bags, I slept in coat and sweaters, with feet stuffed into a rucksack. True, my teeth were chattering when I wakened, but I had

11

enjoyed eight hours' sleep, and four other sets of teeth were chattering in unison . . ."

Alastair Borthwick, on the other hand, had none of John's know-how. On his first big excursion into the Highlands he neither knew the way up The Cobbler nor had he cut down weight for a high camp. Here he is with his friend, sweating his way up the Buttermilk Burn to get away from the crowds of Arrochar:

"The afternoon was excessively hot and the weight we were carrying ludicrous. We had yet to learn that heavy pots and pans, thick ground sheets, raincoats, and much tinned foods are luxuries to be avoided upon a mountain, just as we had yet to learn that there was an excellent path on the far side of the burn.

On our bank, bracken grew with the abandon popularly associated with machetes and tropical jungles, and in some places was taller than we were ourselves. Forcing a passage through it while carrying a heavy rucksack was trying. Also there were flies. The first thousand feet was a purgatory of heavy breathing, sweat, and the forlorn beauty of bracken fronds against the sky . . ."

I could almost smell that bracken and feel the rucksack straps biting into my shoulders for, aged sixteen I did the same, though not on The Cobbler, but up the length of Loch Etive and through the Lairig Eilde to Glen Coe, then north again by the Devil's Staircase. The hardest lift, however, was up over the top of Ben Nevis, after a night in the halfway hut. Somehow we failed to strike the Carn Mor Dearg arête and got embroiled on the crags, where I was in terror as the weight of the pack threatened to pull me to perdition.

Nor was that the end of weight-lifting that holiday. After crossing Rannoch Moor, we finished by carrying the rucksacks over Ben Lui from Tyndrum to Glen Falloch—crazy! Alastair Borthwick's book is full of the same sort of crazy things, not least the trip to Skye for which this Cobbler climb was preparation.

The Cobbler was not only preparation, but discovery, for up there they met Hamish—the hero of the book—who took them under his wing and initiated them into the art of rock climbing. Hamish, an ebullient salesman, with a passion for high-diving, fast motor-bikes and hard rock climbing, can get anybody to do anything. I've known him all my life, and he is an infectious character—still keen on hills.

Alastair soon found himself forgetting the world:

". . . its worries, and its inhabitants ceased to exist, wiped clear from my consciousness; and the only three realities left in the universe were myself, the small niche of rock which was the next handhold, and a passionate desire for union between them. I was not a human being suspended over a fifty-foot drop. The drop had vanished with the rest. I was an animal, exercising all its muscle and guile in an attempt to place five fingers on three inches of rock, thought and action bent on one object to the exclusion of all others, like a cat stalking a bird."

The second chapter is called "Hunger March" and the events took place in 1933, which was the year of my own first visit to Skye. And strangely enough, there is a curious duplication of events—though we entered into our hunger march by deliberate calculation, while theirs was an accident due to ignorance. They were four: Alastair, John, Sandy and William; and having missed the bus from Broadford to Sligachan they decided to strike across country to Glen Brittle to arrive there in time for breakfast.

Their rucksacks were heavy:

". . . crammed with clothes, Primus stoves, boots, a rope, a tent and much else besides, to the tune of forty pounds apiece. The only things they did not contain were the two vital ones—food and blankets."

In fact, they had eight sandwiches and a slab of chocolate, which was eaten by the following morning. Miserably cold, they packed up their tent and set off in the moonlight, their hopes now pinned on breakfast at Camusunary. Spirits revived with daylight when suddenly:

"The whole vast chain of the Black Cuillin, from Gars-bheinn to Sgurr nan Gillean, was stretched out like a curtain before us, with the sun which had not yet dropped to our level, lighting the range from end to end. The mountains seemed close enough to touch. The morning mist was rising from them, softly, effortlessly, revealing first one buttress, then another, of the twenty peaks which stretched for miles, linked into a continuous whole by high ridges, scored by gullies, turreted, pinnacled, heaved up to the sky; rock, rock, and more rock as far as the eye could see. . .

"William began to sing. We slung on our rucksacks and lunged downhill to Camusunary."

Bitter disappointment awaited them down there. The house was locked up. There was no village. The fierce heat made them feel "like four fried eggs in a pan," except that the mere mention of eggs made them groan with hunger, for it was now thirty-three hours since their last real meal—on the train. Glen Brittle was still thirteen miles distant—and hard, tussocky miles without path beyond Loch Coruisk.

I could imagine how they felt. Our similar situation was due to heavy rain making us eat for want of anything better to do. And rather than retreat for provisions we had made do with the last of the tinned fish and brown bread in order to climb Blaven from a camp at Loch an Athain. I remember how mournful the three of us felt breasting Drumhain, to look down on misty Loch Coruisk, inky and boulder-strewn. Glen Brittle and food seemed a long, hard way off.

13

Then suddenly there were spots of colour on the landscape, a bevy of women waving to us, waving eagerly as we approached. But the smiles faded when they saw we were not the relatives they were expecting. They asked us if we had seen any other climbers. We said we had not, and they were disappointed, for they had sailed over from Elgol to deliver a food parcel, and now it was almost time for the boat to leave.

Yes, you've guessed it. We were given the parcel with only one qualification, that we would divide the spoils with the rightful party if we met them. We stood waving until their boat was out of sight. Then we got down to it— new bread, cakes, bananas, butter, jam and a few other things I've forgotten. Even so, we found the ups and downs of that coastal route to Glen Brittle over boulders and screes exhausting. Stiff-necked, we seemed to go on endlessly, until at last we pitched the tent on a dried-up water course within sight of the houses—an unwise choice, but it was the only flattish ground.

I am glad nobody quoted Alastair Borthwick's description of the Bad Step when it was under threat of demolition last year, for their party seemed to find it quite a terror. This is how he describes it:

"The wide, easy terraces which make progress along the wall above Scavaig are cut by a great rock buttress which falls straight into the sea from a point high on the cliffs. Like much of the rock in the district, it is black and utterly smooth in outline, so that it looks like an enormous whale with its tail in the water and its head far up the mountainside. Two parallel cracks slant across its back, about five feet apart, for twenty or thirty feet; and the only method we could devise, rightly or wrongly, for crossing it was to place our toes in the bottom crack and our fingers in the top-crack and shuffle. With forty-pound rucksacks dragging us outwards, this was exciting."

Alastair took twenty minutes to cross it. Two of the others failed on it, and had to take the heathery shelf above— the one now marked by the Army as an alternative. I think hunger and the weight of their sacks must have affected their judgement here, for the Bad Step is so easy that it would be hard to fall off. It only becomes a problem if you follow the cracks too high on the slab, which they may have done and found troublesome.

They now faced their second night out, comfortably on a mat of heather, but now they were unable to raise a cheer or feel light-hearted. Their stomachs were no longer the seat of hunger. I like Borthwick's, "We were hungry all over. Our finger tips were hungry." They found it harder and harder to keep going.

"We just sat down, and having sat down, knew we could not get up. Our legs refused to support us, and half an hour passed in each case before it was possible to go on."

Thoughts of food maddened them. The author kept insisting that his roast beef must be slightly underdone and that the gravy ". . . must be thick, flowing round the rich brown flanks of roasted potatoes." Alas, when they did get to Glen Brittle they ate indifferently, but slept for thirteen hours. How marvellous to be so tired that whichever way you lie you are comfortable! I know I have had a good day when I experience that luxury.

What raised the book to the realm of history is the people he meets— for the poverty of the thirties bred a special race of happy individualists with great qualities of idealism and humour. You could call them unsophisticated. Remember they were the pioneers— the first truly working-class climbers. They travelled light, but there was often a volume of poetry in the sack, and I have heard many a good candlelight reading. They were great readers and talkers. Nor did they bother recording many of the hard rock routes they made on the crags. It was enough to go out and do them.

There was rivalry, of course. And the best of it in *Always A Little Further* is about "Choochter" and "Ginger" on their way to hitch to Glen Coe from the chip shop at Leven Bridge, when they met Wullie and Wee Jock fortifying themselves for the same ploy. So began a "battle of wits, based on the good Biblical truth that the last shall be first and the first shall be last. It must be so, for the immutable rule in the competitive hitch-hiking is that the last man gets the first lift."

I can't spoil this good story by retelling the stratagems adopted to be last, when at one point both parties were travelling backwards. But the tale is hilarious, and I can reveal that "Choochter" was still a keen outdoor man until his untimely death. I was in St Kilda with him a few years ago. His name often appeared in *Scottish Birds,* for he was a devoted observer and recorder, as well as investigator of aberrant humans, for he held a high position in a certain Highland constabulary.

"Choochter" was a pioneer hitch-hiker, among the first to travel on the thumb to distant goals. At least he thought they were distant—after all, Glen Coe or Nevis is a long way from Glasgow. Changed days now, when you can go to Skye for the week-end and thumb your way easily to the Alps or Istanbul, as many do.

How well I recognised that company who found themselves storm-bound in Dan Mackay's barn in Chapter 8 of Borthwick's book! This howff is still in use today, beside Altnafeadh, under the Buachaille Etive Mor. It was the September week-end, Saturday night 1934, and all the keen men of the Ptarmigan, Creagh Dugh and Lomond Mountaineering Clubs were on the road braving rain, sleet and south-westerly gale to make the most of their last holiday. Some had walked from Bridge of Orchy when the lifts ran out.

They all converged on Dan Mackay's barn, including a small tramp, a tall tinker, an itinerant french polisher, two motor-cyclists and a mixture of bedraggled climbing men. Stoves were roaring, the wind was howling,

15

and at 10.30 the stories began. It is the atmosphere which Borthwick manages to capture which is so good. You can feel yourself in the circle listening, straining to hear above the bursts of rain. Everybody tells a tale, but the intervals between them are growing longer.

"The candles were burning low, and the singing had ceased in the malodorous compartment next door. Stories, somehow, did not come so easily to mind as they had done earlier in the evening. The tinker, baulked of his own tales of prowess, had been asleep for half an hour, and the motor-cyclists were nodding. Even the gale had a restful sound.
" 'How about it?' asked Hamish. 'Lights out.' "

That is what I would call "authentic writing"—capturing a mood as magically as the *Farewell Symphony* by Haydn. So does his description of an ice climb and the philosophy which leads a man to it:

". . . the reasoning powers of man are obscured by an inability to distinguish between things he enjoys doing and things he enjoys having done. Sitting by the fireside, dry, fed and rested, he thinks of the struggle he had on the mountains, the elemental pitting of his strength and skill against blind nature, the Valkyrie music that was the wind, and the fact that he—he, John Smith, clerk, blackcoated pen-pusher, by dint of cunning, strength and a compass, outwitted the forces arrayed against him.
" 'By jove!' says John Smith, 'It was magnificent!' "
"Of course, on the mountain he had not eaten for ten hours, had not felt his feet for three, had been soaked to the skin and then frozen solid, and for half the day had wished heartily that he were dead. But he does not think of these things. John Smith is warm again."

You cannot read this book without feeling that Scotland is a land of adventure, where no major town is really distant from the hills, yet vast uninhabited areas remain, Alastair Borthwick does not climb now. His hobbies are trout fishing and sea angling by canoe from his home in Ayrshire.

He lived in Jura and Islay for fifteen years, and he still loves to go north to fish in Stratherrick and Sutherland. He is still lean and sunburnt, and gets a great kick out of being a free-lance journalist. He is a fit senior citizen, and he thinks the youngsters of today are marvellous, "so much more enterprising than we ever were, with tons of skill when it comes to climbing."

When his son was a climber, he preferred not to know what he was doing on the hills. He knows that the climbs he describes, which he thought were hard, are regarded as pretty ordinary now. But everything is comparative. For all we know the same thing will happen to the routes the hard men think are hard now. After all there are plenty of Joe Browns about now, where once upon a time, not so long ago, there was only one.

16

In the end it is the fun that counts, and this is what Alastair Borthwick conveys to us so admirably.

Companion for a Day

It can be winter any day in the year on the Scottish hill-tops. Aye, it can feel summery too any day when there is no wind and unobscured sun like last Sunday, with softness on the low ground, and diamond sharp visibility where the snow lay above a thousand feet in the west.

It reminded me of April rather than November, and an event which took place on Sgurr na Ciche, towering like an alpine spire above remote Loch Nevis, snow encrusted and accessible to me only from Glen Dessary by driving along Loch Arkaigside and camping for the night for an early morning start.

Yes, this is Prince Charlie's country. His escape route from Culloden was by horse to where I was camping, and it was thereafter his mountaineering career began, crossing and recrossing the "Rough Bounds of Knoydart," as it is called, before his final escape to France. I was thinking of him that morning as I left camp in the crisp clear air, frost crystals sparkling in the sunshine, peaks glittering above the blue of the River Dessary track which I was following.

Nobody lives permanently in the wild tangle of ridges and glens between the head of Loch Nevis and Loch Hourn, so I was surprised indeed to meet a fox terrier coming to meet me with wagging tail and placing its chin on my hand when I bent down to it. I could see its nostrils twitching in the direction of my rucksack. I took out my "piece", gave it a wee bite, and when I moved off found myself with lively company.

All the way up to the summit of Mam na Cloich Airde at 1000ft. the terrier was ranging each side of me, sniffing every likely hole and cairn of stones, thinking no doubt it was on a fox-hunting trip by the way its stumpy tail was quivering. Now I had to strike up the rocks of Coire na Ciche to hit first snow, and after a bit of floundering hit the narrow ridge soaring crustily to the summit spike 1600ft. above.

Here was something different from drifted corrie snow. Exposed to the east wind its surface skin had frozen, requiring a good kick with the toe of a boot to make a step; but once you had penetrated it was soft meringue below. The wee dog could scart its way up it at first, but as the angle steepened it began slipping back faster than it could climb. I helped it by coming up behind and giving it a good heave on its backside, which gave it some impetus before it came sliding back to me.

The surface was getting too glassy for this caper, however, and I was having to cut steps with my ice-axe. The wee dog got the hang of it immediately. Born mountaineer that it was, it waited for the steps to be cut.

What a prospect from up there, the silver of the Atlantic stretching to the dark Sgurr of Eigg and the jostling white summits of the Cuillin of Skye. Beyond Loch Hourn lay the Outer Hebrides and nearer hand the Torridon summits. A few more steps and we were on top looking to Ben Nevis and another horizon of snowy peaks, rank upon rank. My photograph shows what frost crystals had made of the Ordnance Survey pillar.

My original idea had been to take in the next peak, Garbh Chioch Mhor, on my way back to camp, but the wee dog reneged. It wouldn't follow me down the first exceptionally steep slope, nor would it let itself be caught and put in my rucksack. There was nothing for it but for me to take another line which began easily in a gully but had a vertical pitch hung with icicles where I was able to get hold of the dog and nurse it down.

Then followed a glorious glissade using my backside like a sledge and my ice-axe as brake and steering gear. I easily outstripped the dog, which took the huff, because instead of coming down to me it struck off to make its own way home, as if to prove to me it had more intelligence than I thought.

Going down the glen next day I made inquiries about that wee dog. It belonged to a fox trapper who had gone away on a trip to Fort William and had been unexpectedly delayed. Glad to report, the terrier was waiting for him when he got back.

In a letter to me acknowledging a photograph I sent him of his terrier on the summit, he told me it was the best terrier he had ever had. I had certainly enjoyed its company.

CALF COUNTRY — LOCH LOMOND

If you were to ask me what has been my wisest move in an active life of travel and adventure in many countries I can tell you. It was buying a wee house below a wee hill overlooking the southern shore of Loch Lomond. That was in 1959, when I got married, and abandoned a base in Glasgow for one on the fringe of some of the most varied countryside in Britain. Since that decision I have had less and less inclination to travel abroad. I recognised early that this piece of country is far too big for any man to know intimately in one lifetime. Readers and television viewers will know that I still travel extensively in Scotland, but in winter I love to be at home to enjoy what the weather is doing right here where the Lowlands give way spectacularly to the Highlands.

The cranreuch resulting from the overnight drop in temperature and the thick mist excited me more than any other conditions as I set off from the house for my morning walk across the burn to Duncryne Hill, a mere 463ft. but sometimes high enough to be poking above the creeping cloud-blanket which has slowed traffic to an icy crawl since daybreak.

Every blade of grass, branch and telegraph pole has an icing sugar coating as I climb through the shrouded trees, stopping to enjoy frost pearls on neatly strung spiders' webs and rimey Balaclava helmets crowning the red rose-hips. I know I am in luck as I come out of the highest trees and I get an impression of a big electric lamp trying to pierce the mist. A step or two upwards and I have blue sky above me and the green bulge of the top of the hill.

Revelation as I come over the crest! Northward stretches a level cloud carpet, unbroken except by Ben Lomond thrusting through, its snowy pyramid softly gleaming as far removed from the smothered earth as a Himalayan peak. As I look I see my own shadow standing out on the mist, ringed in rainbow colour—a "glory" caused by mist particles acting as prisms for the sunlight.

In contrast to the sharp cold below it is warm up here in the windless air and every colour is heightened — yellow grasses, red bracken below my feet. I wait expectantly for the shimmering cloud sea to break — obliterate Ben Lomond but reveal the hidden world below and it begins to happen as holes start appearing. The silhouette of a farm takes shape, skeletal trees poke blackly through the mist. It is a magic hour watching the world take shape and flood with rich colour. By 11.30 the excitement is over.

After a morning like that, it was raining by late afternoon and the air became mild, as happened a few days earlier when I was all set to go ski-ing on the snow-plastered Luss Hills. Overnight the temperature shot up and torrential rain stripped the white blanket. The River Endrick burst over the fields, and floods made driving on the Loch Lomond road difficult.

It was in mild conditions like this that I introduced wild-life enthusiast David Hutton of Callander to the wetlands of the Endrick, which he described as a "revelation". Laden with camera gear he hardly knew where to point his lens as we overlooked from the cover of trees a noisy concourse of feeding waterfowl, rafts of mallard and shoveller with teal everywhere among the reeds, and on the bank two barnacle geese among the greylags cropping the grass with the widgeon.

However the chorus of yelps, whistles, harsh quarks and honks was nothing to the next place we went, barley stubble grey with geese taking off and settling again with a clamour of voice like a cup-tie football crowd. Wherever you looked there were wild geese in the air, greylags, pinkfeet and whitefronts, but I would hesitate to say how many. Perhaps 3000 greylags and a few dozen of the other species would not be so far away.

By the time we came back at dusk after a grand tour of flood-waters, soggy marshes, reedbeds, loch-shore and woods, David was enthusing that he had never seen so much in any one single place in his life. He was lucky. Very hard weather sealing the pools and freezing the river changed the scene a few days later when most of the birds made an exodus to the warmer temperatures of the Clyde.

Which brings me to a sad story following such a cold snap. There had been a thaw, then an overnight freeze-up bringing a china blue morning of absolute calm with a sun that felt warm sparkling on icy loch shores and part-frozen Endrick. "Too good to sleep," I told my wife. "Come down and enjoy it." She did. We had other company that morning, a wee dog called Jock, a neat little half-collie, half-spaniel, he had formed a great attachment to me and got into the habit of seeking me out.

Jock loved the ice and chasing after sticks skited across it. Nor did he stop barking excitedly until you had played with him for a bit, then he was content to rummage about on his own. We enjoyed the fun of watching him chasing the thrown stick and shooting past it sliding merrily, unable to stop. He had calmed down when we went inland along the whins for a mile to look at a great concourse of whooper swans, geese and duck beyond the ice-fringe where the Endrick discharges into the loch.

We were enjoying the bugling of the whoopers and the chirrupings of the teal when Rhona asked me to identify a high pitched squealing sound that seemed to be coming from a distance. I couldn't place it. Then suddenly she asked sharply "Where's Jock?" Her worried glance was enough. The squealing call could only be Jock, in distress. We set off towards the sound at a run.

Half a mile or so up the river bank we came upon Jock in a pitiable state, body in the black water, paws trying to grip the frozen edge, chin on the ice, but slipping back out of sight even as we looked. He must have dashed across the part-frozen river in pursuit of something and, unable to stop, plunged in. All I could do was try to get out to him, getting down on all fours and distributing my weight as best I could until a warning crackling made me retreat at less than half way.

"Branches!" I shouted, "See what you can find!" Armed with two lengths of about six feet I tried creeping out again using the branches like skis. My plan was to try and push them towards the dog as an aid to climbing out, but they wouldn't reach. When I tried launching them like curling stones they went sideways. I tried throwing a short stick to try to turn his head towards safety on the far bank, an easy swim of five yards, but even as I did so he slipped off the ice for the last time, his body going limp, paws outstretched and head down to disappear under the ice.

Could I have done more to save Jock? That was the agonising question. If we hadn't been there on the bank, would he have turned his back and swum the few yards across open water and scrambled up the short slope to safety? I put the latter question to a deer stalker friend, Duncan MacLennan of Glen Affric, who knows much about animals. "No," he said, "a deer or a dog will always try to come out the way it came in. It's blind instinct, not reason. I've had the proof of it more than once. Your wife was wise to warn you not to go out on the ice any farther."

The family who owned the dog were very understanding, and went to the place where Jock drowned, seeing for themselves the branches as far out on the ice as I could reach and throw. They felt I had done all I could but mourned the loss of a great character who in more than a decade of exceptionally active life has sired more pups to the collies of farms within reach than any other dog in the parish. It was he who fathered squirrel-catching little Nell, the wee black semi-collie. She has to be locked up now to prevent her from following me and howls protest as she hears my footsteps pass by.

Animal behaviour is a very strange thing, as Mr and Mrs James E. Smith have been discovering when they put out food for a cat which was living rough in the woods surrounding their cottage in Wester Ross. Their kindly action brought them a most marvellous present, a pine marten, that elusive nocturnal weasel of the trees which few people have seen, but which was to become very familiar to them.

The first sighting happened four years ago. Since then, by putting out food, not just one marten but several came to the window ledge in the darkness, and ignoring the light and faces at the window get on with their eating. One came in the open window one day and allowed itself to be photographed without camera shyness.

Flash-bulbs don't worry them, nor does the sound of music, but they take notice when the radio "pips" and stare through the window at the source of the signal. Their favourite food, the Smiths have discovered, is dead mouse, and if offered an egg they can take it gently in their mouths and leap four feet to ground without smashing it.

What has surprised them about an animal as shy as a marten is its apparent tameness round the house. If Mr Smith goes to put out fresh food they come back immediately. The best acrobatics occur on a feeding pole for the birds which they climb to get at cheese. They can not only walk down the vertical pole, but pass each other without falling off, as one goes up and the other comes down. Mr Smith writes: "I fix the fat meat so that they have to pull at it to get it off and the agility and strength of these little creatures has to be seen to be believed."

By the different shapes of their yellow-orange bibs the observers have been able to identify eight different individuals. Mr Smith thinks the attraction of his house is the long grass in the garden area which is riddled with mouse runs. They grow only wild flowers and native trees which they are allowing to regenerate so there is plenty of cover for the martens.

Writing to me in November, Mr Smith was saying how lovely the pine martens were looking in their fine winter coats, new, sleek and shining the hairs extending even to the soles of the large feet with their non-retractible claws. Small wonder they can out-climb any squirrel, or catch a spawning sea trout when they try.

Mr and Mrs Smith wanted to tell me about the martens because they thought if I wrote about them it might give pleasure to others and arouse a desire to protect one of our most vital wild-life species. Alas, like the otter in Scotland, martens are not protected, which is a sad reflection on our legislators and ourselves for not demanding it. Apparently we will have to wait until these marvellous animals are threatened with extinction before we can have protective measures taken — which is farcical.

Certainly we have more otters on the western side of Scotland than elsewhere in Britain, and pine martens, once confined to one small corner of the far North-west have spread southward into Perthshire and Argyll, and even to the Cheviots, but they are a vulnerable species. They are immensely valuable in clearing up mice and voles, not to mention litters of young rabbits. I hope to respond to the invitation from the Smiths to watch the martens from their window.

In sparkling winter weather it doesn't take much to tempt me away from the desk, so when Pat called me one morning suggesting that I might like a run up to Loch Tay with him. I was delighted. "Just a quick trip to turn off the water in the house," he said. We arranged to meet at Callander, but I was diverted by the police by Gartmore because of a fatal accident on ice on a bend of the Aberfoyle road. It was a warning to keep my eye on the road and not the glowing scenery.

Beyond Callander I had the best of it as Pat's passenger, so I could enjoy the perfection of Loch Lubnaig, its luminous waters reflecting brilliant greens and browns and the grey of rocks and snow peaks more vividly than the actual scene above. Round every bend was a new picture, then the climb over Glen Ogle for the great sight of alpine Ben More and

Stobinian, then the Dochart with the glittering Tarmachan peaks cresting the blue sky above the river rapids cascading under the bridge at Killin.

About the same time as I came to live on Loch Lomondside, Pat built a cottage on the south shore of Loch Tay beside the ruins of a crofting settlement about 600ft. above sea level on the flank of Tullich Hill. This is the bit he has made *his* oyster, and it was grand to explore the home patch with him.

First we went uphill, quite steeply by a gully, to look at the old workings of a copper mine, descending into deep holes, where caves led inward and where splinters of solid rock had holes bored clean through like circular windows to admit daylight. The mine had been worked by the Breadalbanes until 1840, but was not very successful, Pat thought, though enough gold to make a ring had been found.

Then down we went to the shore dropping about 500ft. through birch and hazel and ash to a series of stone structures near the shore perhaps the remains of old furnaces for smelting the copper from the ore. No doubt the local timber on the hillside was used to make charcoal. The stone jetty for loading the boat told its own story.

Exploring Edinburgh's Volcano

"It'll be interesting to see what comes out of that sky," I said to my wife as dawn broke last Saturday morning with parallel air-ships of cloud filling the eastern horizon but never becoming the angry brilliance carrying the foreboding of a shepherd's warning.

It happens we were heading east in its direction to meet up with a man from Montrose. Rendezvous had been fixed in Perth for 10.15. But he didn't arrive.

While we waited, I was regretting being in such a hurry on a marvellous drive by green Strathendrick and the Carse of Stirling. I had merely glanced at the twin points of Ben More and Stobinian glittering white beyond the brown waves of Trossach hills when I would liked to have stopped and paid homage to them, especially with gaggles of flighting greylag geese straggled across the sky.

Yes, my thoughts were up there on the snow, although the drive was continuously interesting by Strath Allan and Strath Earn and across the new road bridge over the Tay, which is a real scene-setter for the Fair City. High up, with the river far below, the impression is of a charming country town ringed by hills. My surprise that morning, though, was to find myself driving through snow-sprinkled fields before I got to Perth, and having to watch out for black ice on shadowy bends.

The message I got in Perth was that terrible road conditions and heavy overnight snow with ice had delayed our friend, so maybe that reddish sky had meant something after all.

But not in Edinburgh where I spent the night after the annual dinner of the Scottish Mountaineering Club. Next morning I had arranged to meet up with three geologists for a ramble over the most studied volcano in the world—Arthur's Seat. Given the 365 days in the year to choose from, I couldn't have picked a better morning after a frosty night with the yellow ball of the sun shining from a cloudless sky.

How marvellous to be taken by such knowledgeable men over one of the best wee mountains in Scotland, tossed up from the sea 325 million years ago, like the one in Iceland when the Atlantic began belching flame and an island began to grow from nothing, as the molten material spewed out, cooled, and formed a great cone, growing ever higher until the activity stopped.

So it was exciting for me to be taken to the strange hexagonal pillars above Duddingston Loch with the descriptive name of Samson's Ribs, climbing from there to the actual vent of the volcano. How did the geologists know the eruption was below the sea?

The evidence is in the fossil fish and other forms of marine life baked in the sediments hardened by the molten lava. In fact there are two volcanic vents on Arthur's Seat, and clear evidence of lulls in activity, which accounts for the varied colours of the rocks which make Arthur's Seat such a real and splendid little mountain.

I learned too that the Salisbury Crags are a "sill," the crags formed by squirts of magma in a horizontal direction. It didn't erupt, but slowly cooled inside the mountain, to be exposed subsequently by erosion of the sediments in which it was embedded. I was shown the rock exposure where pioneer Edinburgh geologist James Hutton was able to prove that changes in rock composition were due to heat, at a time 200 years ago, when scientists were divided as to cause and effect.

What a glitter Edinburgh had that day from the top of Arthur's Seat, below us Duddingston Loch with its marshes giving some idea of what Edinburgh must have looked like when it stretched only from the Castle Rock down the tail of the crag before drainage allowed the town to expand. Cultivation terraces on the steep face of Arthur's Seat shows where the early agriculturists levelled fields to grow crops.

Alas, we could only look at the rocks and not climb them as the fathers of Scottish mountaineering did. Nor are geological hammers allowed. The danger is that climbers loosening rocks could injure citizens enjoying the privilege of walking in the Queen's Park, and generations of geologists since Hutton have had their whack from the Gutted Haddie and the Lion's Head. Now Samson's Ribs are posing a threat to safety for reasons for which Hutton was the first to expound by writing: "From the tops of the mountains to the shores of the sea, all the soils are subject to be moved from their places, by the natural operations of the surface, and to be deposited in a lower situation. . ."

Yes, Samson's Ribs after over 300 million years are breaking up and scaffolders are at this moment making them safe by grouting them with cement.

There is even a chain-net over the rocks to protect the scaffolders who are doing the work.

GOLDEN EAGLES AT EIGHT FEET

I would like to tell you about my eagle. 'An awful stupid place to put an eyrie,' said the keeper when he told me about a golden eagle's nest. I had other views when he took me to the crag.

To get to it involved a walk of over three miles, and a climb of some 1600ft. to the head of a little-used glen where a tumble of black rocks rose for hundreds of feet. The eyrie was in the first tier of cliff, but to reach it from below meant a dangerous climb. We chose to descend to it, by climbing diagonally to a gully which forked down to the eyrie. Under an overhang of the north-facing cliff was one well-grown eaglet, which I forthwith christened Wilkie Bard. And it was well-named, for as I got to know him— I am assuming it is a he, but it might well be a she— Wilkie proved as good a comedian as his namesake.

There were remains of a deer calf in the eyrie on that first visit, and Wilkie looked as if he had just fed. He lay contentedly on his couch of heather and gave us a sideways look with one dark eye. White head-feathers mingling with gold on the ruffled neck gave him an unmistakable juvenile appearance. But the yellow beak hooked to a wicked tip of black was adult. We judged him to be about six weeks old, since he was still showing traces of white down through dark feathers.

I wanted to try photography, but there was no safe place except at the close distance of eight feet from the eyrie, where a notch could be cut in the steep gully. Without very much hope, I decided to put some branches on this spot and see how the parent birds reacted to this sudden growth so near the nest. Within three hours of putting up the branches I had the pleasure of seeing a speck in the sky at about 6,000ft. The dot plummeted earthwards in one terrific fall, flattening out as a gliding shadow on the dark wall of the cliff, then disappearing under the overhang of the eyrie. With such a fearless bird I could begin photography right away.

Two days later the keeper and I started work. First of all we had to cut a platform out of the steep mountainside. Stakes were then driven in and hessian wound round them. Branches were draped over and sewn on with a sack-needle. In the three days taken to do this Wilkie had eaten, to our knowledge, two grouse, one hare, and one rabbit. The hide was completed on Sunday at midday, and within half-an-hour the eagle flew straight to the eyrie, taking absolutely no notice of our construction.

With high anticipation I occupied the hide at ten o'clock next morning. Lying in it was like lying sideways in a coffin, for there was no room to sit up or wriggle about. Pins and needles in the fingers and a crick in the neck were minor penalties. Yet the hours passed surprisingly quickly, Wilkie providing the entertainment.

His roving eye missed nothing on the moor below, if one were to judge from the twistings of his head as a sheep bleated, a curlew called, or a meadow-pipit sang. If I made a sound in the hide, his eye swung straight towards me. Catching flies was his chief amusement. He would watch them crawling on the overhanging rock above him, and as they got near he would stand up unsteadily on long feathered legs and try to pick them off the wall. At other times he would try to snap them in the air. Now and then, tiring of the one position, he would lie on his side and thrust out a yellow talon clenched like a fist.

After three and a half hours of diverting watching, I saw Wilkie suddenly stand up and begin to cheep excitedly. Something was going to happen. It did. There was a sound like a whistling shell, then a vibrant whum, whum, whum of booming wings. Unbelievably, a cock eagle of wonderful fawn and gold sat in front of me, so close that I knew it would be impossible to take a good photo.

I pressed the shutter. The effect was startling. The bird's head swung round to me and two yellow eyes looked into mine. I couldn't believe that the eagle couldn't see me. For fully a minute we stared at each other. I held my breath and kept my eyelids from blinking. The bird turned its head quickly from side to side, raising and lowering itself in curiously reptilian fashion. Suddenly it was gone, leaving me wondering if I had imagined the whole encounter. But there was the evidence in the eyrie—a half-eaten mountain-hare. During the visit of the parent, Wilkie had stood with bent back cheeping excitedly. He continued to stand long after the parent had gone.

My next visit, one week later, was quite unrewarding. I had two days to spare, and on the way up to the eyrie I saw the eagle carry in prey, which proved to be a rabbit. I waited four hours in the hide, but the bird did not return in that time, so I gave it up.

Next day at 10 a.m. I again occupied the hide. Half a rabbit lay in the eyrie, and at midday Wilkie disposed of it, displaying some considerable skill in tearing it to bits. This was the first occasion on which I had seen him eat anything. At 3 p.m. the cock eagle flew past the eyrie and began squealing loudly in alarm. Wilkie got so excited that he staggered to the edge of the eyrie and began flapping his great wings. The overbalancing effect gave him such a shock that he only managed to save himself from falling out of the eyrie by a considerable swerve in space. He then cheeped himself hoarse, a loud musical tee-up, tee-up, tee-up, the 'up' part being on the descending scale. Whatever upset the cock eagle we do not know. It may have been a hiker that the keeper could see on one of the near hilltops. I waited until 6 p.m., and sore and stiff after eight hours in the hide I returned home, long overdue for some food.

There was a marked change in Wilkie when I saw him a week later.

The neck was quite golden and only a trace of white was showing on the head. A little white remained on the upper breast, but the feathers of the general plumage were shining with a new lustre, and Wilkie had taken to preening himself, each feather being whetted on the hook of his beak. Flies and preening were his chief diversions, plus a new habit of standing on one leg with the other thrust out at an angle, the yellow claw clenched to a wrinkled ball. he was now strong on his legs and had acquired the knack of scratching his head with his claw.

My luck was in. I had only three hours to wait, when in came the cock, not from above this time, but flying across the glen on great, slow wingbeats. The sun was on its tawny plumage and a rabbit red with blood hung from its talons. With primaries thrown upwards like a harrier, it lowered the rabbit to the eyrie, the bow of its wings acting as a parachute. The landing was like thistledown.

I pressed the shutter as the bird stood on the prey, but it took no notice, nor did it show any suspicion. It shuffled across the nest to where there was an old bit of bone and fur, picked it up in its beak, and flew off with it. Eyries usually stink with decomposing flesh, and the remarkable sweetness of this mid-summer eyrie had been a surprise. This clearing away of the spoil was the explanation. As before, Wilkie had stood and yelped continually during the whole time the eagle was at the eyrie. The rabbit delivered to the eyrie was the first completely unskinned one offered to the youngster.

With the help of the keeper, I had established certain things by now. First, that the cock eagle was doing the feeding, but that the female was doing the hunting, the change-over taking place on top of a crag half-a-mile away. Second, that the youngster was fed at least twice a day, usually between midday and 2 o'clock and, from evidence at the eyrie, again in the evening. I judged the young bird to eat no more than two rabbits or the like a day. New green branches had been added to the floor of the eyrie since my earlier visits.

In view of the meal arrangements, it was a shock to my calculations to find next morning that a fully-grown rabbit, newly delivered by the look of it, lay in the eyrie beside the remains of yesterday's. It appeared as if I was in for a very long wait.

Both Wilkie and myself were apathetic this morning, the result of sultry air and fierce heat. At midday Wilkie disposed of yesterday's rabbit-remains, but did not touch the new rabbit. An hour later he grew very excited, and I glimpsed the cock eagle flying past. Suddenly it heeled round and came straight to the eyrie. I tried a flight photo in colour as it lowered its legs to the nesting-ledge, but the bird sheered off at the sound of the shutter. I had a premonition that it would return, and, sure enough, in ten minutes it came in carrying a small plucked bird in one talon. As it landed, it took fright, scuttling out of the eyrie with the small bird still clutched in its talon.

28

'What was it seeing?' I wondered. At the risk of not getting a photo, I moved the camera lens inside the hide and waited. In another ten minutes the eagle came flying in again with the plucked bird. Without hesitation it parachuted down, shuffled over to the youngster, looked at it a moment, left the plucked bird, then picked up the remains of the dismembered rabbit in its beak and flew off with them. At that moment I glimpsed the female eagle circling closely, the only occasion when I had seen both birds at the eyrie together. Through the telescope my keeper friend half-a-mile away was able to watch the cock eagle eating the rabbit remains taken from the eyrie.

That day was to be an eagle circus. Within half-an-hour both eagles were back at the eyrie, but only the cock landed. Its movements were peculiar. First it tore a piece from the plucked bird and held it to the cheeping youngster. It wasn't accepted. Swallowing the rejected morsel, the cock then shuffled all over the eyrie looking for something, and not finding anything, it flew away. During this time the female kept watch from the crag a few feet away.

No colour photographs had been possible during this time because of bad light, and I was in the act of changing cameras when in came the cock for the last time. Again it attempted to feed the youngster without success, and again it searched the eyrie. It flew away without any signs of suspicion or alarm. This had certainly been a day of days, worth all the disappointments of the past. When another hour had passed without any reapperance I judged the show to be over and climbed stiffly up the gully.

Next day, in high hopes of a good series in monochrome, I occupied the hide once more. But shepherds were gathering sheep in the glen below and all I saw of the eagle was an inspection flight, during which it skimmed low over the heather like a harrier, its head twisting to the eyrie as it passed. At 3.30 p.m. there was no food in the eyrie and every hope of an early visit, for the voices of dogs and shepherds had quietened. But I could wait no longer. I was already overdue for the road south and reluctantly crawled from my hide. I left with a feeling of frustration in my photography, but that is a minor disappointment. What remains for ever is the mental picture of these great birds soaring over the Highland glens, and landing within eight feet of my watching eyes.

Stan Bradshaw: Marathon Man

I knew Stan was coming. I'd asked him to give me a ring when he arrived in Balloch so that I could pick him up in late afternoon. But when I opened the door to a ring at the bell just after lunch, there he stood, skippit cap at a jaunty angle, big pack on his back, and hand held out. He was stopping the night on the way to Gerry's Bothy at Achnashellach for the second time in a month. The £1 bargain-fare offered by British

Railways to senior citizens was too good a chance for this enthusiast to miss when there were new peaks waiting to be climbed in the north.

Earlier in mid-November's unsettled weather he had back-packed into the hills south of Achnashellach to the remote bothy of Bearnais, adding a bundle of dry sticks to his load. Alone and with a fire for cheer he'd felt on top of the world and the only man in it. From there he trekked north, then after a night in Achnashellach crossed the high Bealach na Lice, striking east from its summit to come down to another bothy half-way along Glen Torridon.

He had told me all this over the phone, and now here he was in person on another ploy to open up some more new country at bargain rates. For canniness you can't beat a Lancashire lad.

He was completely self-supporting with warm sleeping bag, a track-suit as spare clothes, iron rations neatly packed in polythene bags, light-weight canteen for cooking, waterproof trousers and cagoule, maps, electric torch, and jogging shoes. "Tea?" I invited. He said he'd rather go up my wee hill and do the favourite walk along the shore that I'd told him about.

Through my writings he'd read how much I enjoy this gentle country of rolling fields and River Endrick marshes rich in bird life, Lowland in character, but with Highland peaks rising to 3000ft. within easy range. That greyish afternoon wasn't the best time for seeing it, but there was enough dull clarity for me to judge he would get the wonderful surprise that awaits anyone who climbs the hill above Gartocharn called Duncryne.

The easiest way up is by the road behind the hotel striking off left in about half a mile. My own route is by the marsh, then up through the oaks which give way to ash in a steep climb with an abrupt finish which gives it the feeling of a real little mountain. Climbing fast I didn't give Stan the chance to look round until he was on the very top and his amazement was a delight.

"You've got it all beside you," he exclaimed, sweeping his eyes incredulously over the broad base of Loch Lomond and its islands to the peaks. With pleasure I pointed out Ben More Cowal, the Cobbler, and the jumble of the Arrochar Alps, Ben Lomond, Ben Ledi, Ben Vorlich, and the rolling sweep of plateau formations extending south by Dumgoyne and the Campsies to the Kilpatricks and Renfrewshire hills.

Now we went directly down to pick up the right-of-way path which takes off behind the village hall and is the quickest way of reaching the Loch Lomond shore for the walk north-east to a lagoon which is the former mouth of the River Endrick, always good for birds on a winter afternoon. We heard them before we saw them, the sonorous clanging of whooper swans, the whistles of widgeon, the chirruping of teal, and a mighty baying of geese.

It was dark and raining by the time we circled back to the house, and relaxed at the fire, waiting for the fine meal that my wife was cooking up. Afterwards I could see his eyes were closing and he was nodding. But I did him wrong by thinking he was tired. In fact when he jolted awake he wanted a walk and we did a four-mile stretch before he sought out the bed at 10 p.m. and made a request.

"Could you leave the key in the door so that I can slip out at half-past-six and have a run before breakfast? At home I usually do six miles and then I'm ready for my two boiled eggs." He got his eggs and a hot bath too, and he did his run, despite lashing rain and having to use his torch beam to see where he was going. Stan, I have pleasure in telling you, is a youngster of sixty-eight and his visit did me a lot of good.

All this countryside where I now live I knew as a youngster. It was my calf country, biking out from Glasgow at first, then using the bus when I took to hill walking. So much lies within easy reach of the city for short outings. Take last Saturday, not a very good day, but I wanted to see what the heavy overnight rain had done to Loch Lomond, so I took myself to Balmaha and climbed to the indicator viewpoint recently erected above the pier to commemorate the opening of the West Highland Way. The flooding was quite a sight with the marshes inundated where the Endrick had burst its banks in a world bereft of human beings.

It was too windy to linger, but, shelter was immediately to hand by going east along the top and descending to the Rowardennan Road above the Pass of Balmaha. From there I struck hard right over a wooden bridge to climb the forest paths.

There was instant peace among the tall spruces where bullfinches were giving forth melodious feeding calls. I've heard this path unkindly described as an obstacle course, which may explain the two bannisters on a precipitous section leading to a rough plank seat. The view from high above is not to be missed, where, from the rocks of the Highland Boundary Fault you look along the chain of islands to the Luss Hills.

Descending back to the road and across the bridge I now descended directly to the stormy loch to enjoy the white-caps bursting on the rocks in the gusting west wind. Looking at the flood waters again I found myself wondering what the field voles did when their feeding ground became submerged. They have certainly been in very high density these past few weeks, which may account for the fact that we have had a pair of daylight-hunting short eared owls as well as a hen harrier and three kestrels over the river-mouth marches.

Which brings me to a kestrel story I must tell you. One morning a fortnight ago when I was coming back from birding on the marshes I took a diversion to see what was causing such a mighty bit of agitated squealing from a kestrel. It sounded close, but of the bird there was no sign, neither among the trees nor in the air where I thought it might be. Moving towards the sound, my eyes were suddenly directed down to the rough grass in front of me where all the noise was coming from.

At first I couldn't make out what was happening. Then as I got nearer I saw that the squealing kestrel was pinned down on its back to the ground

31

and was being held there by another kestrel, whose wings were spread round its victim. Many birds of prey kill by squeezing their prey to death with their claws; the hooked bill is used for tearing up the kill before swallowing. I think in this case the aggressor was in the act of squeezing to death the squealing kestrel, both of them female birds, immatures I would say by their markings.

Beak to beak, the squealing stopped when I took a few steps nearer and could see the black eyes of both birds regarding me before separating and breaking loose with such agility that I concluded that no real damage had been done. Since then, however, I have been seeing a kestrel with one wing showing a lot of daylight through where it should be tightly feathered and I think it must be the squealer.

Most weeks I manage an outing with Pat the bagpiper, a Gaelic enthusiast who lives in the Stirling area so we usually meet in Aberfoyle for one of the innumerable stravaigs offering themselves from here.

One of our favourite shorties is about a mile west from the Port of Menteith where a track goes up the hill to Nether Glennie to a 700ft. top. Over that ridge of course lies the brown country of the Trossachs and our hill is something of a dividing line between the flat country of the Lake of Menteith and Flander's Moss and the sudden rise of the Highlands.

This is where we went the other day on a none too promising afternoon which gave us a mixture of heavy showers and brilliant rainbows as bursts of sun broke the black clouds. Up on the heathery top we were rejoicing in our good luck, looking east to the Wallace Monument and the hulk of Stirling Castle, as eight blackcock rose one after another, the sun on their white wing stripes and glossy plumage. Showers were still sprinkling the Highland hills gauzily, throwing up the double summit of Ben Lomond above the numerous hillocks behind Aberfoyle which are the moraines of the former glacier which flowed east from it.

I always find this country of the Lake of Menteith sombrely atmospheric, perhaps because of the wide sky and the level sweep of the volcanic plateaux which give it the effect of being in a great bowl with the River Forth meandering like a canal towards the Carse of Stirling, having started its life as a cascading mountain burn such a short distance away on Ben Lomond.

Into the Trossachs itself the best little hill of these bristly parts is Ben A'n, standing grandly above Loch Achray with a car-park at its foot and a marked path to show you the start up the flank of a wooded ravine. The peaklet is a mere 1520ft., no more than a spur of a greater hill, but there is no better true mountain of similar height in Scotland. Not until you are well up and clear of the woods does its full elegance burst upon you, a wedge of grey rock above the knolls of Loch Katrine.

ON TOP OF THE BASS

To make a landing on the Bass Rock you need good luck. We didn't get it on our first attempt. It had seemed that all was in our favour; a bedevilling sea mist had lifted before a light wind, and Skipper Fred Marr was ready at 9.30 a.m. to slip out of North Berwick's tidal harbour. Then disaster! A fishing boat coming in from the sea grounded on the bottom and blocked the entrance until the outgoing tide turned in the afternoon and floated it off.

In his long experience of sailing out of North Berwick Harbour, Fred had never see such a thing happen before. However, he accepted his loss of income philosophically and waved me good-bye as I made off round the corner to the museum. There I learned a lot of things about the old town from the member of the staff who showed me round. The ruins I had passed at the east side of the harbour, I was told, were those of the "auld kirk" for ever associated with witch-hunting trials in Scotland.

James VI began the epidemic when he learned that a coven of witches had carried out devilish practices round the auld kirk of North Berwick, summoning up a storm at sea to wreck the ship carrying him and his bride from Denmark to Scotland. Confessions were wrung from the "witches" under torture with thumbscrews and breaking irons. Their naked skins were pricked with sharp instruments to find any spot insensitive to pain. Then they were strangled at the stake and burned in pitch.

The auld kirk was abandoned because of inroads by the sea at high tides which cut it off from the harbour. A new one was built further inland, but it, too, is now a ruin, and I visited it to locate the grave of another victim of injustice, the Covenanter still remembered in North Berwick as "Bass John". The recumbent slab near the graveyard entrance reads:

> Here lies the body of John Blackadder,
> Minister of the Gospel of Troqueer in Galloway,
> Who died on the Bass after five years' imprisonment,
> Anno Domini 1685.

This brave minister is commemorated in the Blackadder Church in North Berwick, and I was all the keener now to go to the Bass and see his prison. But first I climbed Berwick Law, the 612ft. hill whose building stone provided the walls of the old town. The path goes by the quarry, now a refuse dump, and the grassy zig-zagging path takes you up steeply to the jawbones of a whale which make a pointed arch just below the rocky summit.

It was good to see so many holiday visitors enjoying the pointed top on an afternoon which had become brilliant, with the sun on the harvest fields and the curving sands fringing the glittering sea. The Firth of Forth has great character, with its rocky islets, Fidra, the Lamb, Craigleith, the white hump of the Bass, and away beyond it, close to Fife, the battleship shape of the Isle of May.

And you appreciate from here that the Lowlands are by no means low, as your eye sweeps across the volcanic escarpments of the Ochils, the twin points of the Fife Lomonds, and, nearer hand, Arthur's Seat, the Pentlands and the Lammermuirs running towards the Tweed. Small wonder that in times of trouble and threat of foreign invasion the Law was an important look-out point, with a beacon on its top ready to be lit to give warning as in the Napoleonic Wars. The ruins of the hut the watchers used still stand, as do the whale bones, though they are not the original jawbones erected in 1709. The present ones are replacements put there in 1936.

Yes, a very enjoyable day, which made the Bass Rock even more interesting for me next morning when, within half an hour of leaving the harbour we were bobbing under the big cliffs with a veritable blizzard of gannets' wings above us.

It was as the poet Dunbar described it over 400 years ago:

> The air was dirkit with fowlis
> That cam with yammeris and with youlis,
> With shrykking, shrieking, skyrymming scowlis
> And meikle noyis and showtes.

Fred Marr gives his customers value for money with an interesting loud-speaker commentary. Steering slowly round, he explained the history and natural history of the rock, pointed out the big cave below the lighthouse which pierces right through the rock so that one can walk right through at low tide. And he was just getting on to the story of how the big garrison was conquered by a handful of Jacobites when the moment came for me to hop ashore on the slippery landing step of the stairway that climbs to the top of the rock.

This landing is the only weak point in the girdle of rocks that rings the Bass, and by building a fortress across it those who held it had an impregnable position. The lighthouse occupies the site of the former governor's house, and to reach it you have to go through the thick-walled prison which once held over forty prisoners, mostly men of the cloth, including John Blackadder.

Unluckily, John died just as he was about to be released. But retribution came to his captors only six years later when the prison held four young Jacobite officers captured at Cromdale in 1690. The story is that the whole garrison force was down working at the jetty except their immediate guard, and by a neat action they managed to shut them out of the fortress and threaten the enemy with their own guns.

It was not to be a temporary takeover; they held out for three years against all the might of King William III. They flew the Scottish Lion for King James VII, and they were able to hold out with the help of two French Government boats which kept them victualled. They even increased their fighting strength from four to sixteen, and in the end negotiated an honourable peace settlement.

It is said that they had laid on a banquet for the talks, bringing out their best food and wine to give the impression they had plenty, though, in fact, they were at their last gasp. The bluff worked. Small wonder the fortifications were dismantled shortly afterwards and the guns removed.

Today the only permanent inhabitants are the lighthouse-keepers who enjoy everything about the Bass except the overpowering smell of the increasing gannet colony which creeps ever closer to them. "There's more of them every year, and the whirling beam of the light doesn't seem to bother them," one of them told me.

The Bass Rock gannet colony is one of the oldest and best documented in Britain. Even the Latin name of the bird, *Sula bassana*, is derived from the Bass, and until the 18th century the birds were harvested and sold in Edinburgh "all lawful days of the week, wind and weather serving." Not only were the birds good eating, but their thick plumage was esteemed for feather beds, and their fat valued for waterproofing boots and as a medicine. The more prosperous times of the 19th century saw an easing of exploitation by man at all gannet colonies. Even the St Kildans stopped raiding their stacks. Thus began the great population explosion. In 1902 the number of gannets in eight colonies was estimated at 50,000 pairs. Today the estimate is 142,000 in about a score of colonies. On the Bass, where numbers have more than doubled, gannets spend most of the year on the rock guarding their nesting places. They don't leave until November, and begin arriving back again in December.

Not far above the lighthouse on the grassy upper part of the Bass is a tiny drystane chapel choked with the tall plant known as the Bass mallow. It was built to the memory of St Baldred, who had a retreat on the rock in the 8th century, probably in a beehive cell. The chapel was erected 800 years after his death. During the incarceration of Bass John the chapel was used as an ammunition store.

Gloomy as imprisonment in the cells must have been, the spirits of the prisoners must have risen when they were allowed out in pairs to exercise on the seven acres of greenery forming the apex of the 340ft. rock. The sheep feeding there are said to have excelled in the quality of their mutton, but today the gannets are overspilling from the crag on to the pasture, where they sit row upon row like articles in a shop window.

Even in autumn there were still quite a few downy-white chicks, though most were at the grey guga stage, wing-flapping restively and ready to tumble off the rock at the end of a long-drawn nesting process. It begins with forty days inside the egg, then three months on a ledge of the Bass before the launch-out on unsteady wings to crash down on the sea and not be able to rise again until they have slimmed off their surplus weight. Then they have to learn to fly and crash-dive from heights to catch fish, though it will be years before they establish themselves as breeders on one of the few gannet rocks of which Scotland has the world monopoly.

Sitting on top of the Bass, I could see Fred Marr's *Sula* coming round to the landing. As I hurried to meet him, I found it hard to believe I had been seven hours ashore.

* * * * * *

Once you get a taste of the East Lothian coast you don't feel like leaving until you have seen some more, and the bit I had in my mind to explore was that scenic backwater lying north of the road between Cockburnspath and Coldingham, where the gentle Lammermuirs plunge sensationally into the sea in cliffs over 500ft. high on a wild coast hardly touched by even minor roads.

The beginning itself is unusual when you take the track from Cockburnspath to Cove, and find a tunnel carved through the soft sandstone taking you to the neat harbour; round the corner is the caravan city of Pease Bay, occupying one of the few perfect curves of sand in Berwickshire. Better things lie two miles farther east at Redheugh, where the glowing sandstone suddenly changes to hard grey rock, rising in noble buttresses and grey ribs like something in the Hebrides. Looking along it, my eye caught skeletal ribs on top of a pinnacle—the dramatic ruins of Fast Castle.

This had to be my target, and the map showed a farm track off the A1107 to Dowlaw Farm. At the end of the three-mile track I parked and set off on foot along the grassy footpath traversing north-east and dropping from 500ft. to the hidden precipes of the coast.

I had been here years ago, but not on this path which was built recently by Job Creation workers to encourage visitors to walk this bit of highly scenic coast. The splendid moment is when the stronghold perched on its crag is suddenly before you, loud with the wailing of kittiwakes, and below you is nothing but verticality, with the waves crashing and slunging at the bottom.

This place is all the more fascinating because no one knows who built it, but it was in existence 600 years ago and described as "fitter to lodge prisoners than folks at lybertie." Jamie the Saxt would have been held captive in it if the Gowrie plot had succeeded. And before then, in 1503, Princes Margaret Tudor spent a night in it when on her way from England to marry James IV.

Archaeologists have been at work for years at Fast Castle, and numbered plastic pegs project from various excavations in the stonework. Perhaps they will locate the secret stairway which is supposed to lead down into a cave giving direct access to the sea. Or they may even find the hoard of gold brought from Spain 400 years ago to finance a Roman Catholic invasion of England from the Scottish side of the Border.

Much of the original castle was destroyed and rebuilt, and we hear of its wild occupant, Logan of Restalrig, notorious for theft, murder, treason and rebellion, striking a strange bargain in 1594 with scientist John Napier to search and locate the hidden treasure of Fast Castle. Napier, the inventor of logarithms and the greatest brain of his time, was a firm believer in the occult. But not even the sacrificial gesture of killing a black cockerel helped the mathematical genius to find the gold.

Walking back to the car, we met the shepherd of Dowlaw, who herds cross-Suffolk sheep on these uplands. I asked him if the building and sign-posting of the path had brought a rush of visitors. He said it had, that even the odd busload of school children came now. He felt, however, that Fast Castle was as far as they should be encouraged to go because of the danger of a fall over the cliffs.

I agree with him; the coast eastward is great fun for a rock-scrambler who can enjoy the sensational pinnacle of the Souter and the arête of the Brander, but the ordinary walker is safer keeping more inland. The easiest way to see the best bird cliffs is to go back to the Coldingham road and take the right of way path from St Abbs to the Head.

The perched fishing village of St Abbs with its wee wynds, old houses and busy little harbour, makes the perfect introduction, the walk itself taking less than an hour to the lighthouse built in 1862. Westward rise the highest cliffs in Eastern Scotland, where submerged reefs have caused many a storm-tossed ship to founder.

St Abbs is said to have got its name from a lady who survived shipwreck — St Ebba, a Northumbrian princess. In thanksgiving for her deliverance a monastery was built on the headland. St Cuthbert visited her in 661 A.D., and prophesied the doom of the monastery by fire for the sin of monks and nuns living under one rule. It came true when invading Danes swooped on the monastery, burning and ravishing. The story goes that the nuns disfigured their faces to preserve their chastity.

Talking to Mr Tom McCrow who farms Northfield but has made an arrangement to run the St Abb's Head part of his property as a Scottish Wildlife Trust Reserve, he told me he had done it in the interests of the seabirds, flowers and the shore life in an area which is becoming ever more popular. It is the old problem in the age of the motor car of allowing reasonable access without encouraging an excess of tourists. This first exercise in conservation at St Abbs led it to become a property of the National Trust for Scotland. There is a warden service to help visitors enjoy the place without detriment to the wildlife.

It was there I heard of the Countryside Commission plan for a long distance walkway beginning at Portpatrick in the extreme west of the Dumfries and Galloway Region and crossing through the Border Region to come out at the Cockburnspath. Looking at the detailed map, it took the exact line of the Border Walkway from Moffat to Galashiels, the enjoyable sixty-mile route which I described when my wife and I were given the honour of being the first to walk it, by courtesy of the Border Hillwalking Club.

I've been hearing how the west and east bits link up from Mr Bill Prior, Secretary of the Countryside Commission, who thinks the route could be a fact by 1982 if the Secretary of State for Scotland approves the detailed plan—£150,000 would have to be spent on the 204-mile traverse.

I was delighted to find that I had already walked other bits he outlined, and I think the whole concept is absolutely first class. Beginning at Portpatrick and turning your back on Northern Ireland, with the Mull of Kintyre just across the water, you go through Galloway by the smooth farming greenery of the Rhinns and approach The Moors by Castle Kennedy, enter Glen Trool at Bargrennan and head east by Loch Dee and Clatteringshaws to Dalry.

You head for the Nith at Sanquhar and go by Wanlockhead and over the Lowthers to Beattock for Moffat. Now you are on the Border Walkway for sixty miles. A lonely route which goes by the Wamphray Water and Selcoth Burns to Ettrick Head and over the hills to St Mary's Loch, by Blackhouse to Traquair, then across the Minchmuir and so to Galashiels.

Melrose and Gattonside lead you on to Lauderdale, thence along the Lammermuirs to Abbey St Bathans and by the wee harbour of Cove to Cockburnspath. No other walk in Scotland is likely to take you through a bigger chunk of history or more varied scenery, some of it so lonely that bothies will have to be built. It sounds a great prospect, beginning on the Atlantic side and finishing on the most splendid fringe of Scotland's North Sea coast.

Black Mount New Year

One thing you can be sure of, if you leave the house at 7 a.m. on New Year's morning for an icy drive to Glencoe, is that you'll have the road to yourself. Engine purring sweetly and the car nicely warming up I was looking forward to an exceptional ski-ing day, for the starry sky held not a cloud, and a Hogmanay phone-call had told me of how marvellous the powder snow conditions were on Meall a' Buridh where my two friends had put in about 20,000ft. of downhill ski-ing with no monotonous queuing for chairlifts or tows.

I should have been with them that day but for illness in the family confining me indoors as cook and bed-nurse. It was the patient who persuaded me to leave her and go for a day with my friends. So here I was, swinging round the Loch Lomond bends, between glances at the colour beginning to flush the top of the Ben, just a touch of warm red at first, intensifying to the glow of a red hot poker and changing to gold as the full beam of the sun struck the whole 3,000ft. slope.

As yet I was in shadow, watching for black ice, easier to judge when the sprays of icicles hanging from the rocks sparkled like crystal and contrasted with the brown of bracken and silver of birch. Blue water alive with reflections, blue skies, I had the feeling of seeing the Highlands for the first time. In Glen Falloch my tyres were crunching over frozen snow, the Crianlarich peaks were dazzling. The conditions were as all my friends had said and as I pulled up at the hotel where they were staying at Tyndrum they were outside, strapping skis to the car.

"We'll give you the bad news first," Ian said as I drew up. "The ski lifts have been closed down for the next two days. Not enough trade, they say. Put your skis on my roof-rack and we'll go for a ski-tour. Any ideas?"

We decided on Rannoch Moor. Leave the car just short of the summit lochs and climb west into the Black Mount. Within minutes we were off over the pass to Bridge of Orchy and climbing to the snow-glitter of Rannoch. Now to get skis on our feet and away. It was then I discovered I had left my ski boots in my car back in Tyndrum.

No point in going back for them when I had climbing boots on my feet. I would follow in their tracks, and by so-doing would not sink down too deeply at each step. In fact, while they zig-zagged to avoid bits too steep for skis, I could go directly up, and wasn't so far behind them when we got to the top of our peaklet in time for lunch. With all Rannoch Moor to the east and the whole sweep of Coire Ba to the west and not a sign of any road the feeling of remoteness was out of all proportion to our outlay of energy to get here.

"I'll tell you what I think," said Ian. "That we'll get more out of the day now if we ski down from this point for the sake of having some time down among the old pines of Loch Tulla." Which is what we did, climbing a wee bit above its west end past the ruins of the cottage where Duncan Ban MacIntyre was born, greatest of Highland bards. Straight across from us stood pointed Ben Dorain, subject of one of his greatest poems, a song about the passing of youth and a joyful way of life that ended when the glens emptied of people after the '45.

Duncan would have enjoyed Loch Tulla that day, seeing the feathery frost flowers growing from its surface ice, pink-barked Caledonian pines softly green and backed by peaks stretching from Ben Starav to Stob Ghabhair becoming gold even as we looked. We turned away as the peaks became wan under a green sky where the first stars were twinkling.

Soon we were back at the hotel and I was saying to them how sorry I was I couldn't stay for dinner instead of having to take the icy road. Man proposes, God disposes. That sweetly running engine of my motor car died on me before I was halfway to Crianlarich, nor could a kindly motorist do anything for me except take me back to Tyndrum and rouse my friends out of their hot baths to tow my car into their hotel yard and book myself a bed for a cheery night. My troubles could wait until the morning.

Except there were no troubles. Among the first down to breakfast at 8.30 on January 2, 1980, I was hardly seated before a uniformed Automobile Association serviceman walked in, nodded to me with a "Hello Tom" and sat down at another table. I went over for a chat. He had been called out from Glasgow on a breakdown job north of Fort William which should have been done from the Inverness office. Now he was heading back and his big vehicle was outside complete with ramps and cables for hoisting cars to piggy-back them home.

First though he had a good look at my car, decided that the fault was beyond his skill, and soon we were bowling down towards Balloch. I was in the house by 11 a.m., in time to give my wife breakfast in bed and take her out for a wee local hill climb before lunch. Yes, a New Year to remember, and despite the politics and a none-too-good summer, it was the finest spring in living memory, with exceptional sunshine from early April through May.

SHETLAND FOLK

I am sure it is true to say that the German occupation of Norway in 1940 did a very great deal to focus the attention of young Shetlanders on their Norse origins as refugees began arriving in fishing boats and the flag of "Free Norway" was hoisted on Lerwick Town Hall mast.

Like most folk, I had read about the bold operations of the freedom fighters who crossed and recrossed the North Sea so often that it became known as taking "the Shetland bus." The service did its sabotage work so well inside Norway that it wore down a large force of the German Army and took pressure off other spheres of operation.

Now in Scalloway, the old capital of Shetland, I had the chance to hear first-hand accounts of these adventurous trips from a humorous little man by the name of Jack Moore whose boat-repair yard kept the "bus" going. Down at the slip he showed me the old lathe in his workshop where spare parts of Norwegian engines were turned out to keep the risky crossings going.

He told me about some of the long journeys which began here, sea passages of a thousand miles to the Lofoten Islands and beyond. "The boats used to leave Scalloway at a time that enabled them to enter Norwegian waters under maximum darkness. The intelligence reaching us was marvellous," reminisced Jack, "and from the information supplied we used registration numbers of boats which were safely tucked up in their home ports. We knew even the christian names of the Germans on duty in different ports.

"Our boats would arrive in Norway as if in from a normal night's fishing, but they would be carrying weapons and explosives. They would land saboteurs in Norway and sail back with a new crew to Scalloway. I'm proud of the fact that we have no record of any of our engines breaking down, though the boats themselves took an awful beating and were badly shot up. It was amazing that some of them got back.

"All the woodwork was done by Norwegians of the Independent Force. They were billeted in the old garage just above the slip and they worked in my shed. They were busy times. My wife hardly ever saw me! We've had a lot of the old gang back here since, and we've visited them in Norway. We'll never forget those days of working together."

It was not until I was in Jack Moore's house high above the bay that I saw how he had been honoured with the British Empire Medal and an inscribed plaque from the Norwegian Independent Force. He remembered terrible casualties of that lonely war, but spoke little of his own grief; two years ago his young son, who had just taken over the business, was drowned at the boat-repairing slip while inspecting the hull of a boat—not only a family tragedy but a big loss to Shetland.

Walking along, looking at the boats, I had the good luck to meet a small, thick-set man by the name of Geordie Hunter, who represented the Shetland Fishermen's Association and, as their general manager and secretary, fought for their rights until his sudden death. His thirty years as a skipper were written in his strong face, and I wasn't surprised to hear he had been a whaler in his time in Antarctic waters.

"Without fishing there would be no Shetlanders," he declared. "Fishing was the mainstay of ninety per cent. of the population living on these islands, and our future will depend upon it again after the oil runs out—that is, if there are still any fish to catch. Iceland and Faroe have extended their fishing limits and foreign boats are coming here and scooping up everything. We must have an extension of limits around Shetland if we are to survive. I was one of a five-man delegation to Strasbourg putting the Shetland case.

"The Shetland fleet is eighty boats, employing some 600 fishermen, a fleet that could fish for herring continuously using traditional methods without harming the stocks. But we can't compete with the big, well-equipped foreign boats. We don't want to, for they are using methods that can only result in a future fish famine. As things are, our fish factories in Shetland are facing problems and some have had to close. So while it was a record year for the harbour, the fisheries were down by £1 million."

George Hunter's association has the backing of the Shetland Island Council, who have put money from oil revenues into the ailing industry to help keep it alive. Nor were things helped by an exceptionally bad summer followed by as severe a winter of gales and snowstorms as anyone can remember. One record gust in Unst was recorded at 202 m.p.h.

Yet winter in Shetland is a time to be enjoyed as I saw at Up-Helly-Aa when preparations that have taken a whole year for the Guizer Jarl Squad come to fruition in the torchlight procession and ceremonial burning of the galley ship I described in *Tom Weir's Scotland*. I didn't get the length of the aftermath, however, the night of feasting and revelry which followed in thirteen different halls in Lerwick as Guizer Squad after Guizer Squad filed in to cheers and hand-clapping to perform their "stunt" and choose a dance.

My invitation was to Anderson High School, beautifully decorated, and with a huge spread laid on right through the night until breakfast-time for those with the stamina to watch no fewer than forty-eight stunts performed by the ingeniously dressed teams which would take the length of this article to describe. Protocol demands that they put on their act in each one of the thirteen halls and remain sober enough to perform.

The highlight, of course, was the arrival of the Guizer Jarl Squad marching round the hall, singing their special song and waving their battle-axes. You could feel the emotional uplift. I don't know how they managed to look so fresh all through the night, for they had been on the go since nine in the morning, a twenty-three-hour stint of almost non-stop activity.

I had first seen them marching after breakfast to the British Legion for the customary dram to prepare them for the rigours of the day, then down to the quay with the brass band playing and the first sight of the brilliantly-painted galley *Kveldulf.* Faces everywhere were wreathed in smiles. Their next visit was to the Town Hall to receive the Freedom of Lerwick before an invited audience, with Shetland Council Convener, Mr A. I. Tulloch, and Lord Lieutenant Mr Robert H. W. Bruce as principal dignitaries.

Here, after drinking from the silver quaich in the form of a longship, Jim Nicolson, the Guizer Jarl, told the story of Egil Skallagrimsson, the bold Icelander of the Sagas whom he represented that day. Mr Tulloch spoke of the men who had come after the Vikings and who had kept alive the seafaring tradition.

That was probably the most formal of the day's visits. Now the Squad were off to see the old folk, present themselves at schools, hospitals and call at the Gilbert Bain Maternity Unit to see a very special baby boy born at 12.40 a.m. The parents were Kenny and Margaret Pearson. A fine present for a member of the Guizer Jarl Squad on Up-Helly-Aa Day!

One of the nicest things about the whole Fire Festival is the way everybody is brought in, especially the womenfolk, without whom it would fizzle out, for their behind-the-scenes work contributes so essentially to the annual event. They help with the making of the fancy dresses, they co-operate by letting husbands and sons attend Squad nights week after week, and as hostesses they cook and bake to ensure that every one of the thirteen halls can keep the party going all through the night.

One Lerwick lady I specially sought out was Mrs Rhoda Bulter, mother of seven children and grandmother of three, who started writing poetry for publication twenty years ago and whose two books sold out so quickly that they have just been reprinted in one volume appropriately titled *Doobled-Up.* When I phoned her she warned, "You'll have to take me as you find me, for I've a broken arm. Just give me time to wash my face."

The smiling lady who opened the door made me feel immediately at home. After I had told her how much I liked her poetry, even if I didn't always understand individual words, she picked up the book and with great artistry made music of her own favourite poems, and there was never a doubt about meaning.

"I use the language of the country, which is softer and more expressive than the more abrupt Lerwick dialect. And I'm pleased that the poems are so popular because I feel the language is under attack these days when radio and television are in every home."

Despite the additional threat of the massive invasion of oil folk from outside, she hopes the Shetlanders will keep up the old tongue.

She told me it puzzles her where the inspiration for her poetry comes from. "I can't sit down and say I'm going to write a poem. The inspiration comes at inconvenient moments, often enough at lunchtime when I'm busy cooking, or it wakens me up at three o'clock in the morning and I have to write it down or I'll forget. Or it can come because I'm moved by a natural event."

Contrasts interest her, as in this poem:

WINTER

Da day is juist a blink, short efternun
Fadds awa ta da lang dark night dat shun
Bit whin da fire lowes up and da blind is draan,
Winter can be fine whin night is faan.

Idda moarneen wi da caald snaa and da sleet,
An A'm buskin trow da gutter an da weet,
I think aboot dat lovely simmer days,
Whin da sun shone waarm ower da parks and braes.

Bit dan whin simmer comes, aa green an bright,
An da sun sets ower da voe dat late at night;
An I see da places, whaar for a start love lint her,*
Me hert is brakkin, and I lang for winter.

* lint her—lingered

Rhoda has recorded some of her poems on cassettes, and I really look forward to reading her next collection on which she is now working.

Shetland is rich in people of character, and another one I did not intend to miss was fiddler Tom Anderson. Couthie, rather stern in appearance, but with a quick smile, he was soon in full flow. "Pat Shaw with his tape-recordings of Shetland music was a big influence in 1949, and now the interest is world-wide. When I retired from insurance a few years ago and put an advert in the paper for fiddlers to play together, forty-five responded. This year for the second time I'll be teaching Shetland fiddle style at a Stirling University summer school."

He told me, "We don't have indigenous music in these islands to compare with the Hebrides. Most Shetland music is borrowed—many of the tunes were brought by seamen who were fiddlers, Scots, Irish, English, Norse, but they were given a Shetland twist, so we have tunes for every occasion. I've been collecting with a tape recorder since 1947 and teaching for five years without a text book. But now I've written a book, *Hund me doon da Fiddle,* and its aim is twofold, to revive the Shetland speech by telling the story of each tune, and to explain the technique."

Tom soon had his fiddle out and was playing tunes like "Da Merry Boys of Greenland," for which Bobby Tulloch of Yell wrote some fine words:

44

Da news is spreadin trowe da toon:
A ship is lyin in Bressa Soond.
Tell da boys sho's nortward boond
Ta hunt da whale in Greenland.

Up aloft an set da sail,
Hingin on wi teeth an nail;
We're goin north ta hunt da whale
Da Merry Boys o Greenland.

I wish I could quote the other rousing verses. What a grand afternoon of music and talk it was, all the better when two of Tom's pupils came along, Trevor Hunter, now a teacher himself visiting schools, and little Debbie Scott, who, at ten years old, played me one of her own compositions, "Debbie Scott's Compliments to Tom Anderson," A charming tribute.

Tom recommended me to persuade Bobby Tulloch and his sister Mary to sing some duets for me. And it is something I wouldn't have missed, especially "Da Fetlar Lullaby," with its soothing melody and exquisite words:

Husha-baa Mam's peerie flooer,
Sleep o sleep comine ta dee shon,
Mam sall watch dee ooer be ooer
Till dy boannie sleep is done.

Bide, da Simmer days ir comin,
Dan we'll rin aboot da knowes,
See da bees aa fleein, hummin,
Peerie lambs an muckle yowes.

Rest an slumber shon 'ill come,
Rest an slumber shon 'ill come,
Playin on his plinkie-plinkie;
Rest an slumber shon 'ill come.

Mary is one of a hundred islanders of Yell who cross on the ferry every day to work at Sullum Voe. Wife of a crofter with sheep and Highland ponies as stock, she enjoys her part-time job in the canteen, though she entirely shares her brother's deep concern for the future of the seabirds which are one of the joys of Shetland.

The first big spillage of oil at the turn of the year was bad enough; it could be called an unusual and unfortunate accident. But fresh spills affecting south-west Shetland and Orkney since then have not been accidents. They were the result of tankers deliberately dumping oil, and their pollution slaughtered hundreds of seabirds. It has turned the word oil sour in the mouths of Shetlanders, many of whom fear a major disaster involving the wreck of a tanker. Better controls have resulted however.

Tankers are taking the recommended route west of Foula, and aircraft surveillance has put a stop to illegal jettisoning of oil.

History shows the importance of keen vigilance in these dangerous waters, for around the Shetland Isles lie hundreds of wrecked ships, some of considerable value, so much so that the Shetland Islands Council has taken a lease of the seabed areas where fourteen of the most important of them lie. It was Mr Tom Henderson, first Curator of the Shetland Museum in Lerwick, who alerted the authorities on the need to preserve these wrecks against treasure trove seekers.

Local folk are aware of the lesson of these wrecks, and voices are being raised now to have proper controls exercised, together with the best clean up equipment obtainable to be kept here in Shetland at the ready.

It is this public concern for the environment which is really heartening, for, above money, the Shetlanders love Shetland, the sea, its cliffs, its birds, and a way of life in a hard country which has bred good and self-reliant people.

Winter on Deeside's Heights

In upper Deeside conditions were grim, snow showers blotting out the hills, the wet flakes almost sleet as they swept the Braemar glens.

Standing on the bridge we looked down on what should have been the Linn of Dee, but it was more of a roaring cataract than a fall of white water into dark pools trapped in rock.

Today, however, it wasn't the scenery we had come for, but to pay a visit to an outdoor man who used to live in the highest house in the neighbourhood, Bob Scott of Lui Beg, now retired to an estate house near Mar Lodge. Seated at his fireside with his daughter Eileen in attendance he looked the same Bob as of yore. But the strength has gone out of his hill legs, alas, so now he has to rely on the riches of his memory, and my companion Adam Watson and I had plenty of them to share.

Indeed Adam and I had met each other thirty-two years ago in Bob's house, and many a holiday we have spent there as his guests since that first meeting. Situated below steep Sgor Dubh among remnant Caledonian pines at 1400ft., Lui Beg Cottage was the last occupied outpost before the bothy of Corrour. And in Bob's time climbers made his shed their springboard to open up hard ascents in previously unexplored corries.

In this high place where Bob was king, no traveller went unspoken to. Behind a gruff manner good advice was offered if he thought you needed it; so many people come to walk the Lairig Ghru who have no idea how demanding it can be. Fishing ghillie and deer stalker, Bob once told me what he would do if he had all the money in the world. "I'd buy this place and live the kind of life I'm living now!"

Lui Beg cottage stands empty to the winds now, but I like to think of it when Bob's link with the outside world in winter was by sledge pulled by his horse Punchie.

Bob had been a fishing ghillie on the Dee, and in eighteen years' fishing the Linn of Dee before breakfast never failed to get a fish in season, and always before breakfast. I heard a lot about his army experiences in Italy too, always spiced with humour, during one week of snow and storm when we combined our efforts in daily tasks including putting out food for the stags, sledging timber, and going round the fox traps with Donah the golden retriever.

Rifle slung across his shoulder we came over a knoll to a gin trap as a fox broke free from it. "After it," yelled Bob to Donah as he struggled to get his rifle ready. But before he was ready Donah was sprinting past the maimed fox, to whirl about and "point" while the swerving fox darted past, and Bob's rifle cracked. "That's breeding," he said. "She gave me the chance of a shot, and I hope I hit it, for I don't like to think of it going about maimed." In fact his shot did kill it. (The gin trap is now illegal.)

That week I got some photos of a stag which Bob had affectionately named "Old Beattie" after a famous character at Lui Beg who had been there before Bob. An aggressive and dominant beast it was so bold it would come to the window and take slices of bread from Mrs Scott's hand though it liked freshly baked pancakes better. To bring it down from the hill Bob had only to rattle the handle of an old tin bucket and down it would come to a lure of potato peelings and hold off any intruders until it had wolfed its fill.

I was grateful for Bob's disregard of weather one snowy winter day when I set off from Loch Morlich to cross over the top of Cairngorm, descend, to Loch Avon, cross by Loch Etchachan into Glen Derry, and arrive at Lui Beg before dark. I was fit enough for the big crossing, but blizzard conditions and deep snow wore me down so much that I had made up my mind that I was going to bivouac in the Stone Shelter if I got there.

However once out of the inferno of the tops and into the trench of frozen Loch Avon where all the ptarmigan in the Cairngorms seemed to be sheltering, I felt like pushing on. Up once again into the blowing snow, steering by compass. It was not until I got to the end of 3,000ft. high Loch Etchachan that I realised I had been walking on its frozen and drifted-over surface. Now for the plunge down into Glen Derry and seven miles of heavy going as darkness began to fall.

Then miracle, footsteps in the snow, each a foot deep and ideally spaced for easy walking. All I had to do was put my feet in them. No more sinking in. They led me all the way to Bob's house. He could hardly believe that I had come over the tops that fierce day.

"I bet ye were glad o' the auld keeper's footprints at the heid o' the Derry," he grinned. That was my last meeting with Bob Scott. He died in July 1981 after a painful illness. But his name and reputation lives on.

WEST HIGHLAND WAY

First of all let me say that it was with mixed feelings I read the big report submitted in 1973 to the Secretary of State for Scotland, proposing a long distance walking route from Milngavie to Fort William. This involved the provision of bridges, stiles, waymarkers and explanatory mapboards on a route which members of my generation have been rambling over for a lifetime. Immediate reaction to the expensive proposal was to think that it was being pious in the extreme, when I read that a West Highland Way would offer '. . . an important new outdoor recreational opportunity, both for people who wish to use only short lengths as well as those who want to walk the full route.'

Since fifty miles of the proposed route were already rights-of-way, with the short lengths around Carbeth and the Blane Valley, Loch Lomond and Loch Tulla, not to mention the Devil's Staircase, well known and used, it seemed an unnecessary provision. With a little imagination all sorts of variations were possible, for an experienced back-packer wanting a long distance walk.

I realised however just how times and attitudes had changed when I did a television programme four years ago, following the rough line of the route and got an overwhelming response from people wanting to do the walk. Not only letters but telephone calls from folk ready to up-and-go there and then. All they wanted was information, and I got a bit fed-up explaining where you should start, where you can stay, and how long you should allow yourself for full enjoyment.

The official guidebook with its map on the scale of 1:50,000 covering the whole route on both sides of one sheet of paper, is all you need before planning your exploration.

No problems at Milngavie following the Allander Water up past Craigallion and Carbeth lochs in four miles of classic rambling country, sheltered, wooded and sylvan. Interest mounts when you turn left along the main road a short distance and at the next "thistle marker" turn right on the Tinker's Loan path. You find yourself looking down the sweep of the Blane Valley enclosed by two ridges, the one you are on, and the wee volcano of Dumgoyne, a real "peak" in its own right whose ridge rises eastward to the biggest rock escarpments on the Campsies sheeting down from Slackdhu.

On your side of the valley, immediately ahead is a little echo of Dumgoyne but crowned from bottom to shapely top with trees. This is Dumgoyach and your path winds past a wee cottage to traverse the left side of the wooded knoll beyond which you step on to the grassy disused railway line which used to carry trains to Aberfoyle, but now carries below-ground big water pipes from Loch Lomond to the Central Belt.

Simply follow the railroad, which keeps parallel with the A81 until the cutting which bears you away to Gartness and the old village of Gartness on one of the best bits of the River Endrick. Break off here for a short excursion down to the "Pots", by a wee track going left just before the bridge. Even if the salmon are not leaping the spurting waterfall, you can see the remains of one of the two mills which was the reason for Gartness as a village.

The one by the waterfall was a corn-mill and the most famous citizen of his time in Scotland once asked for it to be stopped when he found it interfering with his thoughts as he strode up and down on the bank opposite. He was John Napier of Merchiston who lived here 400 years ago, mathematician and father of the calculating machine by his invention of Napier's Bones, the only Scottish inventor of world class at that time.

Your "Way" continues along the by-road, and unless you want to break off to Drymen for a meal or bed for the night, continue to the A811 which crosses your path. Now turn right along the road and go left in a very short step, to climb a green rise leading into the Gardhban Forest

Signposting in the Forest is good, and necessary once you cross the old Gartmore Road to continue west with views to Loch Lomond below, where the River Endrick enters through marshes famous for bird life, waders, duck, geese, swans and little islands where terns nest. A high stile where the deer fence ends, and you are in open country with Conic Hill ahead, a triple crown of little summits 1,175ft. high which carries you along the very crest of the Highland Boundary Fault down to Balmaha.

It is here you take official leave of the Lowlands and enter the Highlands as you drop to the shore and follow its windings to Milarrochy Bay, keeping fairly close to the road to the picnic spot at Sallochy where the path takes a delightful short-cut through Ross Wood and along the shore almost to Rowardennan Hotel. You could walk from Milngavie to here in a day, a not unduly hard twenty-five miles, but it would be a pity to pass over so much good country so quickly when there is much to see. Drymen makes a good split for bed and breakfast, and there is a Youth Hostel at Rowardennan.

I would say you want to be fresh for the next bit, fourteen miles of some of the best loch-side walking in the whole of the Western Highlands. All of it on a winding path through oakwoods and grassy meadows, much of it gullied and wild with rushing burns and high rocks along the steep, steep flanks of Ben Lomond.

For the experienced, proficient in route-finding and map-reading and used to steep places let me recommend that you dump your pack at Cailness if the day be fine, and take the sheep path which goes up the south side of the Gorge and climbing in over 1,000ft. to reach the big

49

hollow below the north ridge of Ben Lomond. Not only is it the finest way to reach this most southerly peak over 3,000ft. in Scotland but on the way it is likely that you will have the company of hairy wild goats and red deer. It is also a fine place for alpine plants. As a viewpoint the "Ben" is in a class by itself commanding as it does the whole Firth of Clyde past Ailsa Craig, Arran to Ireland with the great sheet of Loch Lomond and its studded islands as foreground. As for the Highlands, the bulk of Ben Nevis points to where you are going.

Lightly laden travellers could of course traverse Ben Lomond by going up from Rowardennan by the path, and descend to Cailness by the North Ridge and down the gorge. And they could have a bed for the night at Inversnaid Hotel just two miles on from Cailness. Path-storming cyclists have been using the Rowardennan to Inversnaid path for years. Now that the West Highland Way path has been made easier north of Inversnaid, I was pleased to see their tyre màrks when I sampled the new path in October.

To my delight I found the builders had done little more than indicate a good route, by clearing away debris and sawing through obstructing trees, leaving the feet of walkers to make the path. Now you keep more or less to the shore apart from going inland a little at the bay just before the house marked Doune on the map. Beyond that there is another house marked Ardleish. The best way here is to take the western side of the burn for the climb away from the loch into Glen Falloch by a pass taking you to a lochan perched high above "The Glen of Hiding".

This high point is a fine place to be, looking back the way you have come and appreciating the steepness of the flanks you have covered, while ahead of you is your gateway to the north. And now from the bare heights and mountain flowers you plunge down to glen-level, and conveniently situated only a step round the corner from Ben Glas farm is Inverarnain Hotel.

From Ben Glas farm and the big grey-mare's tail of waterfall which thunders down behind it, the "Way" has been cunningly chosen, keeping to the east side of the river for three interesting if rough miles, following the tumbling Falloch which swirls in dark pools and tumbles white over and through the rocks, with a fine mixture of woodland and birdlife. Then you come to the bridge at Derrydaroch where you cross the river and immediately drop to its banks for nearly a mile, until the West Highland Railway forces you to use a cattle-creep and come out on its other side. Now you have to cross the busy A82, leaving it in a few steps for the grassy line of Cauldfield's Military Road which will be your standby on and off to Fort William.

The electric pylon line is your guide in Glen Falloch, with railway and road far below and clusters of 3,000ft. peaks seamed with wild glens to hold your eye as you curl on a short-cut to Crianlarich.

I like the way the West Highland Way gets to Tyndrum by making use of farm roads and bridges over the Fillan, crossing to the ancient Chapel and again at Auchtertyre Farm to reach the Coninish track whose river is really the Tay with source high on Ben Lui. From here the path turns north to reach the Oban Line station at Tyndrum.

Now you are back on the Military Road which heads for Fort William with Ben Dorain heaving into view as you climb above the village, for a glorious impression of the Strath backed by Ben More, Stobinian, Cruach Ardrain and the rest. Cauldfield's road and the West Highland Way keep together, but involve you creeping like a sheep under the line to connect its parts.

Bridge of Orchy is gateway to an even wilder country; the barest yet, with a gentle beginning at Loch Tulla and its gnarled ancient Caledonian pines below the great range of the Black Mount. Classic deer forest country where in the spring you can watch hinds with spotted calves while the stags are growing their new antlers lustrous with "velvet". The walk to Forest Lodge from the first pines is a delight. Then suddenly you face Rannoch Moor, 'Godforsaken, Man forsworn...' For nine miles you have total exposure to the wildest moor in Britain 'A desert wide and wasted, unreclaimed as time'.

In good weather there is nothing to worry about, and the going is easy. You can *see* where you are going. It is a different story in gale-force south-wester or howling blizzard for there is absolutely no shelter, which makes the contrast of its far end all the more astonishing. You have been walking along the flanks of the biggest corrie in Scotland, Coire Ba, with the great mattress of trailing lochs and bouldery bogs stretching as far as the eye can see. Then suddenly the thrust of Buachaille Etive Mor as you round Meall à Bhuridh, a sensational wedge of rock rising abruptly from moor to pinnacle. Perhaps Scotland's finest rock climbing mountain.

Kingshouse Inn looks hardly bigger than a boulder below it, a gleaming quartz pebble, a modern hotel that used to be a cattle drovers' halt. Beyond the snout of Buachaille Etive you turn off hard right, north, by the Devil's Staircase for Kinlochleven. The ridge of mountain ahead is the highest point on the West Highland Way at 1,800ft. The distance is only nine miles, zig-zagging up to the cairn on top, then a marvellous plunge down to the sea at Loch Leven, an aluminium town at the head of a narrow fjord between steep mountain walls.

Fort William lies fourteen miles ahead, easy walking on the climbing Military Road by the Lairigmor to outflank the great range of the Mamore ridges; coming into Forestry Commission territory on the last stretch of seven miles or thereabouts, when it is something of a relief to get off the road and get rougher walking in a north-easterly change of direction for Glen Nevis. You are embarking now on your last climb. From the valley top you come face to face with Ben Nevis and the home stretch.

High Wind — High Water

Even for the notoriously bad weather of Hogmanay, 1981 produced some unpleasant surprises. A blizzard blotted out the road as I drove from Tyndrum to Dalmally where I was meeting some Scottish Mountaineering Club friends. It was this storm in the Cairngorms which killed twenty-two year old Neil Baillie when he went through the snow into the freezing March Burn above the summit of the Lairig Ghru.

Then another tragedy came with the thaw on 2 January, when torrential rain and melting snow filled mountain burns and caused rivers to burst their banks. It was with a sense of shock, that I read in the papers of the death of a mountaineering acquaintance swept to his death while crossing a rope fixed over a stream at the head of Loch Nevis below the peak of Sgor na Ciche.

Donald Mill was a tough man with thirty years' experience behind him, including time in the Himalayas. But no matter how much you think you know about the Scottish hills, New Year is a particular time to beware of. So many people have lost their lives then in innocent places.

Take the Corrour tragedy of 30 December 1951. Four young men and the wife of one of them set out from Loch Ossian to bring in the New Year at remote Ben Alder Cottage. It was 8.30 p.m. when they left the lodge on a reasonable night, but after 2½ miles three of them, feeling tired, decided to bivouac. Two of the men decided to push on, but after half an hour they too decided to bivouac, rather than go on with their heavy rucksacks.

The weather had changed dramatically for the worse when the advance pair awoke at 6 a.m. A gale force wind was blowing, so they got up and went on, since it was on their backs. After a while, however, they decided to turn about and make contact with the others. United again, but in some disarray after a wretched night, they all decided to return to Corrour, one of them dumping his rucksack because he wasn't feeling well. He died shortly afterwards as they struggled against the terrible wind and hail.

In a short space of time all four men were dead. Only the wife survived. She had stayed with two of the men, one of them her husband, while the fourth man tried to reach the lodge for help. He had died just half a mile on. The wife waited, but as no help came, she made her own way to Corrour Lodge, reaching it at 2.30 p.m. These members of the Glencoe Mountaineering Club were regular weekenders, were very fit, and were personally known to me.

This New Year's Day, after the whirling blizzard of the night before, our plan was to drive from Dalmally to the Pass of Brander and decide there whether to climb Ben Cruachan or abandon it for something less ambitious if the overhead conditions were unpromising. In fact there was a glitter on Loch Awe and shafts of sun sparkling the lower slopes of our mountain, so up we went by the Falls of Cruachan to the big concrete dam of the pumped storage reservoir.

Playing safe in this grim spot, where we felt the full strength of the gale force wind, we decided on traversing west for shelter before striking directly up to the 3,689ft. peak, whose head was in faster moving storm clouds. We knew we had been wise as we got up to 3,000ft. where the gusts were stopping us in our tracks and blown powder was giving way to grey ice gullies, demanding careful placing of the foot.

Fighting that wind gave you a curious detached feeling, like seeing your disembodied self in a dream. Then sudden reality, and a stab of elation, as our world of private storm suddenly opened up and above us was our summit glittering in the sun, our route to it up a staircase of enormous ice-encrusted boulders.

Magically too the wind had dropped, and now we were getting the true reward of being up there above the moving cloud where everything was fragmented, edges of mountain, gleaming lochs far below, sparkling ice below our feet, and huge masses of weather advancing.

The climbing was exciting too, picking our way up the ice-encrustations, using ice axe to chip steps for hands and feet, then the last airy move to the summit. Just in time too, before we were enveloped once more. A few whoops to celebrate what we hope is going to be a Guid New Year, and we were on our way down, this time by another ridge and a direct descent towards the Pass of Brander.

JOCK NIMLIN: THOUGHTS OF AN OUTDOOR MAN

"I suppose I can fairly class myself as one of the pioneers of the outdoor revolution. I had been camping and climbing before 1928, but after that time I was away every week-end summer and winter. The escape to the outdoors had become so compulsive that for years I never spent a Saturday night at home.

"At that period I was a salesman in a music shop, working until 9 p.m. on a Saturday. As soon as I was free I dashed home to Kelvinbridge, changed into climbing gear and caught the last bus to Drymen or the last train to Helensburgh. My shop-worker pals did the same.

"Although we had been on our feet all day we could, if necessary, walk all night to catch up on the luckier ones who stopped work at noon and consequently got a much greater distance between themselves and Glasgow. We could keep up a four-mile-an-hour gait hour after hour. We carried no tents, and some of us carried no blankets or sleeping bags. It hardly seemed worth while, as we had so little time for sleep.

"Nowadays, when I cover some of these routes by car, I am astonished at the huge distances we walked just to get to the hills. My boss used to swear that I didn't wake up until Wednesday—which was gross libel—I was always wide awake by Tuesday. One night round a camp fire we solemnly enrolled the twenty members of our first mountaineering club, the Ptarmigan. I am still in touch with three of them, and wonder what has become of the others.

"In my early years I think I was luckier than most city children, in living beside the River Kelvin. The river was lined by belts of natural vegetation; a wilderness of sorts within the city. Here we had our early adventures. The Kelvin must have been relatively unpolluted in those days for I swallowed a fair amount of it in accidental immersions without any ill effects. The outward progression was from the Kelvin to the Cadder wilderness, the Campsie Hills, Ben Lomond and the Arrochar bens. When I graduated from hill-walking to rock-climbing, the range soon extended to the Lakeland Fells, the Welsh hills and the bens of the North.

"But in these early days Ben Lomond had a special place in our hearts, for you could get within striking range of it on a Saturday night, whether you came from Drymen or Aberfoyle off the last bus. We had howffs on each side of it, and the shepherd and his wife at Comer, below the north face, were great friends of ours.

"They always knew when we were coming, for we carried a bugle, and a few sharp blasts long before we hove in sight assured us that the pancakes

54

would be on the girdle and tea on the go by the time we arrived. The Campbells were great folk. They had an old horn gramophone, and many a parcel of gramophone records I carried over for they were very fond of music and so were we.

"We once decorated the house for the Campbell's carrying the stuff over from Loch Lomondside, across the big gorge above Cuilness in a wet snowstorm. It was a right soaker of a day, but the paper was still crisp and dry when we got there, for we had it wrapped in an oilskin. Our boys were good tradesmen, and they did a good job

"Funny how things stick in your mind, like the dark night we passed Ledard Youth Hostel on our way to the "Ben," when we happened to notice that one of the windows had been left open. So Dougan got out the bugle and let out some horrible blasts. What a din! And as we made off, dogs were barking and lights were going on.

"But retribution caught up with us next day when we met a party of climbers who noticed the bugle on top of Dougan's pack. They were a Holiday Fellowship party, and after they had calmed down we became great friends.

"Aye, we were a bit harum-scarum, I suppose, delighting in caves where we slept wrapped up in newspapers like tramps, taking a pride in hard living, but being as comfortable as circumstances allowed. Not for us the kind of equipment that people take for granted today. These were weekends of simplicity I would not have missed.

"The early thirties brought hard times, unemployment or dead-end jobs. Just to have a job was happiness. Yet people had hopes for the future. They discussed utopias and political solutions. Fellow climbers went off to fight for the republicans in the Spanish Civil War. We had protest slogans in these days, too. A frequent one was "Hands off China!" when the Japanese were embarking on their expansionist ventures. Having seen the vast territorial and political changes in the forty years since then, I would never predict the changes another forty years may bring.

"Climbing was a healthy outlet at that time. We climbed for adventure because we needed it. My first real rock-climb was in 1930, a solo route on the right-angled Gully of the Cobbler. It gives a certain satisfaction to know that the route is still graded "severe" in times when most original ratings have been down-graded.

"We were quite idealistic in our approach to the rocks. We never made elaborate plans to conquer a route, and we never used artificial aids. Rather, we set out in receptive mood, open to the inspiration provided by the situation.

"In 1937 five of us made the first ascent of Raven's Gully on Buachaille Etive Mor. When we set out from our camp at Coupall Bridge, our aim was to climb the well-trodden Crowberry Ridge. But it was a grey, misty, damp day, and our chosen route looked so wet and gloomy that we decided to traverse round to the north side of the mountain to look for something more inviting. We came across the gully which was even gloomier.

"But the gully held out the lure of the unknown. I tied on the rope and started up the first few feet of the crag. As the first rope-length ran out, the next man started into motion, then the next. It was like the carriages of a steam train jerking into action at the first pull of the engine. Before we realised it we were committed to a hard day's tussle. We were exploring the gully for the first time, a tiny corner of Scotland, so well guarded that the line of least resistance never fell below the grade of "severe," and ranged to "very severe."

"Night was falling as we topped the last pitch to face the long descent of the steep, rough hillside. Our sense of elation was boundless. Raven's Gully is still rated "Very severe in rubbers," although our original ascent was made in nailed boots common to the time. Perhaps only a climber could find inspiration in such a formula.

"Looking at the present, I feel that the smooth community life of today builds up more frustration in youth than we ever knew. The males try to find satisfaction in sport-watching. If their team loses, they blame the referee or the opposing team, and work off their frustration in brawls and vandalism. They pay professionals to exert themselves on their behalf. With machines constantly decreasing the amount of physical exertion required to earn a living, more and more young people are under-exercised. Yet facilities for recreation were never so readily available.

"I consider mountaineering to be the most fulfilling recreation of them all. No sport is less competitive in terms of contest between individuals. Yet no sport is more intensely competitive in terms of the individual's struggle against the defences of mountain gradients and extremes of weather. It can bring one to the highest degree of physical fitness, not through the discipline of recommended exercises but purely as an incidental to the full pursuit of its pleasures.

"Marriage and a family modified my climbing ambitions, but my wife is also a climber, and the children—carried in rucksacks in their early days—were familiar with the hills before they could walk. We recall this as a time of hard labour, when we carried loads that might have worried a Sherpa.

"Nearly twenty years ago I became interested in the lapidary craft. It occurred to me that the terrain I had been wandering over for the previous twenty-odd years was productive of semi-precious stones. I had never noted any in all that time, simply because I wasn't looking for them.

"I also discovered that I was an unfulfilled prospector. Instead of hunting for new routes on crags I was hunting for new sources of polishable stones.

"Hunting smoky quartz crystals in Arran and the Cairngorms is often more toilsome than conventional climbing. No climber would tackle a scree-slope if it could be avoided, but a rock-hunter seeks out the screes as the most profitable source of materials. Likewise, no climber would show preference for the friable rocks of a lava exposure, but I have chipped out many a fine agate from the same shaky rock. Load-carrying is another consequence of rock-collecting, and the heavy rucksacks of my climbing days are nowadays equalled by loads of angular rocks.

"In my visits to the remoter areas of the Cairngorms I am perhaps selfishly pleased to find them no more visited than they were in the thirties. The increase in leisure and car ownership has certainly brought more people to the countryside, but they come to look at the landscape rather than to explore it in depth. In the thirties, people travelled by train and bus, stayed in each area for a week or two, and made thorough explorations of the countryside on foot. Today's expeditions are planned with an eye to the nearest driving road and parking place.

"In 1963 I joined the staff of the National Trust for Scotland as a field officer, just as the shipyard in which I had worked for many years was due to close down. At an age when many of my contemporaries were thinking twice about breaking into a trot to catch a train, I found myself stepping up my climbing activities to meet the demands of the new job. Soon I was climbing in Arran, Glencoe, Kintail, Torridon and St Kilda, with parties of hill-walkers from the Trust's adventure camps and adventure cruises.

"It gave me a new lease of life. But I had to adjust my approach to the situation. Unlike the early days, when my companions were experienced, self-sufficient climbers, I was now leading parties of largely inexperienced people, most of whom would never have ventured into the hills without guidance. But it has turned out to be most rewarding. There is a great satisfaction in sharing the delights of wild, impressive places with people who are seeing them for the first time.

"I think the most rewarding experience is to lead Trust work-parties to St Kilda. This group of Atlantic islands, fifty miles west of the Outer Hebrides, offers remarkable contrasts. The great encircling cliffs are true primitive landscape, kept thus by the gouging, boring action of the waves, but the cliff tops on the main island, Hirta, give way to green pastures, grazed by large herds of the wild Soay sheep. Scattered around are the many stone structures erected by the long generations of people who inhabited the island until its evacuation in 1930.

"I have climbed in Norway and in the Alps. I have been tremendously impressed by the situations encountered on mountains such as the Matterhorn, and by the vistas from its summit. But nothing I have seen beyond Scotland has diminished my appreciation of the hills of home.

"People ask me to name my favourite place or mountain, but I refuse to be judge in that kind of beauty contest. Choose one and you diminish the claims of the others. How can you reach a conclusion when you realise that you will never complete your exploration in a lifetime?

"I find new, fascinating places every year. In gem-hunting the prize stone is the one you have still to find. The best view is the one you have still to see."

Eagles' January Display

This January day the bitter wind is north-east and everywhere on my horizon, hills sparkle after overnight snow, blotted out by more showers from time to time, but revealed again whiter than ever above 2,000ft. Even on our own 463ft., Duncryne Hill, it was eye-watering on top this morning, yet a hundred feet down on the slope I could enjoy the heat of the unobscured sun.

As I sat down to my desk, a robin flew to the glass to look in the window at me, fluttering immediately to the bird table as I looked up and fixing me with a beady eye, in a "where's the grub?" look. Now it is perched on a saucer of bacon fat, starlings and blackbirds having rushed off with the crusts. Rivals for the fat are now arriving—tits, blue and great, with a pied wagtail running below.

No doubt about it, spring is on the way. On Loch Lomondside I've seen the first expanding hazel catkins stretching yellow. The first snowdrop is blooming, the tits are "belling", but there was an even better proof yesterday when I went to first-foot a friend and we watched two golden eagles in courtship play high above the rocks.

Sweeping on long broad wings to a height, the smaller male, higher than the other, would quick-turn and come diving at the female, almost collide, and swing away, followed by the female. Soaring, cavorting almost to touch each other in the air, their mastery of movement was wonderful to behold, especially their gliding speed. Maybe eyries, deserted last year, are going to be occupied.

That hill-walk on Sunday was very different from an outing I made with Pat on the Friday, along the north shore of the Forth from Culross to Crombie Point on a day to delight the heart. It was sunny and warm, giving the illusion of May in the greenery of the inland meadows where oyster catchers by the dozen were probing red bills into the earth.

Pat treasures this area as one of the least spoiled sections of the Forth, and it had a new shine that day of light and colour on pink rocks and gleaming houses of the Royal Burgh, with bird sounds everywhere coming from the shore—burbling of curlews, flighting calls of redshanks and turnstones, "skrakes" of dunlin, and mellow calls of ringed plover.

The tide was beginning to favour us at lunchtime, as we sat on some rocks, backs to a stone wall, enjoying a celebratory glass of sherry as we ate our "pieces". Our heads went up when a mob of cavorting peewits hurtled over, flashing black and white as they swerved and curved about in perfect unison, with attendants in the form of about fifty golden plover whirling about at twice their speed, miraculously changing level as one bird.

Now we betook ourselves to the causeys of Culross to enjoy the feeling of stepping back four centuries, since this is the best preserved sixteenth century industrial town in Britain. Yes, a town, for it was once as big and important as Glasgow. The connection between the two cities is St Mungo. He was born here in Culross.

However it took a man-inspired deepening of the River Clyde to make the dear green place the great city of Glasgow. The Forth on the other hand had a direct outlet to Scandinavia, Germany, and the Netherlands. Ships plied quickly and easily between the Lothians and the Fife shore.

Industry at Culross began with the monks driving shafts into the hill to extract coal and use it to get salt from sea-water, a basic commodity which ensured the future wealth of Culross.

Climbing the narrow wynds, up past the Mercat Cross, you arrive at the ruins of the Abbey, dating back to 1217, with a fine view over the Forth and a feeling of being far from the mainstream of the modern world. In preserving Culross the National Trust for Scotland and the Department of the Environment have done a fine job. The feeling is of elegance, but what of the life conditions of the labourers who created the wealth?

No doubt about it, the serfs who worked in the mines and saltpans suffered slavery. Professor T. C. Smout describes their conditions as ". . . a degradation unparalleled in the history of labour in Scotland". They were even bound by an Act of Parliament of 1606, forbidding anyone to employ a collier, coal-bearer, or salter unless he could produce a certificate releasing him from his former employment.

As for the actual long hours of work, wife had to help husband by carrying the baskets of coal he hewed to the pithead. Nor did their children escape. At six or seven they were added to the workforce, so they were "born" slaves. We left these "good old days" behind us with no regrets.

150 YEARS OF THE CALEDONIAN CANAL

To trace the beginning of the Caledonian Canal we have to go back to 1773 when James Watt reported on the practicability of a shipping canal through the Great Glen. Studying the full sixty miles separating the Atlantic from the North Sea, Watt had seen that the Watershed was a mere 115ft., and that nature had already provided a waterway of ribbon lochs for all but a third of the distance. He estimated that for a cost of £165,000 the coastal ships of the time would be able to avoid the unfavourable winds and strong currents of the Pentland Firth. Fishing smacks would have east and west coast waters open to them, and the Baltic and West Indian trade would be stimulated.

But the Government did not act, not even when John Rennie had drawn up another scheme in consultation with Watt in 1793. Then in 1801 it commissioned Thomas Telford to visit the Highlands and report on what public works would be most likely to benefit the natives and teach them the habits of industry. Telford was asked to look into every aspect of communications and trade, suggest where roads, harbours and fishing stations might be built, and advise on the possibility of a canal along the route surveyed by Watt and Rennie.

The energetic Telford—son of a Border shepherd and time-served stone-mason—was forty-four years of age, with behind him the solid achievement of connecting the Severn, Dee and Mersey by the Ellesmere Canal. He had fought his way to the top, moving from Eskdale to Edinburgh, then to London, learning dock and wharf construction in Portsmouth to become surveyor of public works in Shropshire by the time he was thirty.

In his Highland survey for the Government, Telford saw that the various aspects of his remit were ". . . not only practicable, but are capable of being formed into one intimately connected system, which would evidently have a striking effect upon the welfare and prosperity of the British Empire".

It resulted in his being sent back to the Highlands the following year to report more fully and extend his survey. Exhausted by his travels, he spent the winter writing up a staggeringly detailed plan, for a 20ft.-wide Caledonian Canal linked to a road programme covering 920 miles of new construction, together with harbours and churches. The Government acted with unusual decision, agreeing to pay the full cost of the canal and accepting half the cost of other works.

The canal had taken on a new importance to the government because of the danger to naval and coastal ships from attacking French privateers. This, and the road programme, would also help to stem the tide of emigration from the Highlands. Asked to report on the emigrant situation, Telford had stated that 3,000 were in process of leaving, and thrice as many preparing to leave the following year. The Government feared that if too many Highlandmen emigrated they would lose their finest source of recruits.

Telford was appointed principal engineer of road and canal works at 3gns. a day plus travelling expenses. William Jessop was the consulting engineer, a man with whom Telford was to associate happily during the next twenty-five years. And from the Ellesmere Canal he brought another two outstanding superintendents, Matthew Davidson and John Telford, who began work before the end of that year on the Caledonian Canal eastern and western terminals.

But even as Telford collected his gangs of stone masons from the shores of the Moray Firth, and gathered his labourers from Lochaber, Lismore, Kintyre, Skye, the braes of Morar and elsewhere, an event was taking place on the Forth and Clyde Canal that was to have world-wide significance in altering the course of shipping history and outmode the Caledonian Canal long before it was built.

That event was the trial of the first steamship, using James Watt's revolutionary discovery of the principle of the separate condenser, which is still regarded as being ". . . perhaps the most basic invention of modern times". Telford was being pressed to make more building speed, but the canal that he thought he could build in seven years was to take nineteen, by which time ninety-five steamships had been built in Scotland, and Clydeside had become the world centre of a new industry.

Government interest in the canal had lapsed long since, owing to the ending of the French wars and the continual expense. Yet even in the urgent days when Telford was being pushed to make more speed, he was having to pay off some of his badly-needed work force because the Government was alarmed at the cost of his labour bills. It was a false economy, because wages and costs of materials were to escalate all too soon. For Telford, engineering problems were so great that nothing the railway builders did later eclipsed them.

It took five years to build the three lowest locks of the Fort Augustus flight, with steam pumps going—James Watt again—to get rid of the water and allow the work to go on. In fact the lower lock had to be 20ft. below the level of Loch Ness because of the loose gravel. But the most difficult piece of engineering was at the Clachnaharry sea lock on the Beauly Firth where the mud was 55ft. thick and the entrance had to be carried 400yds. beyond the shore line. The eastern section from the Beauly Firth to Forth Augustus had been open to traffic for four years before the first through passage from sea to sea was made. Henry Bell established his steamship service in 1820, taking six hours to Fort Augustus, where a diligence took

61

passengers down the military road to Fort William to board another ship and sail for the Clyde through the Crinan Canal.

In the end the canal was opened before it was ready, and the depth of 20ft. envisaged by Telford had dropped to 12ft. owing to the costs of getting greater depth by dredging and tearing a way through a tangle of giant oaks embedded at the entrance to Loch Oich where they had been carried down river in distant times. However, there was plenty of water on the official opening, after days of torrential rain when Loch Oich was over 5ft. above its normal level.

The violent criticisms of the costly canal died down as 800 vessels passed from sea to sea in the first eighteen months and a new service of steam boats plied between Glasgow and Inverness. And at the same time as the Caledonian Canal was opened, Telford had completed his great Highland road-building programme, achieving more for his country than any other single·man had done before him.

Telford died in 1834, disappointed in his outmoded canal, but it was being brilliantly successful in one of its main aims, as a source of employment to destitute Highlanders, for its banks and walls kept collapsing. Also it needed deepening, and after being closed for three years it was reopened in 1847 with a depth of 17ft. by which time it had cost the Government £1.4 million— nearly three times as much as Telford had estimated.

The deepened canal did not attract more revenue, though it was popular with visitors to the Highlands, and 15,000 passed through it by steamer in 1863, just two years before the Perth-Inverness railway opened, ushering in an era of increasing speed. By 1909 a Royal Commission dismissed the canal as "antiquated", yet it could pass ships 150ft. long and 35ft. beam, drawing 13ft. 6in. of water, whereas the successful Forth and Clyde canal could accommodate ships no more than 68ft. 6in. long by 19ft. 8in. beam. The difference was that the Forth and Clyde canal was serving an industrial area, whereas the Caledonian Canal had virtually no local trade.

The Government had to act to save the canal, no longer important to coastal shipping, just one year later when Laggan lock collapsed and banks at Corpach, Banavie and Fort Augustus crumbled. The reconstruction proved its value in 1914 when war broke out and vast quantities of explosive mines and military stores had safe passage by avoiding the Pentland Firth. Not so much use of the canal was made in the second World War, though it did perform a valuable role in the later stages.

Revolutionary changes have taken place on the canal since these days. Mechanisation of all locks was completed in 1969, and the building of a Pulp Mill at Corpach resulted in the basin having to be enlarged to accommodate timber ships. During this period of renovation the canal was closed for ten months between 1964 and 1965, when drainage revealed some of the original Telford workmanship. The bigger basin has resulted in a good turn-round of ships and a general increase in canal trade. The passage time has been reduced an hour or two by mechanisation, and the general future of the canal seems more assured.

The most heartening aspect of the Caledonian Canal traffic is that it had greatly increased over the fifties and sixties, with a steadily mounting number of yachts and cabin cruisers adding to the fishing boats who are the main users. It seems certain that the recreational use of the canal will increase with more leisure, since the broad waters of the canal provide sporting sailing against a background of peaks rising as high as Ben Nevis over Loch Lochy, which is a height differential of over 1,300ft. No pleasure ship operates the full length of the Caledonian Canal, but there is a daily sailing from Inverness in summer to Loch Ness by the converted ice-breaker *Scott II,* which has accommodation for sixty-five passengers.

The eastern approach is a very ancient sailing route, since long before there was a canal there was a naval vessel in service victualling the garrison at Fort Augustus. And as long ago as 1651 Cromwell's forces used Loch Ness as a waterway. No doubt the first users were the early men using dug-out canoes to penetrate the hostile forests where wolves, bears, great elk, caribou, northern lynx, beavers and even bison roamed.

The paradoxical thing about the Caledonian Canal we know today is that Telford's great engineering work would have been in vain but for the steamship, for navigation of it proved too difficult for an age of sail. Captain Edward Burt had foreseen this in 1726, forty-nine years before James Watt's revolutionary discovery. Watt in fact made his discovery only two years after he had surveyed the Caledonian Canal.

Ice on the Cobbler

Conditions on top of our wee village hill on 19 January were almost exactly those which sent two of us to the Cobbler for our finest-ever traverse of Glasgow's nearest equivalent to an Alpine peak.

The rapidity of the passing squalls, the flashes of sun, and the sight of the three-pronged peaks solidifying challengingly out of storm, reminded me of the morning when Roger and I set off to tackle the Cobbler.

We needed our resolution to keep going once we got to Arrochar, for it looked for a time as if we were merely pushing our noses into a settling blizzard. No sight of our peak until we were high in the corrie, then suddenly out of the flying murk it was there, even more heavily encased than we expected. There was disappointment too; a pair of climbers had beaten us to the south-eastern arête. The clink of their ice-axes had led our eyes to them, like black sticks against the verticality of the white wall.

Well, you can't have everything. We lost sight of them as we came under the steep start and began to get geared, uncoiling the rope, tightening our boot laces, sorting out our slings, and eating a sandwich as gusts of wind whirled the snow down our necks. It was then we heard voices very close and they seemed to be a bit concerned. "How's it going. What's it like up there?" I called out.

"Pretty hopeless, actually," came the answer. "Everything's iced up with loose snow on top of it. We can't get up, and it's hard enough to get down I can tell you." We were able to safeguard them down the steep bit that was worrying them, and no wonder, for they were in rubber-soled boots. Now it was our turn and I soon saw what had stopped the other pair, a vertical crack plated in ice and glassy as a bottle.

In fact, it was ideal for placing a running belay to safeguard what was a tricky bit of moving. The weather had turned grim again, but we were warming to the interesting work and all too soon we were on top looking down at something more problematic. The steep wall which drops abruptly to the main ridge was encased in water-ice and every ledge banked in snow.

There was only one way to find out if it could be descended safely and that was to go over the first vertical step and test the thickness of the ice and its reliability. I anchored myself securely so that I could hold Roger in case of a slip and down he went, out of my sight, the rope moving foot by foot as he shovelled away snow and cleared rock holds for hands and feet. Then a cry for me to "come on" and follow down, taking great care, for nothing would stop me for a very long way should I slip.

United, it was now my turn to go down first, but it was the "tapmaist elevation" I was thinking about for the summit pinnacle was clear of squall and looking very daunting. We could see climbers looking at it and expected to be pipped at the post for a first ascent. However, they moved away without trying it, so it was ours, and as marvellous a surprise gift as a Scottish climber could have. Surprise because the climbing was so easy.

We didn't even wear the rope for it, so perfect was the frozen-hard snow for yielding to a well-directed kick or slitting neatly open with the ice-axe. It proved the old story that there is only one way to judge the difficulty of a vertical-looking place, that is by rubbing your nose against it. Up there we had a rare feeling of pleasure from looking at the line of our descent from the south peak. It looked positively suicidal.

However, there was no time to stand too long staring. A red glow on the mist showed that time was running out for us if we were going to climb the north peak and complete the traverse of the three peaks, and once down off the pinacle we hurried down to the next col and swarmed up the steps which a previous party had made.

Our plan now was to get to the lip of the north corrie and use our backsides as sledges for a fast swoop to the foot of the bowl. The twinkling lights of Arrochar beckoned, and behind us as we looked back the pinnacles we had climbed were deep in a misty nightcap. Leaping and jogging we made such good speed that we were down without having to use our electric torches.

I can't remember the phrase that Mummery used to the effect that

"Happiness may baffle pursuit, but it can be surprised on the granite crags or beating the ice slopes into submission," which at the end of the day is why we climb I suppose.

CROSSING THE CAIRNGORMS ON SKIS

It was the eleventh day of sunshine in Aviemore, and I knew that the time had come for me to put into operation a plan I had to ski across the great plateau that rises over 4,000ft. between Spey and Dee. The conditions were perfect, with long snow tongues shooting like gigantic waterfalls from glittering cornices, which overhung the edges of snow-smoothed summits. The hard frosty sky held not a cloud, and robins and hedge sparrows were singing round the houses as I wheeled out my bicycle to tie my skis along the cross-bar, taking care that the handlebars would not jam.

I was not fooled by the springlike weather, however. I knew I was going to climb into winter, so into my rucksack went a light groundsheet, four candles, a little shovel, a supply of concentrated food and a solid-fuel cooking stove in case I were caught in a sudden storm.

With these necessities, and my ice-axe to dig a trench in a snowdrift, I was equipped to make a bivouac and survive a blizzard. The candles were carried as a source of warmth to raise the temperature inside my igloo once the drifting snow had sealed the cracks.

That was the theory, but I was not expecting to use this survival kit. I hoped to be sleeping that night in the keeper's house of Lui Beg, twenty miles across the mountains, if all went well. So off I went on the bicycle, pedalling up the stony track that leads into Glen Einich. Soon I had to walk, and I was glad to rest my binoculars on the handlebars to watch crested tits raising and lowering their barred head-feathers as they gave out the sharp vibrating trills that distinguish them anywhere. Louder, more metallic sounds came from the crossbills feeding on the top-most pine cones. I was lucky enough to hear one warbling sweetly for several bars—the most musical sound I have ever heard from this Scottish species.

Where the pines thin out I was in a different world of snowdrifts on the road, but I could ride for much of the way to Coire Ruadh of Braeriach, below which I dumped the bicycle and set off up the steep slope that leads to a narrow ridge between two horseshoe corries. It was a mountaineer's choice rather than the easiest line, and I paid for it by having to hang my skis on my rucksack while I hacked a way up a glassy section, before the ice gave way to more easily-cut hard snow leading to the open summit.

What a wonderful reward it was to be up here, with miles of sparkling snowfields before me, none of it below 4,000ft! "This is worth all the hard work," I thought as my eye ranged from the top of Braeriach round to Cairn Toul where I was going. I was in a world of utter silence—a polar waste but for the warm reds and pinks of the Lairig Ghru pass far below.

The River Dee rises close to the summit of Braeriach, near the sweeping precipices of Garbh Choire. There was no sign of the "Wells" that day as I swooped past the place, enjoying my wild situation on the lip of the great cornices plunging into space. Down there I could see frozen Lochain Uaine hemmed by Ice-Age bulges. I was moving fast over the ups and downs of the Garbh Choire edge; so was a subtle change in the weather. Visibility was closing in, and the distant sky was grey, not blue. But I was still in a brilliant world, tinged with gold now, the snow appearing almost warm against a violet sky. It was also a sign of approaching night and time I was down off the top of Angel's Peak.

Which way should I go? I could shoot down to Devil's Point and drop to Corrour Bothy; or choose the longer and steeper slope, which plunges directly to Glen Geusachan. I chose the latter and felt almost dizzy with the succession of linked turns that brought me helter-skelter to the last tongue of snow fanning into the heather. I abandoned my skis by sticking them upright in the snow and fixing in my mind the various landmarks that would take me back to them. All I had to do now was follow the glen down to the Lairig Ghru path, but it was dusk by the time I leapt across the Dee and my last three miles to Lui Beg cottage were in starlight.

"It's yourself," said Bob cheerily when he opened the door. "You'll be ready for your dinner." I was, and I was soon sitting down to it in borrowed clothes. Although they did not know on which day I would make the crossing, they were ready for me. I had of course written explaining my intentions if the weather held. "I must go back in the morning in case a change comes," I said to Bob. I had a shock coming when I looked out next morning at seven. Mist swirled round the house and the air was mild. However, I had risen with the object of making back to my bicycle, so I decided to try it. Unfortunately the mist did not thin out as I had hoped, and it was snowing on the plateau as I steered a compass course, pausing every few moments to take a bearing in the white-out.

Far out on the Monadh Mor I was forced into a decision: whether to risk being overtaken by darkness before I was off the plateau, or ski back along my tracks to Bob's cottage. I chose the way of safety-first, and was glad I had done so when at the edge of the snow line I met a fox walking slowly in my direction. The lolling gait and grey mask almost touching the ground showed that he had no clue of danger. I stood quite still, and on he came, closer and closer, the sheen on his red coat and long brush showing he was in fine condition. Then with a foot in the air he froze, ears up, nostrils twitching. We were eye to eye, and I swear I saw his expression change as he noticed me and spun round, diving behind a heathery knoll to disappear into the mist.

What was he doing up here? After the speckled ptarmigan, no doubt, since these birds are unable to fly safely when the world is opaque. I had seen a pack of twenty or so sitting in neat little holes in the lee of a cornice. The cunning fellow was no doubt going up to take a look. The only other birds I had heard that day were snow buntings, tinkling out of the mist, veritable sprites of the blizzard.

It was black darkness by the time I pushed open the door of Bob's house. "Well, well. I'm glad to see you back, I can tell you. We've been worried about you all day, for it's been wild here." Bob was to give me hospitality for the best part of a week, as the temperature shot up and the Dee rose to a brown flood impossible to cross.

It was no hardship—not with this keeper who lives in the highest and most isolated house in the Cairngorms. With the Labrador we went visiting fox traps, and watched the hungry deer foraging in hundreds among the newly uncovered heather. We saw the return of the golden plover to the moor and the oyster-catcher to the river—happy sights and cheering sounds. More unexpected was the sight of three yellow hammers outside the bedroom window: strange birds up here, strange as the robin I was to find perched beside my skis later that day. The partial migrants were on the move, and so was I—back to my bicycle.

The thaw had changed the face of the Cairngorms in the week since I had crossed them. The great plateau was now at the rags-and-tatters stage, but there was still more snow than bare ground, as I saw from the top of Cairn Toul, enjoying a mighty view of peaks stretching from the North Sea to the Atlantic. This time I intended to go back to the head of Glen Einich by way of the Monadh Mor, so I left the top on a long traversing line, taking Carn Ban Mor as my guide, then striking out towards the dip that marked Coire Dhondail—a long, long way, and an ample opportunity to watch the many pairs of courting ptarmigan crowing their creaky cries from many a snow patch. But gradually the brown crags of Sgoran Dubh were drawing close, and soon I was on the lip of the plateau, looking down what at first glance appeared to be a sheer drop.

Getting down posed an interesting problem. The drop was not sheer: the illusion was due to the snow cornice that overhung the steep face between me and the corrie. The cornice itself had been split by the thaw all along the plateau edge, but it was still managing to defy gravity. I could not risk climbing down anywhere here. There was one place, however, where it was uncracked, where the angle was less than vertical, and down it I lowered myself, ice-axe driven in to the shaft as I kicked steps downward, hanging on to my axe. I took it carefully for 200ft. then I considered it safe to relax.

Below me now was Loch Einich, with no obstacle between me and it. Indeed, there was a magic highway in a ribbon of silver ending in the blue water, and soon I was swinging down there on snow as smooth as silk. The ski-ing was over, but looking back to the great bowl of the corrie shining against the blue sky I could hardly believe that only half an hour ago I had been up there. But the evidence was there, in the black dots leading over the cornice, and the flowing curves left by my turning skis.

"It's not really so far," I thought, as I visualised the way I had come since morning: the pines of Glen Derry, the traverse round Cairn à Mhaim, then over the Dee to Glen Geusachen and the plod to the top of Cairn Toul, peppered with rocks where everything had been smooth snow a week before. Then out over the Monadh Mor, alone in the great depression between Bheinn Bhrotain and Carn Ban, a strange place at over 3,000ft., where I once met a dipper. Here, too, is a nesting-ground of the dotterel, my favourite bird.

Now I was down in the glen, with only two miles of walking to reach my bicycle. After twenty miles on foot and ski I was in no hurry, especially when a merlin rose from a heathery moraine and with squealing cries skimmed low over me. And before I reached my bicycle there was a sight of a splendid goosander, white-breasted and streamlined, followed by its mate. All too soon I was twisting down the stony track to Speyside, enjoying the effortless travel of the downhill run. In the evening light, the green of the Caledonian pines shone with a golden light, and the bark glowed with an extra touch of pink. Down here was a rich overlapping of bird sounds, of echoing curlews, drumming snipe and whooping lapwings, while from the trees came staccato songs of chaffinches, mistle thrushes, blackbirds, coal tits and goldcrests. Coming from the arctic heights of the tundra country to the fullness of spring down here gave me the feeling of having encompassed two worlds.

I chose the western plateau of the Cairngorms in preference to the east because the whole terrain is undeveloped. There are no chair-lifts or ski-tows to make the summits easy. I prefer my mountains lonely. Those wishing to gain the summits more easily should go in from Glen More, where there is a ski-road and lift to a point close to the top of Cairngorm. This has the time-saving advantage that splendid cross-country routes are possible in one day on foot or ski, from Cairngorm across to Ben Macdhui, or to the Shelter Stone and back by Ryvoan to Glen More. All this is splendid country for the naturalist, but the distances are long.

The important thing to remember when you branch out on this plateau is that it is potentially dangerous country. The plateau is featureless; storms rise suddenly; mist descends quickly. It is easy to lose your way, but difficult to find any house in this greatest expanse of mountain-top in Britain. Too many people have died in the Cairngorms because they did not keep a careful check on their route, or have the clothing and food necessary to withstand a storm.

Hunting Forest of James IV

The sudden thaw brought gloom to the brows of climbers and skiers but set the mistle thrush singing lustily last week. No mere tentative note either, but shouting bursts hurled from a top branch for minutes at a time—"the storm cock" indeed.

Robins were warbling too even before the footprints of the water rail in the snow had melted. But the dipper was silent, perhaps because its ouzel-singing-stones were under the water of an over-full burn.

Just how dramatic the thaw had been we didn't see until the hills emerged last Friday after four days of mist and murk.

That very timely clearing put me in the mood for an outing with Pat, and the morning was even better than the weather forecast as I sped east for Stirling to meet up with him, pausing below the grey crag of the castle where a grey mat of wild geese were grazing on the green.

"Where should we go?"

"Why don't we go to where the Stuart kings used to hunt with the Earls of Perth, away by Torlum Hill where there's still a bit of the old forest. It's very rocky. I think you'd like it."

In no time it seemed we were looking across to the sparkling houses of Crieff perched under the Knock, and Pat was pointing out to me the hill road that would take us over to Glen Artney.

It's always great to get into a new bit of country with ancient forest. "James IV used to hunt here," explained Pat. He used to stay at Drummond Castle just near where you can see the loch. He was intending to marry Margaret Drummond, a daughter of a Royal house. But she was poisoned so that it couldn't happen. At the age of thirty he married Margaret Tudor who was only thirteen. He was a Gaelic speaker and a great horseman. He was a much loved man, and fond of the lasses, with four mistresses by whom he had five children—six by his wife too."

We walked on the bones of the long-gone forest where he had hunted to the most unusual feature of these highland foothills, a sill of volcanic rock girdling the slope like the hoop of a barrel in a face averaging 40ft. and mostly vertical.

But before we got there we sank down on the heather to glass a large soaring bird that was quickly joined by another—a pair of ravens one of which went into a tumble with half-shut wings, straightening out to catch something in the air with its bill—a twig of heather we thought.

At the same time the other bird dived down to ground, picked up a white stone, flew high with it, dropped it, and began tumbling about with the other bird. Then came a third raven and all went to ground, the intruder bird sitting apart.

Into the air again and we had some real acrobatics from the paired birds as they swooped and twirled about, shaking themselves from side to side, letting their legs dangle as if to see how mad they could be and croaking hoarsely as if to say, "Look at me."

Ravens are the first birds of the hill to nest and the hardest to photograph because of their wariness. The Norsemen carried them in their longships and released them when in doubt where the land lay. They followed the direction where the raven flew.

Certainly it is a bird with a sense of humour. A friend of mine who gave houseroom to a lost young one found he had a real "character" in the house when it grew up. The first thing it proved was its intelligence when it learned how to twist the lid off the rubbish bin. Then for amusement it would tweak the cat's tail as it slept in the sun, croaking with glee as it flew off.

Nor did it take it long to discover that my woollen hat could be snatched from my head so long as it swooped down silently from behind. Leave a car window open and heaven help your upholstery.

He was great fun, and there was sadness in the camp when he took his freedom and flew off to the wild.

ERISKAY: THE UNDESERTED ISLAND

It was a July morning to cheer the heart, sun shining on a grass brilliant with flowers, and from our tent door a view over rock-speckled knolls, each by a crofthouse above a sea-scape stretching to South Uist. Peat smells vied with the scents of clover and thyme. A corn bunting was an unexpected songster among the twites perched on a nearby fence. Beneath us terns fished in the clear green water, and the rough sail from Oban to Lochboisdale, less than sixteen hours ago, was already a distant memory.

Waiting for the kettle to boil for some tea before setting off on a first exploration I read a poem written on 13 February 1898, by Father Allan McDonald, who was Priest on this Island of Eriskay until his death in 1905. Translated from the Gaelic into prose it goes something like this:

"Rough, gloomy weather, as is usual in early Februrary; white spindrift off the sandbanks driven everywhere; spray like ashes driven across the Sound; sod and slate loosened by the quick blows of the wind. Fierce squalls from the north shaking every gable, hard hailstones which would cut the top off one's ears, men so chilled with cold that they cannot look outside, huddled indoors at the edge of the ashes. The head of yonder hill above is sheathed in a shroud, since the cold has killed her natural virtues. She has lost her appearance entirely, the sleep of death has come on her, and there is no likelihood of her moving until the warmth of spring unbinds her."

Eriskay is only 3½ miles long by 1½ miles broad, and few people were aware of its existence until Mrs Margaret Kennedy Fraser visited the island in 1905 and brought back *An Eriskay Love Lilt*, one of the best-known Gaelic songs today. Miss Amy Murray, an American, took down about 100 other airs in Eriskay at about the same time, thus the world became aware of the marvellous oral tradition of these islands with words and songs going back hundreds of years.

Of all the islands in the Hebrides, Eriskay seems one of the most unlikely for habitation, consisting of little more than two hills whose rocks go right down to the sea. Looking down from the highest of them I marvelled that it should support a vigorous community of 200, when so many islands of better soils lie empty, their ageing populations having given up.

Eriskay had no more than a miserable hovel or two on it in 1745, when Prince Charles Edward put it on the map by making his Scottish landfall there on his way from France in the ship *Du Teillay* to raise the clans and march upon England. Typically, his arrival on Eriskay was an accident,

72

due to panic at the sight of a ship which they took to be an enemy frigate. By dodging among the Barra Isles they managed to give it the slip. So in the wind and rain of 24 July, the Prince was put ashore and taken to a smokey hut where he sat miserably on a pile of peats, waiting impatiently for the Laird of Boisdale, who had been summoned from South Uist for help.

It is likely that Eriskay would never have been settled if the Prince had listened to Boisdale who, meeting the Prince, advised him to turn about and go back to France. But while they argued, the hostile-looking ship reappeared off the coast, in company with another. Conversations were cut short. The *Du Teillay* set sail east to Loch nan Uamh. The adventures of the Prince had begun—and he was a beaten man when he came back this way after Culloden, desperate to get a ship to France.

The settlement of Eriskay dates from the clearances of the mid 19th century and the mass evictions of South Uist and Barra crofters to make way for sheep. To escape being rounded up like cattle and shipped to Canada, some took refuge on Eriskay, and were allowed to stay, because the thin soil was too poor, even for sheep.

Wandering about the island in the next few days I could only marvel at what the descendants of the downtrodden settlers had made of their island, as shown by the well-built houses glittering in the neat whitewash and roofed in colourful blue or red. Perched on the bedrock, you had to go looking among the boulders to find their cultivation patches, no more than a few rigs of soil built up with the spade and given treatment of sand and seaweed for growing potatoes.

The islanders say it was the big shoals of herring and mackerel in the seas around them that enabled their forebears to survive. They fished with such vigour that they were better off than South Uist crofters who had been forced off good *machair* land and depended for a living on the burning of kelp. The Crofters Act of 1886 enabled the Eriskay people to rebuild their thatched single-roomed cottages into something better, and today they are among the best-housed people in the Hebrides, thanks to the sound financial base of their fishing.

Arriving on a Friday, it was a surprise to find so many motor cars on Eriskay's three miles of narrow road which connects the linear crofts. "It's only weekend traffic. It'll be quiet enough when the men put to sea again in the early hours of Monday morning, and the cars will be in the garage for another week", explained one of the islanders. I learned that a new boat had been added to the fleet of six, fishing for prawns and herrings, while two lobster boats worked the shores.

My visit coincided with a "Sale of Work" on the island which brought a great traffic there on the Saturday afternoon. Boats came over from Barra and Uist, and the people packed the village hall, filling it with happy Gaelic tongues. Two priests worked the Wheel of Fortune, and a visiting nun won a prize. Eriskay pullovers with tree-of-life designs, and waves and furrows were bargains at £12. Incredibly the amount gathered was £1,450—good going for an island with a population of 200; it was to pay for chapel repairs.

Sunday was a happy day, as family parties in their Sunday best converged in the chapel for morning Mass. "You should come", said one wee girl. "The Priest will give you a paper to tell you what to do." The chapel perches on a westerly spur above the main settlement on the north tip of the island, and was built by the islanders, who dug the foundations, cut the quarried stones and carried up sand and cement to create something beautiful for their beloved priest, Father Allan MacDonald, who died just two years after the church was opened in 1903.

I saw how well balanced the present population is at a ceildh held in the hall on the Sunday evening, when the entire population turned out in a healthy scattering of ages from young to old. The missing ones were those in the merchant navy or girls away working in mainland hotels for the summer season. The Gaelic singing was a joy, and so was the naturalness of it all, as the audience waited to see who would be called next when the last chorus had faded away. None refused their call and my only sorrow was that I had no Gaelic to follow the humour or the pathos of the songs. There were alcoholic refreshments too, and a great sweeping of the floor for a dance which began around midnight and finished only when the fishermen stole away to join their boats and go off for another week.

An islander showed me where to look for the Prince's flower on the shell sand beach known as Coilleag a' Phriennsa. I was advised to search the dunes just above it, among the silverweed, ragged robin and lady's bedstraw. It took three hours to find the pinkish trumpet flowers of *Calystegia soldanella,* the sea convolvulus.

The islanders believe that the plant grows only on Eriskay, and that it was planted by the Prince to celebrate his arrival on Scottish soil. It is a romantic notion, upset by the fact that there are twenty post-1930 records of *Calystegia soldanella* from various bits of the Scottish coast, though Eriskay could be its most northern location in all Europe. Alone, in the rain, I had a strange moment, almost a re-run of history, when an old-fashioned schooner, square sails stretched, hove into view off the bay. It was not "second sight" but the top-gallant-yard schooner *Captain Scott,* with an "adventure" crew on one of its island voyages.

From the 609ft. top of Ben Scrien, highest point of Eriskay, you get a truly mountain-top view, out over Rhum, Canna and the Cuillins to the peaks of Ross, while just across the water the dark hulk of the Barra Isles stretch southward, with the sands and crofts of North Bay no more than a short sailing distance away. Northward between Eriskay and South Uist is the smudge of a small island called Calvey, enshrined since 1941 in the pure gold of Hebridean memory.

Sir Compton MacKenzie, who lived on Barra at the time, has enshrined for us in his hilarious novel *Whisky Galore* what happened after the cargo ship *Politician* struck a reef off Calvey that February night without loss of life, or too much damage to the 20,000 cases of export whisky which formed her cargo. It was certainly the happiest event in a grim war, all the better for the whisky being of thirty-two different brands. Songs are still sung about it—and it would appear that the oral tradition has handed on more than has been written down—if you have the Gaelic.

Isolation has kept alive old ways and customs on Eriskay, and it has enabled the special Eriskay ponies to retain their purity as a primitive breed. Used for bringing peat in panniers down from the hills, the docile and sure-footed breed is regarded by experts as being closest to the old Celtic horse. But lack of stallions was causing it to die out. The situation is healthier now, since the formation of a Preservation and Development Society. Owners on Barra, Eriskay and elsewhere have a Stud Book now, and the intention is to breed selectively and attain a surplus which could be sold as riding ponies. At this stage it is necessary to dilute the breed, but in a few years it should be possible to breed back to only pure Eriskays.

At a time when there is so little belief in crofting and fishing among Hebrideans, it is heartening to see one well-stratified and balanced community who believe in the old way of life. What father Alan MacDonald wrote about Eriskay at the beginning of the century may sound romantic, but broadly speaking is still strong in right values. Listen to his words, the first line of which refers to a 17th-century MacDonald.

> "Eriskay of the Mac Iain 'ic heumais
> of the speckled knolls
> and the bright white strands;
> 'tis there one finds strong men
> who are not afraid when the sea rises,
> and kindly, tunefully, diligent women
> who sing more sweetly than the birds on the trees."

St. Valentine Fervour

There was a rare ambience about last Monday that made me impatient to get away from the BBC Studios in Glasgow at 10 a.m. and back into my old togs for a walk in the warm sun along the Endrick shore of Loch Lomond.

No doubt about it, there was a St Valentine fervour from the birds proclaiming the nesting urge. A starling, its throat puffed out and head to the sky was trying to be a curlew, a goldcrest was stringing together a jingle of hurried needly notes, hedge sparrow and chaffinch were trying their impatient songs, tit-mice and wrens were in shrill voice. Best of all was the arrival of our common song thrushes, absent all winter.

While listening to the songsters I was glassing the water to see where the soft talking of the Greenland whitefronted geese was coming from.

Yes, out there among a sea of Picasso colours reflecting the hills upside-down, the rich browns of Conic Hill, the snow patches of Ben Lomond, the tawny shoulders of the Luss Hills, green of shores, dark spludges of wooded islands on pale china-blue water spattered with the white of tiny lambs' wool clouds.

Spying north in the direction of Balmaha I got a shock of pleasure as I ranged with the binoculars along the top of the oakwood where the herons nest. The big grey birds which are always first to nest were in occupation, a pair standing up and wing-flapping on one nest, while another five nests had single birds.

Walking back west I hear a shrill mewing that is unmistakably buzzard but it has an agitated note. Is it being attacked by something? I can't pinpoint the direction, then I see it is almost immediately above, yelping and diving for the sheer joy of being alive and looking forward to the nesting season apparently, its last dive being a real bobby dazzler as it closes its wings like a peregrine falcon and lets itself fall hundreds of feet under gravity, putting out the broad wings again and gliding down to land on the top branches of a tall tree.

With me is an uninvited companion. You would take it for a miniature collie but it is a farm-dog mongrel about 2½ years old which I have known since it was a pup and which attaches itself to me whenever it can. Immediately on joining me little Nell thinks she is out on a squirrel-catching expedition, running from tree to tree hoping to see a bushy tail.

I bet she dreams and squeals in the barn where she sleeps, of her one great success— and failure. The events occurred at the edge of the lagoon where I saw the herons when instead of being frightened by the barking dog and staying on top of its lone hawthorn tree a grey squirrel leapt on to the ground. In twenty yards Nell pinned it, picked it up, and shook the wildly squirming animal, and the next thing I saw was the squirrel clinging to Nell's back, riding like a jockey while the dog searched the ground, weaving back and fore looking for it.

Too late, she realised where it was when the squirrel leapt off and shot up a tree leaving the excited bitch squealing.

ISLES OF ENCHANTMENT

A fine thing to be landed on a desert island with food for a week and little possibility of being disturbed! The island was Eilean-an-Tighe, one of the Shiants, in the Outer Hebrides, and down beside its only habitable dwelling we pitched our tent, while the fishing-boat that had brought us heaved its way back to Stornoway over the North Minch. Grey as the four-hour crossing had been, we were now in a pocket of sunshine, emerald sward gleaming, orange-lichened cliffs vivid against the dark sky. With two boxes of food and a gallon of paraffin for cooking we knew we were going to enjoy ourselves, as we climbed the crag above the tent and surveyed our island domain.

The Shiants lie in the wide space of sea between the north end of Skye and the bulge of Lewis. Over the glittering west we could see rain showers sweeping the blurred hills of Harris. Mist hid the distant mainland and Skye, so we knew we were in luck, escaping the main deluges, as do so many of these small Atlantic islands. Indeed, we had mainly dry weather for a week, while Stornoway had torrential rain. Eilean-an-Tighe is shaped rather like a mile-long bottle, its neck pointing south. Attached to it, except in spring tides, is Garbh Eilean, more bulbous in shape but about the same size. Just half a mile across the water and inaccessible to us was Eilean Mhuire, shaped like a boomerang, and from our position on the main island we could see that its whole summit was etched by the lazy-beds of former cultivation.

The Shiants were inhabited until near the beginning of this century, but now they are used only for sheep grazing, and visited occasionally by shepherds or island-loving naturalists. From our high viewpoint we looked down on the piles of stones that had been houses, their surrounds greener than the turfy furrows of former cultivation. We were to find lazy-bed ridges in every corner where potatoes or oats could be grown; for these small islands totalling only 500 acres supported no fewer than ten families.

The name "Shiant" is derived from the Gaelic *sidh*, a fairy; so these are the enchanted islands. We found that this was not so far from the truth, when we came to the Miannius, where the Sgeir—the tooth—plunges into the sea in a fretwork of pinnacles. Here, on the end of the island, was perched a twite, as if awaiting us, while above the noise of fulmars and growling guillemots floated up the shrill vibrations of a wren.

For such low islands I had not expected very exciting rock scenery, but this is the northern limit of the columnar basalt—a formation of pillars like giant organ pipes dropping sheer from summit to sea. The cliff was impossible to traverse, but the jumbled boulders below it were firm and safe for scrambling, so we could creep across to guillemot ledges and razorbill grottoes, or creep stealthily up on sitting fulmars. The Miannius reminded me of Ruival, on St. Kilda, except that the plants were infinitely richer here, hanging in splotches of colour. Red campion and ox-eye daisies jostled with purple vetches and masses of buttercups; while the orange rocks were peppered with the white stars of stonecrop. Ravens barked, shags snarled angrily from caves, and great black-backed gulls declaimed monotonously round us, because they were being disturbed on their nesting territory on top of the cliff.

Eilean-an-Tighe was easier to get to know than Garbh Eilean, across the strand from us. At low tide we crossed to it, traversing the enormous scree of jumbled blocks that litters the base of the finest columnar cliffs in Scotland. We found the boulders an absolute warren of birds, puffins, scurrying out by the endless stream and razorbills peering out at us from every stone. In one burrow it was amusing to find a puffin and a razorbill within 18 in. of each other, the puffin in the rear, so that it had to brush the razorbill every time it went out or in.

In June we were at the period when eggs or young were at every stage, from new-laid to new-hatched, though shags showed the greatest variation, many with clutches of five fresh eggs, while other nests contained almost fully-grown young. Of all the auks I find the razorbill most endearing, so gentle and unafraid as it broods its single egg or guards its silver-grey young. We apologised for having to disturb these birds, since we required to borrow their eggs to measure them and record their volume as part of a growth-study.

The highest point of the Shiants lies right above this great boulder field, soaring up in great pipes of pillared rock. One way to it we favoured was by rock-climbing to a hole pierced by the sea through a headland, to make a natural arch. On sound rock we could traverse above the plunging sea, then climb rapidly to a viewpoint that proved finer than from most mainland peaks six times higher. One day was especially thrilling. Showers skirmished over the Minch, revealing the insubstantial islands around us like lumpy billows of the sea, as unreal as a weird stage setting shot through gauze. There to the west were the blue hills of Harris trailing to nothingness beyond Uist, while out of the black rain showers eastward leapt other shapes, the summits of the Torridon hills and An Teallach.

We could have been out in space, except that a wheatear fed its newly-fledged young with much tchick-ing and tail-bobbing round us, while under a nearby tussock a skylark brooded four heavily-speckled eggs. It was on this point that we saw our only golden eagle—a visitor that wheeled on broad wings, looking gigantic as it beat over a pinnacle where the last sea eagle, or erne, in the Western Isles nested on the Shiants until 1890—five years longer than the human population, who had never known an erne kill any sheep or lamb on the island.

Garbh Eilean had many things to recommend it, especially the floral paradise of its south-western shore. This was difficult to traverse because of deep gullies, but worth the trouble of all the up-and-down work involved in visiting its herring gulleries and boulder fields of auks. At the far end of the shore was a line of jagged skerries known as the Galtas. There the sea pinks were in late display, like a fringe of red carpet, and here we sat, happily counting kittiwakes and working out the proportion of bridled guillemots to the ordinary kind, while below us from resonant depths sounded the wailing songs of Atlantic seals, drawn up like brown slugs on warm shelves above the green water.

That evening we found ourselves cut off from our home island by the spring tide. Hungrily we waited for the water to subside, but the inconvenience had its own reward when we saw a little party of chequered waders trip past, swing round and touch down with a flash of pinkish shanks. They were turnstones, some in chestnut breeding-dress, others not. I imagined them to be non-breeding birds, remaining in Scotland rather than migrating to Iceland or Greenland, where they should have been at this time. Curiously enough, the only other visiting wader was a common sandpiper, heard at 2 a.m. as we searched the cliffs listening for stormy petrels which occupy burrows here.

From midnight onwards we traversed the great cliffs, picking our way across the face, stopping now and then to listen to the cries of gulls, using the darkness to hunt the stones, on the lookout for unguarded eggs or young. But it was the sounds beneath our feet that were most compelling— the extraordinary mixture of squeals, croaks, groans and snores from the countless thousands of birds in the eternal process of creating new life.

Gradually the luminous sea cutting the dark curve of cliffs lost its contrast. Dawn stole upon us. Colour was gradually apparent where there had been none, as we climbed the cliff to the highest point of the island. The larks were singing as we came home, back to the tent. Summer on the Shiants is a delight, but when the storms of winter roar they must be sombre indeed.

Harvesting History

Have you ever heard of the "Glesca Buchts?" I had not, until Bob Mackay told me it was the principal feeing fair for the West of Scotland, held near Queen Street Station.

Bob had run away from home in 1912 and at the May term was feed, contracted to a Gartocharn farmer for a lad's wage of the time, £6 the half year. On holiday from England with his wife, he'd come to see me and show her East Cambusmoon Farm where he had unloaded his kist all those years ago.

His chief memory was of the gaffer who showed him a cubby-hole at ground level with a window looking out on the clairty yard. "A grand view disnae pay the rent," said the gaffer by way of explanation. Things looked better in the kitchen where the farmer was tucking into a tasty looking meal, but all Bob got was a bowl of brose and a girdle scone.

Bob certainly got a fine welcome from the present farmer and smiled his surprise when she led him into the cubby-hole, now a nice wee bathroom in the modernised old house. Mrs Wilson was as delighted as I was to hear the old man's memories.

"Up at five in the morning, it was into the byre to milk the kye, and without a bite to eat yoke the horse and cart and take the milk to Balloch where I bought half a dozen rolls and ate the lot. The breakfast when I got back was a bowl of porridge and a herring with a slice of bread. Then out to sow turnips. At lowsing time there was more brose, but before bed I went for a walk to find the railway line and the nearest place where I could get a train.

"I never took off my clothes, I just dozed, waiting for the grey of the morning, eased the window, and in stocking soles crossed the yard and got the dung barrow. The yard was cobbled then, so I tied wisps of straw round the wheel and tried to slide my kist from the window on to the barrow, but bang went barrow and kist on the cobbles. I held my breath, but nobody wakened.

"With tackety boots round my neck I warsled the kist and barrow bumpety bump over the cobbles, often keeking over my shoulder. On the loan, puffing and blowing, I came to the level-crossing I had seen the night before and knew I would come to Croftamie Station if I kept along the line. Pushing the barrow on to the platform I found some old newspapers and was cleaning my kist when out came the station master.

"'Where do you hail frae?' says he. I named the farm. 'Cambusmoon, I thought you might be frae the Moon. But what about the filthy barra on my platform?'

" 'Right,' says I. So I took the barrow outside and shoved it through the hedge. 'Are you hungry laddie?' says he. 'I could eat you,' says I.

"The workman's train came a half hour later, and soon I was in Stirling. That day was Stirling Fair, and between penny reels at the Corn Exchange I was feed to Rab Armstrong at Cambus near Alloa."

Fascinated by his total recall I asked what happened next.

"The war. I joined up in the Argylls and went to France with them in 1914, got seriously wounded in 1917, and in and out of hospitals until 1921. Then four years later I married one of the fine girls who had nursed me in Chichester, and there she is. I retired after twenty years with the Duke of Richmond and Gordon at Goodwood, in charge of the forest, racecourse, and motor circuit.

"We have a house on the Duke's estate and I have a good pension, so in our old age we are quite comfortable. My mind has often wandered back to Gartocharn, wondering if the farmer got back his barra, and what did

Companion for a day, the fox terrier on Sgurr na Ciche.

The infamous Bad Step on the shore path to Loch Coruisk. There is nothing to it if you avoid the smooth upper bit.

Crowberry Gully in February, a major climb of the 30's in W. H. Murray's time.

The broad base of Loch Lomond from Ben Lomond.

Frozen Loch Tulla in January, part of the route of the West Highland Way.

Wilkie Bard the eaglet on the left with the tawny parent bird.

Wilkie ready for his first flight.

Tom Anderson with two young Shetland fiddlers.

Lerwick, the capital of Shetland.

Rannoch Moor abuts on Coire Ba. The West Highland Way follows the middle distance.

Jock Nimlin (L), on the Isle of Canna, with a work party bound for St. Kilda.

Corpach Basin of the Caledonian Canal, and an east coast boat heads for the Hebridean fishing grounds.

The edge of the Braeriach Plateau, looking to Cairn Toul as bad weather begins to develop.

Bob Scott of Lui Beg in his prime days.

"Old Beattie" the stag takes a slice of bread from Mrs. Scott but it preferred pancakes.

Tom Weir in the Blane Valley stretch of the West Highland Way, heading for Gartness beneath the Campsies.

Descent into the Blane Valley on the West Highland Way at Arlehaven Cottage. The route traverses left round the wooded knoll of Dumgoyach.

An osprey touches down with a fish on the Loch Garten Eyrie.

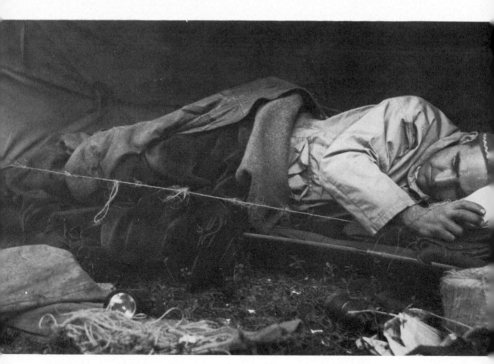

George Waterston sleeps with an alarm cord on his wrist guarding the Loch Garten ospreys. Tom Weir was at the other end of the cord.

The Pools of Dee on the Summit of the Lairig Ghru before the descent to the Dee.

On the summit of Lochnagar. The lochan is 1,200ft. below.

The Ballochbuie Forest which Queen Victoria saved from being felled.

Stormy weather at Troup Head on the Moray Firth.

Gardenstown, a prosperous fishing village on the Moray Firth.

Summer on Beinn Bhrotain, one of the remotest tops of the Cairngorms.

Glen Lui Beg on the Lairig Ghru path. Beinn Bhrotain centre.

From the high Glam road on the Island of Raasay looking across The Narrows to Braes in Skye.

Loch Trool in Galloway from Glenhead.

The winter crags of Lochnagar which Tom Patey made his own.

Superb powder snow conditions on the hills above Tyndrum, Beinn Dubhcraige.

he think when he saw the bed empty and the laddie ower the hill."

At Cambusmoon you don't need a barrow now. The byre has press-button automatic cleaning, and the milk from the cows extracted from them by machine is piped direct into a bulk tank for collection. And with extra grazing on another farm the stock of cows is 180, 62 of them milkers.

TWO LUCKY PEOPLE

How would Waterston or Purchon
Like a bird to do research on
The way in which they propagate *their* clan?
Thank the Lord the bugle's callin'
And they'll have to go and fall in—
Now for twenty minutes' love life while we can.

These lines, written in a prison camp in Bavaria in 1943 made George Waterston smile when I quoted them to him. "Where did you dig that up?" And recollections began to flow when I told him I quoted it from *Bird Watching— The Song Of The Redstart*, written by fellow officer R. D. Purchon to cheer up the camp inmates who had been pressganged into all sorts of ornithological services.

"I'm the luckiest chap in the world," said George. "Even when taken prisoner after the battle of Crete in 1941 I landed on my feet amongst a fine bunch of naturalists. Purchon was studying swallows and field crickets, John Buxton wrote a book on redstarts as a result of his work, Peter Condor, now Director of the R.S.P.B., was studying goldfinches, and I was busy on wrynecks. In fact, some of my wrynecks were driving out the redstarts from nest boxes we had made for them."

I prodded George to tell me some more. "Well, it was there that Ian Pitman and I began thinking about Fair Isle, and how marvellous it would be if we could get a bird observatory on the island. Planning to buy Fair Isle and do some real scientific work up there to unravel the mysteries of bird migration, was a way of escaping from the camp into the freedom of the future.

"Getting a chance to do so much birding in the camp whetted our appetites, for so relatively little was known about the detailed lives of individual species. Even in camp we made contact with German ornithologists. I had records of German bird notes sent to me by Professor Erwin Stresemann. I sent him my notes on the birds of Crete, and when he published them along with his own in the middle of the war in a German journal he acknowledged the help of a certain Lieutenant Waterston.

"Funny how things work out. When Crete was retaken by the Allies, Heinz Seilmann, the great German cameraman, was captured. But when he explained he was filming the life of Eleonora's falcon, he was allowed to go back and finish his work.

"Imagine it, years later in America, Professor Stresemann, Seilmann and I faced an audience from the same platform at an International Ornithological Congress. And when Stresemann stood up to give his address, he introduced us: 'On my left George Waterston, and on my right Heinz.' Then he told the story of our adventures in Crete and how our friendship through birds triumphed over the stupidity of war."

George's brown eyes fairly sparkled in his dark gypsy face as he spoke of how the "ups" of life so wonderfully make up for the "downs." It was ill health which caused him to be sent back to Britain for hospital treatment in 1943. His homecoming was by way of Sweden and the coast of Norway, then west across the North Sea.

"I think the most emotional moment of my life was when somebody shouted 'Land ahead,' and there, only two or three miles off, was the Sheep Rock and Fair Isle standing out in the sunshine. The tears ran down my cheeks—I knew it so well, and it had been so often in my thoughts."

George's interest in the three-mile-long island lying midway between the Orkneys and the Shetlands had begun in the mid-thirties when it then held 130 folk. "Oh, they were great fun, always good for a laugh, and really keen on birds, for it's such a marvellous place for migration. Anything can turn up there."

But Fair Isle had to wait meantime, as the ship bore home and he went into hospital for kidney treatment. He was expecting to be given a Home Guard command when he came out, but instead found himself being persuaded by ornithologist James Fisher to undertake a study of rooks to assess their effect on agricultural output at a time when Britain was desperately short of food.

So from being a prisoner ornithologist, George was now a free professional, meeting farmers and leading scientists and building up a picture of the rook population and their feeding habits. Evidence that has built up since George's confirms his finding that any harm that the rook does to crops is counterbalanced by the pests it eats.

The end of the war saw George back in the Edinburgh family business of stationery and printing, but his heart was not in sales management. The Fair Isle dream was as fresh as ever. Typically he had prepared a careful memo stating the ornithological objective and presenting it to friends and likely people to win their backing and some of their cash. The purchase price of £3,500 was raised and George became the owner of Fair Isle.

There was a hutted camp on the island, built for the Navy, which was to become home to the noted ornithologist Kenneth Williamson. His work there soon proved that the island was even more remarkable for migration than anyone suspected. Visitors stayed at the observatory and stimulated the demand for knitting Fair Isle patterns. The "laird" who had stayed in every croft, was "George" to all the islanders through his hundreds of visits. However, he could not close his eyes to the fact that, even since the purchase of the island in 1948, it was running down: crofts were deteriorating as young folk left and the population eventually dropped to under fifty.

Money would have to be spent on it to prevent it from becoming another St Kilda. Houses needed modernisation, a better harbour was an urgent need. The island needed a new boat and better roads. The solution was to offer Fair Isle to the National Trust for Scotland since they were in a position to launch an appeal to charities and the public.

The Trust took it over in 1954, with George as their official "visitor" or adviser, and great work has been done since then, thanks to financial help from the Scottish Office, the Highlands and Islands Development Board, the old County Council, and National Trust for Scotland staff, not to mention the field work done by Enterprise Youth workers and the International Voluntary Service. An air-strip has been built, renovated houses have electric light and the new island boat can come into a deepwater pier for the first time in history—previously a flit boat had to be used. Better still, there has been a drift back to the island by the young, and the population has stabilised at around seventy.

And in the year the National Trust for Scotland took over responsibility for Fair Isle, George broke with the family business of George Waterston & Sons to become secretary of the Scottish Ornithologists' Club and Scottish Representative of the Royal Society for the Protection of Birds. "Yes, there was some opposition, for I was the sixth generation in the oldest family firm in Edinburgh—it was established in 1752. I can understand their concern, for financially it didn't look very wise.

"Nobody could have foreseen then the rapid growth of bird interest or the urgent need for action to combat toxic insecticides which were poisoning our birds of prey. And the nesting of the ospreys on Speyside did a lot for us. Remember, you helped to guard the original pair in 1959 when we could muster only six watchers. Last year we had over a dozen breeding pairs, and we have had over 70,000 visitors at the Loch Garten hide in one year.

"Look at the Scottish Ornithologists' Club. When I helped to found it in 1936 we could muster only sixty members in the whole of Scotland. Now we have 2,700. It's fantastic."

I remembered the young black-haired George of these early days on the occasions when meetings were held in a Glasgow hotel. A hearty laugher with the gift of puting everyone at ease, his drive and enthusiasm was persuasive. Even at school in Edinburgh Academy it was natural that the bird club should meet in his house, talk ornithology and plan week-end outings. The accent was on conviviality.

"After the stir of Edinburgh we really enjoy living full-time in the country. Irene and I are both fond of gardening. Planting things and watching them grow until you can eat them, satisfies something deep down. With the green-house we are trying to be as self-supporting as we can. Come and look."

I was impressed by the amount of work they had done between them as we looked at the orchard, the neat vegetable plot and the flower garden. "This place used to be a croft with a cow and hens on three acres. Part of the house was a wee shop. We bought it eighteen years ago for Irene's mother with a view to having it ourselves eventually. We moved in last year after she died at over ninety."

I congratulated them on their foresight, with country house prices the way they are now, when the setting can cost as much as the house. "Yes, we got it for less than £1,000 and look at the view!"

I told him I had never seen a more rural corner of East Lothian, with a burn meandering at the foot of the garden slope, and a swell of green hillside rising on the other side of the little valley. No sound of traffic or any other house in sight.

"I'd be nowhere without my wife Irene. We've worked together on everything, and we have had so many tricky problems and exciting times. Last year was terrific. We had the good fortune to be asked to go as guide-lecturers on the *Lindblad Explorer* for two months on a sail of 7,000 miles." And as he spoke he took down from the book-case a fat photographic album, showing me colour prints of the ship beset in the pack-ice of the North Magnetic Pole.

"The passengers were paying up to £1,300 a month to be taken to the remotest shores of the Arctic. It cost us nothing and was a fantastic opportunity to see new places and revisit old Greenland haunts. I won't forget the sight of the calving grounds of the beluga whales where about a hundred of them swam about with their six-foot calves. We enjoyed every minute of it even if it was a different kind of scene from what we would have chosen for ourselves."

The album pages flicked to Ellesmere Land. "Now that really was to our liking; just Irene and myself and the nearest humans to us seventy-five miles away. That was three years ago, when the Canadian Wildlife Service put an Otter aircraft at our disposal and asked us to carry out for them a seven week ecological survey to report on what effect oil developments there would have on the musk ox and caribou lands. Irene found two plants new to Ellesmere."

Other photographic albums were pulled out, one of a West Greenland trip in 1965 with a Danish expedition when they visited Cape Shackleton where a million pairs of Brunnichs guillemots form the biggest seabird colony in the world. "We ate some of them, too," grinned George, "but we liked the tystie best, stewed in an iron pot."

There were photographs in which I had played a part, at the Ospreys' eyrie in 1959 when there were only six of us to do a round-the-clock watch. A photo shows George with a string attached to his wrist as he takes a nap. The string was attached to me in the hide. At a tug from me he would raise a general alarm, since a tug meant an attempt was being made to rob the nest. Alas, that first nest was robbed despite our safeguard, and the raider got away after substituting hens' eggs in the nest.

It was after that robbery the hide was thrown open to the public. "Colleagues thought it was a rash decision when I said we should invite visitors to come and see the ospreys. Response was fantastic. It did more good for conservation than almost anything else we could have thought up.

Wonderful how Irene has shared his experiences with him. She, too, is a keen ornithologist, but has been taking more and more interest in Arctic botany, perhaps as a relief from constant birds since her job was secretary of the Scottish Ornithologists' Club when George took over full-time Directorship of the R.S.P.B. in Scotland.

I remembered her with a big book on alpine plants at the hide in Fetlar when the first pair of snowy owls nested, making it a first for Britain. Protection was vital, so George was there mustering a guard of helpers, as he had done with the ospreys. Glad to say the Arctic owls are still nesting after eight years, and the Fetlar hill has Reserve status.

We talked about the ten R.S.P.B. Reserves which he has helped to set up in Scotland. "Yes, it is a great pity we have to find money to buy reserves and put in wardens to organise the public. But in an overcrowded Britain it has to be that, or constant disturbance by large numbers of people would drive away what bird watchers want to see. And valuable habitats are so vulnerable to commerical exploitation. Right now the Society are trying to raise £290,000 to buy the whole 1500 acres of Loch Garten to protect the total forest environment of that wonderful bird country." And with a swift motion he passed me an "appeal" form. The old fund raiser was still very much in action!

It was for outstanding services to ornithology and conservation that George Waterston was awarded the O.B.E. in 1964. Then in 1980 this modest man was flabbergasted when he was capped LL.D. by Dundee University for his outstanding work. It came just on the eve of departure on the *Lindblad Explorer.* Alas, things were never to be quite the same afterwards, for around last Christmas he had a return of the old kidney complaint, suffering pneumonia and pleurisy as well.

For two months he lay in Edinburgh Royal Infirmary, weak and depressed. I knew he was seriously ill, but I also knew that he didn't want anyone to hear about it. He cannot go on any long trips now for he is tied to a kidney machine in Edinburgh Infirmary, which he has to visit three nights every week for five hour stints. "A tedious bore and very time-consuming," was all he would say about it.

He looks upon the restrictions imposed upon him as an exercise in adaptation. Depression has gone and his natural ebullience and enthusiasm for life has returned. "I have a lovely place to live, plenty to do and I can lead a pretty normal life. I'm lucky," he says.

Lucky he is, certainly to have achieved so much in his most active years against a background of the kidney trouble which has plagued him since boyhood. Lucky to have retained his youthful enthusiasm for all the things he holds dear. Not so many manage to do that to the age of sixty-four. His beloved Fair Isle has been uppermost in his mind recently, because he sees a threat to its survival if the Loganair inter-island service is withdrawn as is being suggested.

George explained to me why the present air service is so vital to the Fair Isle community. "The economy of the island depends in part on the visitors who fill the twenty-four bed hostel, which is part of the new observatory we built in 1969. To keep the hostel filled we need the Loganair service, since the boat could never carry enough passengers to make the observatory pay its way. Because of the observatory the islanders have a good market for their produce. It is also their community centre. It cost £50,000 to build."

Explained this way, I could see why he was concerned. He had just written out a personal appeal asking people to support the National Trust for Scotland in giving a donation to further the work of bettering the island for the crofters, who are putting the land into better heart by reseeding the rough pastures.

Speaking about the future for himself, he is keeping his eyes on a glimmer of light. "My hope lies in a kidney transplant, and I am pressing hard for it."

The problem is to obtain somebody's kidney. "I know of transplants which have restored people to complete normality once the body has adapted. Meantime, I can do most things except heavy work. I drive myself from here to the Unit in the Edinburgh Royal Infirmary and connect myself up to the machine. And while my blood is being changed I watch television. It's about all you can do, for you feel too light-headed for reading. I go to bed in the Infirmary after it, then drive home."

I declined their warm invitation to stay the night, knowing that George has only one clear day to himself between drives to the Infirmary. I made up my mind, however, that I would dedicate my own kidneys for use to help someone like him. Even as I made the decision I had to chuckle, for such is George's power over people, that I could almost have passed him my kidney there and then.

* * *

George was given a transplant operation but it did not "take". He died on 20 September 1980 but not before he had some brave days in the Highlands and on Fair Isle, thanks to a mobile kidney machine and the support of his wife Irene who shared his great days. Whatever his suffering, his life-long enthusiasm for wild places and wild life never dimmed.

Sunshine After Flood

The first thing I heard when I opened the door last Sunday was a new sound, the squeaky whoops of peewits tumbling over their nesting field. As I stood savouring the balmy air on my cheek a yellow hammer was wheezing out its anxious request, "A little piece of bread and no cheese."

I made my own request to the guidwife: "Make up a piece, fill the flask, and we'll go to the hill once I've had a wee walk down the marsh." Down there was another new sound, loud, vibrating, whinnying. Yes, the singing of the curlew, and there was the grey bird gliding over its nesting ground, big curved beak open and the glorious sound spilling out as it sailed.

Listening to it I was enjoying the warmth of the unobscured sun which was lifting the mist from the bens, revealing how effective the blow-lamp of the balmy wind had been in shifting snow. Even at 3000ft. only patches remained of the big plastering which was lying eight inches deep on the hills on Friday morning. On Saturday the Endrick was running red with silt and every hillside was spouting.

Now everything had a benign look, the lower fields emerald green backed by tawny reds of bracken and grey rocks, the bark of trees shining silver, and alder catkins showing their pollen. Bees were buzzing, in full employment again, and woodland birds were rejoicing, but were not able to drown the torrent of skylark song spilling down from the sky.

Now we set off in the car for Aberfoyle. My thoughts are on the Craigroyston shore of Loch Lomond to visit our retired friend John who leads a solitary life in a cottage with no road to it but is never lonely. He has his garden, his boat for crossing the loch, the wild goats which are his neighbours, the birds which come to his table, the badgers which snout over his lawn, the singing dippers at the water's edge, and the sheep on which he keeps a weather eye.

The floods are worse than we thought; with a considerable lake where there are normally fields near Aberfoyle. Loch Ard is brimming over. The big waterfall above Loch Chon is leaping down in grand form, while Loch Arklet can't hold its catchment and spills it over the whole length of the concrete dam in a white cascade.

Just beyond it is where we take to the hill, round the shoulder of innocent looking Cruachan which suddenly changes character and becomes an apron of rock in a mile, falling from the Craigroyston skyline to the oakwoods and seamed with four gullies of spouting water.

This is where Rob Roy's Macgregors lived, and where later, the charcoal burners harvested the oaks.

Just a little further on as we drop towards the shore we see a pair of wild goats among the trees, black, hairy, and impressively horned. A movement near them, and I notice a kid, black but with a white bit on the head and white markings on the back. Near John's house we see another two animals, a white Billy and black kid.

John is in great form, and as we take a walk up the edge of the finest gorge on Loch Lomondside he tells me I should have been here yesterday. "As well as the thaw, we had 3½ inches of rain, and the whole thing was a marvellous sight."

A WELCOME IN LEADHILLS

In the warm light of the mid-morning sun the Nith Valley was looking better than I had ever seen it, with fields curving on each side of the river and sleek cattle dotting them, bright as in a painting. I was comparing it in my mind to the Kentish downlands until the high ridges of the Lowthers heaved above Sanquhar, and gone was my tranquillity. I had to get up there, and before me was the Mennock Pass, seven miles of magic climbing from the beauty of a man-made landscape into brown heather hills, closing in to a trench with snow under my wheels, and round a corner, Wanlockhead, the highest village in Scotland looking like something out of Switzerland.

The strung-out village houses on each side of the burn lie just below the 1,500ft. summit of the pass, with a branch road leading to billiard-ball radar domes occupying the top of Lowther Hill, 2,377ft. Twenty years ago a party of us had used that road to begin a February ski tour over Green Lowther and down the ridge of Windy Knoll to Leadhills, but I didn't expect to be remembered when I met the shepherd, Jake Elliot, out with his dogs, but "Aye", he said "it was jist up there I met ye last time. There's no sae muckle ski-ing done here noo".

Jake's house above Leadhills is on par with the top-most in Wanlockhead, and I was soon in the snuggery of the fireside, resisting an invitation to have a cup of tea, but enjoying a chat with this Ettrick shepherd and his wife, who is a local lass and went to school in Leadhills. I told them I couldn't stop for now, but I was going to come back for a week and get to know something about this countryside of which they are both so fond.

And back I went a week or two later to make good my promise, to walk immediately into another co-incidental meeting when I knocked at the door of a house to ask for information. You are never kept on a doorstep in Leadhills, and before I had asked my question I was inside and seated at the fireside in a cosy wee room and invited to have a cup of coffee by the smiling old lady who was saying that the last time I was in the house was when her brother was occupant.

I immediately felt an impostor. She is mistaking me for somebody else, I was thinking, when she cleared up the matter by saying, "You brought your mother here once with Mrs Hamilton and her daughter Mary when they lived next door to you in Glasgow". Now I remembered. They were Leadhills folk, and when I bought my first motor car in the mid-fifties we made an outing which my mother never forgot. That wee cottage made a powerful impression.

Life keeps catching up with you. I now had the perfect introduction to a lot of folk in Leadhills, and when I said I would like to spend an hour or two in the Miners' Library I was touched to find that four of its committee— Mrs Cameron, Mrs Kay, Miss Holly and Mrs Smith had the place warmed up, a fire going and tea and sandwiches for me, assisting me at the same time to find books and information I wanted. The ladies were proud of their library founded by the miners in 1741, and the first of its kind in Britain. It was the miners' hard-earned money which bought the books.

One of the ladies told me, "It's called the Allan Ramsay Memorial Library after the Leadhills poet who wrote *The Gentle Shepherd*, but there's no doubt that the mine manager, James Stirling, had a lot to do with it. He provided some of his own books, and the reading-room. But the idea maybe came from Allan Ramsay, who set up the first circulating library in Britain at the Luckenbooths in Edinburgh. James Stirling, curiously enough, is of the same family who set up the Stirling Library in Glasgow".

I was to hear a lot about James Stirling — known as the Venetian — who became mine manager at Leadhills in 1734, and as a social reformer pre-dates David Dale and Robert Owen at New Lanark. Stirling took over the mine when it was losing money and in a bad way. His own fortunes were none too good, for he had been thrown out of Italy for trying to uncover the secrets of Venetian glass-making so that he could bring them home and set up in competition. His life would have been in university circles, for he was a noted mathematician and scholar, but this was denied him because he had the unwelcome taint of Jacobite attached to him.

Stirling was forty-three years of age when he came to Leadhills to try out a job for which he had no training. He made his influence felt from the very beginning by appointing the best men he could find as overseers and working out a system of book-keeping based on piece-work bargains with the men. We would call them "productivity agreements" now. He also cut the hours of any shift to six and drew up sensible rules and safety regulations. Always he was concerned for the welfare of the miners, for whose intelligence he had great respect.

"These are the bargain books," said Mrs Kay, unlocking a special case containing dozens of large ledgers containing the entries of the overseers. To my surprise, I kept coming across my own name, for one of the writers was a Thomas Weir, who detailed his supervising visits to the various lead veins to measure and record work done. Another Tom Weir was a notable goldfinder.

Research in the Miners' Library revealed that as early as 1260, the monks of Newbattle Abbey were leadmining in these parts, but that big scale developments did not get off the ground until 1640.

Progress must have been swift, for Thomas Pennant, visiting the high villages on his famous "Tour", describes the mines as "inexhaustible" in 1772. But he was not enchanted by what he saw — a population of 1500 souls living in what he describes as mean houses in gloomy surroundings, "with neither tree nor shrub, nor verdure, nor picturesque rock, to amuse the eye". The workforce then was 500.

I was to spend a few more delightful hours in that library, but when I was shown Old John Taylor's blackthorn stick, and told that he had lived to be 137, I asked if I could take it for a walk to the cemetery to look at his grave.

The recumbent slab tells us he died in 1770, but of his birth in Cumberland there is no record. What is known, however, is that he was an old man when he came from Strontian to work in Leadhills in 1732. The question is, was he ninety-five? The folk around here believe he was, and that he was a mere 133 when he died and not 137.

The evidence on which this is based comes down directly from Old John, who had the date 1652 impressed on his mind, for on that "Mirk Monday" there was an eclipse of the sun and he remembers being called up from underground to witness day being turned into night and birds falling from the sky, (the birds were probably diving down to roost, being fooled by the sudden darkness). To have been underground and working as a miner John must have been over fifteen, the minimum age for underground work at that time.

The chronology of his life squares with this, for he travelled widely, working in various lead mines, prospecting in Ettrick, in Islay, at Strontian, where he contracted scurvy because of the monotonous diet of salt beef and whisky; he even worked in the Royal Mint in Edinburgh, converting Scottish coin to English. By reason of this wide experience he was a self-taught mining engineer when he came to Leadhills. Astonishingly he still had thirty-two years of working life left in him.

He was 5ft. 8ins. tall, a spare man with a ruddy complexion, and he said his teeth fell out when he stopped chewing tobacco, though it was more likely due to scurvy. He could eat at any time of day or night, and one story shows his exceptional hardiness and spirit. Out fishing in the hills, and following up two burns after trout, he got caught out in a blizzard and failed to make it home. The curfew bell was rung, a search party went out and found him in the snow, still alive. As soon as he recovered he was away back to the hill to recover his rod, which he had left upright to be sure of finding it again. He was 116 at the time.

Senility came to him in the end. In winter he felt the cold and would stay in bed, taking a wee glass of brandy to warm his stomach. But four years before he gave up the ghost he walked the two-mile gradient from his cottage to visit his children and grandchildren, and then walked home again.

John Taylor's grave is just over the wall from the Symington monument, commemorating the most famous son of Leadhills, born in 1764, son of a mine manager who put his talents to use here on steam pumps before turning his mind to ships and steam navigation. And one who helped him greatly to realise his ambition was a grandson of Old John Taylor, university-trained and tutor to the children of Patrick Miller of Dalswinton, who became Symington's patron.

Success attended their partnership on Dalswinton Loch in October 1788 when the first working steamboat took the water, watched by a big crowd among whom was Rabbie Burns, who was farming at Ellisland, nearby, at that time.

The practical steamship on which the engineering reputation of Symington rests had to wait for a bit while the inventor put his skills to use inventing new steam pumps for the Wanlockhead and other mines. The *Charlotte Dundas* was named after his new sponsor, and made its debut on the Forth and Clyde Canal in January 1803. This was a steamship which did its job perfectly, towing barges efficiently and speedily. But there was prejudice. The canal shareholders feared that the water disturbance caused by the paddles would erode the banks and the boat was never used for anything except dredging — and without its engine.

Symington, alas, was no business man. Nor did he have that magical ingredient — luck, Henry Bell in Scotland and Robert Fulton in America operated the first commercially successful steamships. Symington didn't even get the state pension he hoped for. All he got for his discovery was the sum of £150, and he died a poor man at the age of sixty-seven. His greatness lives on.

Now I moved up to Wanlockhead, and had the good luck to meet industrial archaeologist Mr Geoff Downs Rose, one of the leading lights of the Wanlockhead Museum Trust. He gave me a conducted tour of the walkway which has been devised to show visitors the layout of the village in relation to the mines. It proved so popular last summer that the little pamphlet and map which goes with it were sold out.

First we looked at the museum in a wee cottage of Gold Scars Row, containing just the right amount of exhibition material and a model showing the veins at different levels inside the hills which penetrate to a depth of 600 fathoms, good graphic stuff, with wee figures of miners at different levels, giving it scale. A constant problem of working underground was flooding, so there is a working model of a beam-engine showing how the early engineers used water from above to pump out water below ground by the use of aqueducts and buckets.

The minerals, in the form of silver, lead and gold, and the tools used to extract them, are all here, together with photographs of great historical interest. Next we visited the library, founded in 1756 as a reading society like that in Leadhills.

And we had a look at the very first school built in 1750 a scheduled building which is now a thriving community centre doubling up as an outdoor centre in summer. Farther down we came to the mine workings and went underground — crawling 400 yards inside the hill by torchlight, following the dank twists and turns of a rock passage blasted out of the hill by gunpowder and cleared every inch of the way by shovel.

It was good to straighten up and breathe fresh air again after an hour inside. We had a look at the smelt mill, where Job Creation men and boys were restoring the foundations to show ore hearths and the water-wheel pit. I wanted to talk to some old miners, and was introduced to Joe Scott, who took me to see his father and his Uncle Wull, who had begun together in the Wanlock mine at the age of sixteen.

Sanny Scott, who is now nearly eighty, described the work in one vehement word. "Slavery!" I wish I could write his pure Scots Doric, but I can't. "What else was it?" he demanded of Wull rhetorically. "You even had to buy your own gunpowder, blasting, shovelling, hauling, hard, dangerous work for 27s 6d a week, and on constant shift system, day and night."

Wull nodded his assent. "So you've no good word to say for it at all?" I asked. "What about comradeship?"

"Aye," he said, his face lighting up. "There was plenty of that. In the mine you had to depend on your mates. You worked as a team of six, and you were on a piece-work bargain so you had to pull your weight. There was always danger, and you had to trust one another and depend on each other."

"What about Wanlockhead as a place to live?" I asked them. "There's no place like it," they both agreed. "You're never lonely, and you never weary. We've a club. There's always something going on, even if it's only the weather. You can be in the clouds and you can be above them in this place. We had a great time when we were young, quoiting, fishing, curling, looking for gold in the burns, wandering the hill."

Sanny's son Joe shares his enthusiasm for living in Wanlockhead although there are snags. "We've no school in the village now. My son goes to Leadhills, and there's not much in the way of work. Most of the people in the two villages commute by car to their jobs. I'm lucky — I work at the Radar Station. It's great to be back here for I was a long time away at various jobs, some of them in Glasgow. My wife's from Cambuslang but she'd far rather live here."

We went up to the Radar Station to look on what Joe regards as the finest view in Scotland, down the narrows of the Enterkin Pass to the Nith. "The Deil's Chair — that's where I'd like to take you. Do you know its story?" I didn't.

"Well, you know about the Covenanters. This was a hot-bed of them, and they were determined to rescue a minister by the name of Mr Welch who was being taken from Dumfries jail to Edinburgh for trial. In these days of the 17th century, the three ways across the Lowthers were by the Dalveen, the Mennock and the Enterkin Passes, so the Covenanters had to watch all of them since they didn't know which one the dragoons would use.

"It fell to the Enterkin lads to carry out the rescue just above that very narrow bit you can see from here, where the hills squeeze down on the burn. The mist was in their favour that day. They could hear the dragoons but couldn't be seen and they took the troops by surprise, ordering them to give up their prisoners. The officer refused, but changed his mind when a shot sent a man and horse into the ravine. The Guard of twenty-eight gave up nine prisoners, and I can just imagine it all when I am down there."

I had the pleasure on a later visit of seeing it in the conditions that Joe likes best, when the hilltops stand above the clouds and the effect was of a white polar sea covering the entire low ground stretching unbroken to the south, while the hills of Beattock and the Clyde were clear.

Spectres in the Mist

Crisp, clear, settled weather in March is not all that common in the north-west Highlands, and here we are in an empty house under the rock ridge of An Teallach. Across the wide river are tracks that cross the wildest bit of roadless Scotland to Loch Maree.

At 6.30 a.m. I look out on mountain tops flushed crimson in the first glow of sunrise, but the shadowy glen is white with frost. I shout to Iain to come out to see it. He tells me to take its picture and show it to him afterwards. I get the ham and eggs on and we are away by 8 a.m., removing our stockings but wearing our boots to wade the freezing river.

Our path takes us into Gleann na Muice Beag and a no-man's land of small lochs then climbs to the crest of a pass where we have a snack before turning into the corrie of the Fuar Loch Mor—the big cold loch—which sure enough has ice-floes on it. There is a bit of mist on the tops now, showers are developing, but we don't think there is anything serious in them. Anyway we both like effects of mist and sun.

We get them, and Brocken Spectres too as our shadows are projected on the drifting mist, each of us inside a personal halo of rainbow. We wave to ourselves and our shadows wave back, keeping pace in space as we stride along. The mist swirls and vast shapes come and go, peaks of Torridon and Loch Maree.

From the main summit precipices plunge steeply down, mostly Lewisian gneiss, the most ancient of all rock formations, clean cut and reliable for climbing. We have to search to find a gully down which we go to traverse back under the challenging buttress. We rope up and lead alternate pitches up a succession of interesting features, arête, groove, overhanging wall, and chimney, bringing us out exactly at our rucksacks.

We are reluctant to descend from such a wild spot. I think back to the family of MacRaes who used to live right below us, working the croft in the loneliest house in Scotland called Carn More. I stayed with them

95

forty-six years ago, and remember it as a house of fun and laughter.

The sun dropping westward warns us that it is time to cut the talking, descend, and move back along the track if we are to ford the big river before dark. We make it comfortably, and with the fire lit in the grate and the soup and tinned stew warming we anticipate our meal with a relish that the best hotel chef could not improve upon.

Loud cracks from the tin roof as we lie in our sleeping bags tell us it is another frosty night, but we are snug, and the sun is up when we shoulder our rucksacks in the morning.

We had seen quite a few new things on our trip. The meadow pipits were back in the glens, the snipe was "drumming", a woodcock was "roding" and we'd watched its batlike flight. But the most thrilling sighting was reserved for the last, when a couple of little grey birds rose from the stones and I heard the jangle of song which says "wheatear", the first true summer migrant of the year.

ALONG THE SOLWAY

Now and then comes a day off sheer perfection, when the sun shines from sunrise to sunset. Against the red sky, a fantastic aerial display was taking place by what could only be called a cloud of starlings. The thousands of them were so tightly packed that they made a black, wavering mass through which no light penetrated.

Back and fore went this wavering shape like an enormous rugby football, far bigger in size than the trees and knoll below. You would not have guessed it was birds but for its ragged outside edges, until the football punctured and starlings began dropping out of it like air from a ballon as birds fell on trees and fields and covered telephone wires like strings of black beads. Only once before have I seen such a spectacular gathering of cavorting starlings and that was in Norfolk over the reed beds of Hickling Broad.

On that day when I saw the starlings I had travelled the whole length of the Solway coast from Ruthwell in the east by Caerlaverock and Kirkbean to Kippford. Nor was it all just for pleasure. It was a pilgrimage to the birthplaces of Jimmy and Ethyl Baird who lived in Glen Lyon, Perthshire, when I knew them. Jimmy was head deerstalker at Meggernie and was in his prime when he died suddenly. He always regarded himself as a "gooseman" because he was from Bankend, Caerlaverock. Ethyl was a Ruthwell girl, and she died six months after Jimmy.

I had never been to either village, though I had talked about them with the deceased often enough. Jimmy was a haaf-netter as well as a good shot and he loved the Solway. Ethyl was proud of the fact that the Ruthwell Cross in the village kirk is regarded as one of the finest early Christian monuments in existence.

Ethyl left Glen Lyon to take up house at Ruthwell with her young son, but died before she had a chance to occupy the white-washed cottage in the village street which was to be hers. It was while looking at the village in its quiet setting of fields where the public road ends, that a cottage door opened and a pleasant faced man asked me if I wanted to come in and look around the museum.

He was surprised to hear that I didn't even know there was a museum in the cottage which in the early nineteenth century became the very first penny bank.

He was suprised to hear, too, that I had never heard of Dr Henry Duncan, Parish minister of Ruthwell who began taking savings money from the parishioners and paying them interest on what they saved in this cottage which was the Friendly Society Hall. The date was 1810, and this museum celebrates the fact that it was the first savings bank of its kind to be based on sound financial principles, for until that time public banks would not take deposits of less than £10.

Mr Reid, the custodian, showed me the wooden box, like a little cupboard with drawers inside for holding the money, and he showed me some of the coins of the period. The census of 1811 shows the parish had only 1,184 people in it, but £151 was saved in that year, £176 in the next year, £241 in the third. By 1814 the bank had £1,164, which reveals how the savings habit caught on in an agricultural community where the average wage was under 10s. a week.

Henry Duncan, a son of the manse, was emerging for me as a very exceptional man, for he had studied banking in addition to attending three universities. He chose Ruthwell because the quiet life suited him, but with a sharp mind like his he was almost fated to become the Moderator of the General Assembly in 1839.

A lover of literature, writer, poet, antiquarian, student of banking, he was also Captain of the Ruthwell Volunteers when the Solway was a place of possible invasion by the French. It was also Duncan who rescued the Ruthwell Cross which had been cast down at the Reformation and lay in bits in the churchyard.

Duncan gathered together the pieces of the cross and had them erected in his manse garden. I knew the cross was now inside the parish church within an apse, specially built to enshrine it in the oldest building in South Scotland still in use as a Parish kirk. Collecting the key, it was a great moment when I stepped inside and saw for the first time this 1300-year-old cross. Lit by daylight from three roof-slits, the delicate sculpture on the tall tapering cross had a glory beyond my expectations.

Hewn from local sandstone and sculptured in panels, episodes of the life and death of Christ are portrayed. Scholars cannot account for its extraordinary quality, with its runes and vine-leaf tracery created in an age of barbarism. Blessings on the Rev. Gavin Young who disobeyed the order to destroy it in 1642, but let it fall into a specially prepared trench so that it would not be forgotten.

As for Henry Duncan who collected the thrown-out pieces and stood the cross up in his manse, he abandoned the Church of Scotland at the Disruption, and at the age of seventy gave up his living, moved into a tiny two-roomed cottage and preached his sermons in the open air — an individualist to the last.

It was an event for Ruthwell when in 1974 there came to the village the great, great, great grandson of their most famous man to open the Duncan Savings Bank Museum as a tribute to the Father of Savings Banks. Afterwards the party made their way to the old kirk and paid homage to the Great Cross he had rescued. For this occasion the local children dressed in 19th century costume and sang two of Dr Henry Duncan's popular songs, one about the joys of curling, and the other about the Ruthwell Volunteers. He was a lad of parts indeed.

Dr Duncan of Ruthwell was eighteen and was studying banking in Liverpool when another great lad of parts of the Solway died, John Paul, known to the world as Paul Jones, son of a gardener, who 133 years after his death, was elected to the USA's Hall of Fame. Motoring west along the sunny Solway coast that afternoon I suddenly remembered that Jones had been born at Kirkbean.

A villager told me to drive up to Arbigland and near the gate to the big house I would find the cottage where he was born. "Come in," said Mrs Dugan who occupies it. "This is the room where he was born, and we still use it as a bedroom. The house is to be taken over as a John Paul Jones Museum when another place is built for us. My husband works on the estate."

The gardener's son who was to become the greatest naval commander of all time went to sea when he was twelve, making voyages to America. He sailed on a slave ship for a time, then he changed his name from John Paul to Paul Jones. In 1775 he embraced the cause of the American colonies and began raids on Britain, taking or destroying merchant vessels, capturing the *HMS Drake* and founding the legend of a sea-faring Robin Hood.

Nor did he forget the Solway, for he knew all about the ports and landed on St Mary's Isle. It was the last time he was to set foot on Scottish soil, but he did return the family silver that his officers took, and in a letter to the Countess, explained his love of liberty and desire for peace. The latter sentiment is at odds with his determination, fearless courage and ferocity in battle.

From his family cottage at Kirkbean I followed the road round to Kippford where the tide was ebbing visibly on the narrow fiord of the Rough Firth. In the late sunshine of afternoon, the white houses of the village street and the gentle hills across the water had a tranquil quality peculiar to the Solway where fields and pastures of cattle go down to the sea. Tides here run with such speed that even as I looked I saw boats that were afloat become high and dry. Kippford is one of the best centres for sea-angling on the coast.

That delightful week-end on the Solway happened because I was at a wedding in Dumfries. A duty visit to Troon Arts Guild a fortnight later saw me down in that neighbourhood again, this time in exciting conditions of gale-force wind and rain. It was the transition from wild storm to bursts of sunshine which made it thrilling.

The change came at Turnberry, as we hit the coast, and a rainbow formed over a sea churned white like buttermilk, above which rose the black hulk of Ailsa Craig, looking infinitely higher than its 1,100ft. After that it was magic all the way, waves bursting on the rocks like shivered crystal, glimpses of Arran peaks, Ballantrae village sparkling on its headland, bracken rust-red on the hills. Then the next squall would blatter the windscreen.

In Glenn App, though, it was suddenly winter, as the rain changed to ball-bearings of hail, a blizzard of them blotting out visibility and forcing me to switch on headlights and reduce to a crawl. When it passed, everything was white.

Soon I was pulling into Bob Grieve's house at Cairnryan, where, from his window perch, he had been enjoying the squalls.

Next morning he introduced me to the most sylvan piece of country within easy reach of his home, Castle Kennedy and its White and Black Lochs, ringed by gently swelling hills and parkland. Here is elegance, in well-maintained lawns and woods, with paths wandering delightfully in a man-made landscape full of birds. Even on a windy day you could pick out the white pencil-stalk necks of great crested grebes on the water, and greylag geese which have sanctuary here.

Scotland is full of inexhaustible little worlds, and wherever you go there are stories. Take my quest for the grave of Jimmy and Ethyl Baird. I found it at Bankend, near Caerlaverock, but the man who directed me to it was a gamekeeper in Ruthwell. "Aye, Jimmy Baird," he said. "He was a keen haaf-netter, and he was very good. I used to buy salmon from him. His wife, Ethyl, used to live in that house over there before she got married. Her father was a farmworker."

In a wee country like ours, few country folk are forgotten.

An Old Arab Proverb

My friend Iain hates motor cars. He likes their convenience but doesn't begin to enjoy himself until his rucksack is packed with tent and food and he is on his way into roadless hills.

Now we were on our way along the wild eastern shore of Loch Maree where he was quoting me an Arab proverb that a man's soul can only go at the speed of a trotting camel. I could hardly hear him for the gale force wind and the noise of the waves.

The gusts were helping us along though, buffeting our backs, a big advantage when our packs weighed about 30lb apiece, containing tent and all the stuff you need for March camping. We were soon warmed up and enjoying the white horses on the water and the winding path lifting out of Glen Bianasdail past rickles of stones and green patches among the rocks which told of past crofting.

The target we had picked out on the map as a possible camp site was a narrow inlet of the loch. It was just a hunch Iain had that it could be a good spot. We were forced to climb high by the broken nature of the ground and suddenly it was below us, seen through a screen of oak trees stretching right down, giving perfect shelter and a turfy platform close to a burn. Tent down and the stove purring, we got the soup and the chops on, as happy with ourselves as a couple of scouts.

We were away by 9 a.m. in the sunshine of a perfect morning, threading silver birches and startling a herd of wild goats. Now and again we had to stop to pay homage to the new sights opening up across the loch, the skyline of the Torridon peaks above the Caledonian pines of Beinn Eighe; a sudden blizzard of white wings as over a hundred snowbuntings swirled in the air ahead of us musically calling; then a picturesque group of Highland ponies gazing down on us from knolls of red bracken

Next we came to the place marked on the map "Furnace", site of the first known ironworks in the Highlands. Dating back to 1600, it used the forest oaks to make charcoal and smelt the ore shipped from Cumberland. It was the beginning of an industry that swallowed up the woods of Loch Maree until ". . . the trees of it were spent." The only trees that remained were those too difficult to extract. The oaks of Loch Maree are the most westerly in Scotland.

Later as we climbed into the corrie formed between Slioch and Ben Lair in a short-cut to Loch Fada, we walked on the decomposing roots of trees strewn in the sphagnum moss, easy walking because the normally soft ground was frozen hard. Our idea had been to traverse round to the north side of Ben Lair and climb its great rock face. But the coldness of a strengthening wind changed our minds since we could use its force to help us to the summit from this side.

Soon we were forgetting the wind in the joyful clarity of grey rocks, bright lemon grasses, and island-spattered Loch Maree opening below us. It was even more perfect when we found a sheltered spot to have lunch, comfortably warmed by the sun. Neither of us had been on Ben Lair before, so it was a moment of revelation to top the crest and find ourselves looking on to the face of A'Mhaigean standing above the Fionn Loch, the remotest of all Munros.

This peak is short of Munro height, only 2,817ft., but it is built of Lewisian gneiss with huge buttresses of this clean climbing rock. On the north skyline stood the serrated skyline of An Teallach, with only footpaths penetrating the wilds between us and it, the sternest bit of true wilderness country remaining in Scotland, where the young Sir Frank Fraser Darling did his pioneer studies on red deer.

SUTHERLAND'S LAW

I had an intriguing letter not long ago from a place I had to look up in the gazetteer—Abriachan, Inverness-shire. In it there was a phrase about the wild rugged precipices of Loch Ness which caught my interest, for I didn't know of any. The letter read:

"I suppose I am mainly a small farmer or crofter but I do other things. I have created a small farm out of the wilderness, have built the house, steading etc. myself but the whole setting I think is rather unique. The house is separated from most of the land by a very fine and spectacular ravine, and to cross this I have rigged up a cable from which is suspended a little platform attached to a pulley.

"Every morning to feed my cattle I launch myself in space across the gorge and pull myself over. It occurred to me the other morning that I must be the only person east of the Andes going to work like this and thought that perhaps this unusual life style would be of interest to you, since the only other crossing of the gorge is by steps and a rope abseil which gets very iced up in winter and needs an ice-axe.

"This crossing is in the stronghold of the pine marten. Their tracks show up very distinctly, but I have only occasionally seen one. Badger and wildcat are here, and the fox is all too common. I'm not mad about publicity, but I really think it would be interesting for your readers to see how some people are living in remote places."

The letter was signed "Gordon Sutherland", whose name was familiar to me by repute, for I had heard of him often enough through one of his friends, who had time and again said I must meet him. "You'll have a lot in common," he had reiterated. "He's a keen cross-country skier. He's lived with the Lapps north of the Arctic Circle in the coldest months of the year. He speaks Norwegian fluently, he's a keen amateur botanist and geologist. As for Scotland there's hardly a corner he hasn't been in, Lowlands and Highlands."

I was intrigued, not only by the prospect of seeing a new place and meeting a mighty unusual crofter, but by what I learned by looking up Nigel Tranter's description of Abriachan in his *Queen's Scotland* series. ". . . a surprising place, in more ways than one. To be within a dozen miles· of Inverness, it is remarkably remote, in fact as in atmosphere. . ."

Perhaps I wouldn't go so far as to call it remote, but it certainly feels it the moment you make the awkward turn off the main A82 and face an abrupt climb on a single-track road where a gorge cuts the steep flank above Loch Ness. "Gordon's ravine," I registered in my mind, and when I saw a rough road leading over a make-shift cattle-grid with an unusual timber house beyond I thought it must be his. As I crunched along the drive, out came two barking dogs, a Border collie and a wee white terrier, followed by a tall rangy-looking man in a Norwegian pullover.

The voice that greeted me was soft and Scottish, the manner slightly shy. We walked over to the ravine for a look at his cable-way. "I got the idea from a colour photograph in an article about Peru in *The National Geographic Magazine*. I thought what a good thing it would be for me to save carrying fodder right round the gorge to the cattle. First I abseiled down into the gorge and made a ladder and fixed a rope. Then I found the best trees to take the wire cable. The idea then was to fix a winch and a pulley, attach the platform, then I'd be able to pull my hay over and cross back myself on the platform.

Gordon made it sound easy, but it looked pretty daunting to me with a drop of 80ft. or so below and a fair sag in the middle of the cable. "There's a wee bit of a trick in it," he said as he pulled in the platform and seated himself on the rough boards about the size of a kitchen table. At this point the wee terrier Lapka leapt between his legs, and away slid the pulley at a rare old lick with Gordon pulling hard on the thick manilla rope for the uphill bit on the far side. Then back he came smiling. "You can have a shot in the morning. It's time we had something to eat."

I volunteered to do the cooking while Gordon lit the fire and finished off a few chores. I liked the long low timber house, with its rooms all facing out beyond the plunging gorge to Loch Ness. The knotty pine wood lining gives it a typical old Norwegian log cabin finish inside, snug and practical with an open fire in the living room and a kitchen with a choice of gas or electric stoves. "It's all very home-made," grinned Gordon, "including that oak dining-room table we're going to eat off."

Over the meal and with a dram at the fireside I heard how he came to be here. "It was all very accidental. I was chatting at a gate with a very helpful local man, talking about crofting and saying how much this place appealed to me with its oak and birchwood gorge and steeply sloping fields, when he suggested I should make contact with the owner and try to buy the place since it wasn't being worked.

"The man who told me—Willie Grant, he's a good friend now—did me a good turn, for I got the place, fifty acres, and I was able to rent another fifty acres. There was no house on the croft, so I lived in my Land-Rover while I set about building what I thought was the cabin which would be my home. That's it across the drive on the higher site—I use it as a store and museum now. It would have done fine, but the Planning Authority didn't think it was up to standard. They said I would have to submit a plan for a proper dwelling house.

"It was quite a struggle to get them to agree to a timber house. They wanted natural material—concrete blocks, would you believe, but I

103

persisted, with the help of an architect friend, Calum Anton of Fortrose. They allowed it in the end, but wouldn't let me have the eaves I wanted which they thought unsuitable for the site. I dug holes in three feet of clay and rigged up a jib to lift Douglas firs from Atholl as uprights for the frame, and I got much of the timber from my old farm, Boreland at Kirkmichael, for six rooms, kitchen and bathroom, plasterboard and timber-lined.

"I've always been good with my hands, but I had great help from my friends, Jimmy Rattray and Dan Webster from Strathardle. Dan is a wonderful mason and Jimmy a first class joiner. A brilliant carpenter.. Jack Lowe came up from Strathardle too, in one of the worst weeks of January blizzards in 1976, to fix the roof structure. It was a killing job. We were soaked and frozen, but the difficult outside work was completed and on 1st April I moved in to a wood-lined house snug with a stove. A friend put in the electricity and I piped in water from a spring."

I asked him how the crofting had been going all this time. "I think you could say I was living on the breadline hoping I would get a break. I had made over my farm in Strathardle to my son, and I was working in sort of partnership with him. I would go down there, help with the hay and the sheep clipping, and take from his farm about two dozen suckled calves, yearlings, and buy another ten or so up here. I'd keep them for one more year and sell them in Inverness at quite a good profit. It's beautiful shelter here for the outwintering of cattle, not so good for sheep.

"That's what I've been doing over the last four years, but I've also been doing a bit of fish farming. I started breeding Arctic char in conjunction with the Highlands and Islands Development Board. The original stock came from Canada and it was quite successful. The method was to put fish into the tank for spawning, and in the autumn have a few thousand young ones to mature. Lots of fish were sent away from here, and I found out the pitfalls and disasters that can occur, attending the fish, feeding them, ensuring the pipes weren't choked or frozen, for it's death to the fish if the oxygen supply is cut off for as little as ten minutes."

I had a look at the big tanks in the morning and the water-supply pipes connecting them above the gorge. With the aid of a net Gordon lifted out a big fat char to show me. "They give a good return for the food expended, and I even put the midges to good use by placing a light over the tank. Thousands fell in.

"What I'd like to see in Scotland is a real char fishing industry as in Norway. Loch Ness is full of Arctic char, but being deep water feeders they have to be netted, and nets are not allowed by the land-owners. It could be a great cottage industry for crofters, if they were allowed to net the fish and raise them in tanks like mine. Solensjoen in Norwegian is just like a big Scottish loch and farmers there produce twelve tons of char every year, and it has been going on for centuries.

"I've got some eels in this other tank. If you look closely, with your eyes right down on the surface of the water, you'll see them draped round the pipes." I could see them clearly. "Eels could be another good crofting industry. Catching them is no problem, but the cost of getting them to the market alive is prohibitive. As you know, smoked eels are very popular, and if we had a place for smoking them we could do a bit of exporting."

I asked how they were caught. "You use conical traps about three feet long, and have long nets as leaders on the bottom to direct the eels into the traps. I can sell eels to local hotels, and char, too, if I have them. As a crofter fish-farmer I can make just enough to keep going with another side-line, geology. We can have a look at my mineral collection once you've had a walk around Abriachan."

So across the ravine we went, and I had the pleasure of swinging over the gorge in the swaying box, a lively swoop downwards into the dip, then a strenuous haul on the rope with Gordon assisting on the far bank. It was trickier to manage than I expected, because of the strength needed to hold the platform in place as you get off. Also, you have to steer round a tree jutting out from the steep gorge wall.

Behind us was an opening view over the deep slit of Loch Ness with the bulging peaks of the Monadliaths rising in the distance.

At roughly 750ft. above the loch we were in a big open sweep of high country dotted with crofts and covered with new forestry plantations, quite different from the snug corrie-like formation lower down. "The way I describe Abriachan is this," smiled Gordon. "On top are the hard-working crofters struggling hard to make a living. At the bottom are the retired crofters, and in the middle you have the stock-broker belt, those who live by commuting to Inverness, or who have holiday homes.

"I'd like you to meet Mrs Katharine Stewart who wrote a book about crofting in Abriachan twenty years ago and it's just been issued again. She and her husband had the dream of being crofters and gave up everything to buy a high place on the moor above the loch and for ten years they had a marvellously happy life which she described in *Croft in the Hills*. In the end the economics beat them. The financial returns were too low, and they had to let the fields while Mrs Stewart went back to her old job, commuting to Inverness to teach French."

What a pleasure it was to meet this lively little lady whose husband, sadly, died three years ago, but keeping her company were her two granddaughters. "Squeeze in through the books," said Mrs Stewart, who runs the tiny post-office and library, and whose life-time collection of books seems to occupy every corner of the house, including the floor.

"Yes," she said, "we were lucky to come into crofting when we did, when so many of the old crofters were still working in the fields. We saw the end of an era, when survival depended on ripened crops and fattened beasts. Now so much of the farming land is neglected or ploughed for forestry. My book is a tale of other times when this was a crofting community."

105

Sad thoughts, but she is not a sad woman, for she keeps her mind busy, writing dramatised history scripts for the BBC Education Service, and reader's of *The Scots Magazine* will have read her poetry (November 1979). Before we left we had a look at the nearby Folk Museum dealing with the crofting life of Abriachan which was a joint effort on the part of Katharine Stewart and the pupils of Inverness High School. What a fascinating collection of household and farming implements has been assembled from this crofting community, gathered together just in time!

Back at Gordon's house I was staggered at the range of his own geological collection, the result of travels from the Borders to Shetland and every hill district between. "The whole thing snowballed when I discovered I had a nose for minerals. It's a terrific thrill when wherever you go you can find things if you know where to look; in road-cuttings, scree slopes, eroded peat hags, quarries, mines, etc. I sell specimens to schools. I've taught at field centres and done work for museums. With the exception of Wavellite, found only on the Shiant Isles where I've not been yet, I have found pretty well every mineral that has been unearthed in Scotland and several new ones. More will be found, though, for half the Highlands hasn't been fully surveyed geologically."

It was the desire to find a Cairngorm stone which set him off, and the sheer beauty and variety of different forms of crystal he found were a revelation. He reckons his greatest bit of luck was finding the Heddle Boulder on Ben Bhreac near Tongue. This had been a mystery for a hundred years and was thought to be a legendary thing no longer in existence.

."One summer evening I thought I'd have a look for it. Five minutes from the road I saw a rabbit dash into a hole and went over. There was a little piece of rock showing and I recognised it as Amazonite. I scraped away the turf and heather and there was the Boulder containing more minerals than any other ever found in Scotland. The Amazonite was a clue because it doesn't occur anywhere else in Britain. I made the mistake of telling various people about it, including museums, which accounts for the boulder having been demolished by geological hammers."

Botany was his first love, and he feels a great affinity with his ancestor, Dr Robert Brown, who went to Australia as an unheard-of botanist and returned with a collection of over 4,000 plants largely unknown to science. He became the President of the Linnaean Society. "Yes, he climbed Lochnagar at the age of eighty-three," added Gordon. "Hope I can do the same if I ever reach that age."

Gordon's father was a farmer on Stronsay in the Orkneys, and Gordon has a memory of one gale which lifted the henhouse, blew it into the sea and left the hens sheltering in rabbit holes. Then, when he was eight or nine, the family moved to Old Meldrum to farm 250 acres of arable with a grieve and three pair of horse. "Up at four to take the cows in for the milk to be collected at six, it was extremely hard work," he recalls.

In 1938 he joined the Forestry Commission with the intention of taking a degree, but 1939 saw him in the Gordon Highlanders, training for war, and he recalled his first sight of Norway, a cliff towering blackly above the sea in the moonlight on a pre-dawn raid on a whaling factory with a task force whose job it was to blow it up and give cover to Norwegians they were taking off.

It was in hospital in Blairgowrie in 1948, being treated for a knee, cut open while timber felling with an axe, that he met his future wife and went back to his beginnings to become a farmer. He was first at Tom Breac on the slopes of Ben Lawers working with sheep mostly, then moved to Boreland to 60 acres or arable and 70 acres of hill at Kirkmichael. "It was quite a struggle, ploughing by horse, using a water-mill for threshing. Lots of hard work haymaking, cutting corn with the binder. But fuel was cheap and potatoes were a good cash crop.

"I had wonderful neighbours, and a wonderful wife, but I had also terrible mental frustration. So much of farming is tedious, mentally frustrating. My bent is towards biology and geology."

It raised a question in my mind. At Abriachan, Gordon has built a homestead for himself, planted trees, broken new ground, experimented with fish-farming, established a crofting routine. "Won't the old mental frustrations re-establish themselves, or do you think you can find complete satisfaction here?" I asked.

"I don't think I could say 'complete satisfaction'. I think crofting is a rewarding life in all but monetary return. I believe more and more people appreciate this, and I'm trying to find a way of making it pay. Sweden, Norway and Finland have done more to keep their small farmers going than we have. I think there is a future in crofting allied to such things as contract work thinning timber for the Forestry Commission, or fish-farming, Norwegian-style. At the moment it's tourism which helps, but it is seasonal. There has to be a way of earning enough cash to supplement the income from the croft."

Glissading Frogs and Hungry Herons

There I was with my old friend the shepherd, praising the wonderful warmth of Sunday and Monday, two of the warmest March days I have ever known, but he was shaking his head dolefully.

"We'll pay for it. I've seen it before, with the snow over my boots at the lambing time and myself wearing two jackets to keep out the cold," he said. Grudgingly however he admitted that there was a good growth of grass and he had never seen his ewes in better tid.

He brightened even more as a skylark began to sing and a curlew sent out its shivering notes as it planed down to land. He loves wildlife and many a talk we have had about it. He had a story for me today.

"I was standing there, and the dogs were at something in the bracken, when out came a wee red squirrel, straight to my leg and up my trouser to sit on my shoulder. I wondered if it was going to have my ear off, spitting like an angry cat at the dogs. I put my hand up and it didn't even put its teeth in me as I put it over the wall."

Frogs were the next subjects which cropped up when I bumped into a climbing friend who wanted to bet me that he had seen something which I had never seen. "Have you ever seen frogs glissading ten feet down a snowbank on their bellies?" I could only shake my head. "Well, that's what they were doing, one after the other to slide into a wee pond full of mating frogs, all burping away."

In fact the frogs were sliding down out of control, not doing it for sheer fun like playful otters who will go out of their way to find a glissade.

Which brings me to another query—this time from a keen bird man who had seen something entirely knew to him, twenty herons in a tight group all busily feeding in a marshy spot near the village of Campsie. "I've never seen so many herons together, what would they be getting— puddocks?" No doubt about it; they would be filling their pouches for regurgitation to their young in the nests near Lennox Castle.

Yes, early as it seems, the herons hatched their eggs in mid-March, having laid almost immediately on arrival in mid-February when the weather was mild, and no doubt they were heavily dependent on puddocks as food. Of course they eat all sorts of other prey as well, including watervoles and young rabbits. And in time they will be eating lots of young birds.

But what animal eats the herons? Golden eagles for one, as naturalist Dick Balharry discovered in the wild country of the Fionn Loch. Birds with an eyrie not far from a heronry showed a distinct appetite for the big grey birds, which are as big as themselves, and decimated the colony.

It was another contact, a vet from Blanefield, who set me thinking about another fish-eater, that most jewel-like of blue-green water birds, the kingfisher. He told me of one of these uncommon birds frequenting a little lochan near where he lives. I didn't go there, but decided to check out a section of the River Endrick where a pair nested successfully last year.

So this morning I took a walk down river, seeing dippers and grey wagtails, redshank and nesting mallard, but no kingfishers, until I followed the flight of an unknown small bird which led me to a perched kingfisher on a bare branch. I was watching it when it took off, whirring downstream, a stumpy short-tailed bird with a dagger bill sparking like a diamond in changing colours of blue and green and orange.

BUACHAILLE TO BEN LOMOND

"Where do all these people come from?" said Len. "You would think nobody did any work." "Including us?" I asked, since the day was Tuesday, in the middle of the June heat-wave, and here we were speeding north to Buachaille Etive Mor for the second time in four days. His remarks were evoked by the sight of so many sun-worshippers by every burn and bay from Loch Lomondside to Rannoch Moor.

Len had managed to snatch an additional day because he had been working over the May holiday, and the marvellous warmth and clarity of the previous Saturday had whetted his appetite. After the wettest May in meteorological history, we had almost given up hope of dry rocks. Then had come our good luck, to be on Buachaille Etive on the first day of summer.

This looked as if it was going to be a repeat, and car windows down, we were enjoying the fresh scents wafted into us from bluebells, May blossom, rowan and gorse, all at their brilliant best together, in a world of shimmering birches, oaks and beeches. I've never seen anything better than this!" exclaimed Len. He was almost running out of exclamations by the time we reached Ben Lui, rising above us with a thousand feet of unbroken snow in its corrie.

Then to Loch Tulla, floating snowy reflections from the Black Mount peaks; and when we stopped to pay homage we could hear the vibrant "reeling" of dunlin, and surprisingly, the "tuleep" of ringed plovers, the first time I have known them here.

Buachaille Etive Mor, its rocks shiny pink in the morning light, looked invitingly clean and face-washed as we slung our packs and started towards Great Gully.

The good weather and dryness of the past four days had filled Len with ambition. After our climbs on the Saturday he had talked longingly of Guerdon Grooves, a very exposed and delicate climb, so sustained at one point that the leader needs 150 feet of rope to reach a stance. He had asked me to bring my long Perlon rope.

I kept my apprehensions to myself as we scrambled up the rocks below our route, remembering that some of the best men known to me have retreated from this climb, indeed have had to "rope-off" it when failing to find a way. Len had done it once, and I did not know whether to be sorry or glad when, after scrutinising the buttress rising smoothly and without break for over 500ft., he pronounced it "hopeless." I could see why. The rocks were stained with gleaming patches of wet, on a route which has to be absolutely dry before there is any hope of ascent.

"Let's do 'Ledgeway' on Great Gully Buttress," Len suggested. "You take the first pitch. I'll lead the crux." Rock climbing has been rightly called "a baleful sport." I always find it so, especially when the first steps of a pitch are hard and unrelenting and I have to fight an inner voice of fear. Yet I never climb well without this "inner voice." It is rather like the moment of getting up to give an after-dinner speech. You may feel a sense of inadequacy for the task, but if you have given thought and preparation to the subject, then you will forget yourself as you begin to talk.

On the rocks, the mind takes over from the nerves, as the whole of your experience and training goes into the control and balance of the body, with an effect of exhilaration on your whole being. This pitch does not let up for forty feet, and when he joined me for his lead, I was glad to hear Len say he found it hard.

"Marvellous rock. The best in Glen Coe," he said as he traversed rightward from me. He could have added that it is also some of the steepest rock, and I saw the route was none too easy to find as he explored right and left before committing himself to a line that left the rope hanging clear in space behind him. Then he vanished from sight, behind a bulge, and in a short while I heard his "Come on."

The crux was where he had disappeared, a daunting place with an overhang pushing you out with its beak, and no holds for a pull-up until you make a delicate move up the smooth right wall, then you can swing boldly on to the nose and enjoy the thrill of your body tilting over the long drop below.

The next pitch was mine, right over Len's head, for a hundred feet of sheer climbing delight, never easy but never too hard. The route had us purring with pleasure, and after it we crossed over to Rannoch Wall, to the foot of the Grooved Arête, first climbed by John Cunningham and Bill Smith twenty-one years ago.

It was this amazing pair of climbers who pioneered Guerdon Grooves, setting a standard of achievement hitherto unknown on Scottish rock. Wherever their names are linked to a route, you can expect something technically exciting. This one is particularly elegant.

Len took the edge of the arête, which soars up for ninety feet of small holds, where every move depends on fine balance. The crux lies above, and this fell to me. The problem is to get round the crest of the arête into the groove beyond. I enjoyed it, but made the mistake of keeping too vertically to the crest above, until I found myself unable to proceed, so I had to climb down again—which was very much harder than the crux.

Now we coiled the rope and followed the Crowberry Ridge over the Tower to the summit of the mountain, basking in a sunlit world of peace and silence. Boots off we gave thanks in silent contemplation of the Lost Valley snows, still filling the cream jug between Bidian nam Bian and Stob Coire nan Lochan.

All too soon we were scrambling down the Curved Ridge, marvelling at the changes which four days of sun had wrought in the hanging garden beneath it, with clusters of buttery globe flowers, sprays of yellow roseroot, starry saxifrages amidst red campion and the white flowers of fleshy scurvy grass. We felt the world was a pretty good place as we took the winding track along the foot of the crags, stopping now and then to look up at the pink edges of soaring rocks which have given us such intense delight over the years.

I was hardly home before pressure was being put upon me by the village children to take them on "the climb." They were eager to take advantage of the good weather, and remembering the mist and drizzle we had on Ben Lawers last year, I felt their enthusiasm should be rewarded. So arrangements were made for Ben Lomond, and on the Saturday morning thirty-six of us set off for Rowardennan, one a mother of ten children making her first-ever climb.

We were away early, and the freshness of the air was a delight as we made up through the woods where wood warblers and redpolls were singing, then into the realm of skylarks and the thin piping of golden plover—a sort of dawn chorus, for the Ben was still wearing a night-jacket of cloud.

It disrobed just as the first of us reached the summit ridge, and within the next three-quarters of an hour the whole party were seated along the top, trying to capture any fragment of breeze to blow away the midges and clegs making the most of an unexpected feast. The visibility was getting better and better every moment as new peaks broke the morning mists.

Everybody was feeling pretty fresh, including Neil Brennan, aged four, who made so light of Ben Lawers and Ben Ghlas last year, then we all sang *Happy Birthday* for Gordon Barclay, who had just made six, and down we went, anticipating the pleasures of a dip or a paddle in the loch. Halfway down we began to meet toilers on the way up. In fact, we must have met well over a thousand potential "summiters" of all ages and sizes which shows the popularity of Ben Lomond on a fine day.

We were glad to get down and get hot feet into glittering water, to splash about while water-skiers twisted in silvers of curving spray as they made swings round sailing dinghies and sent waves bouncing over the bobbing heads of swimmers. Ah, yes, a scene of idyllic tranquillity with deckchairs spread in every bay, and on the warm rocks white skins burning red in their first frizzle.

It was a big moment when the paddle steamer, *Maid of the Loch,* drifted in, shining in new white paint and packed with passengers. These people had the right idea for a fine day which you might think of copying. But here is an even better one. Catch this boat, sail to Rowardennan, climb Ben Lomond, and board the boat again as it returns to Balloch. There is plenty of time for the climb if you catch the first sailing; and it involves no road walking or twisty lochside driving.

Five hours is ample for the path from Rowardennan to the top of Ben Lomond and back, but do not under-rate the hill. If the weather is bad, leave it for another day. It can be cold and stormy up there.

The Tarmachans

I wish I could find the words to describe the perfection of last Saturday at over 3,000ft. in the Tarmachans, enjoying warm sun and a refreshing wind along a mountain spine surrounded north, south, east, and west by the best of Central Scotland—lochs, bens, and glens.

My friend, the sheriff, who had not had such a day for some time, was enchanted by the brilliance of it all, the vividness of the light on the lemon grasses contrasting with the clean grey of mica schist, the sparkle of the snow ribbons under our feet, and the high lochans still frozen white.

I had set the sheriff a problem of judgement that morning. Since decision was his forte, I left it to him to decide whether to go rock climbing on his favourite mountain Buachaille Etive Mor, or accept the more liberal alternative of a hill wander beginning at the Lochan na Lairige high above Loch Tay offering a neat cirque of peaks.

So our first peak was Meall nan Tarmachan, 3,421ft., just two hours drive from Glasgow, and within minutes of setting out we were in the company of singing wheatears and parachuting meadow pipits under the steep rocky gully which I expected to be hanging in clumps of purple saxifrage, the first of all arctic-alpines to bloom on Scottish hills.

Yes, they were there, and so was the summer migrant I associate with this face of grey rock, the mountain blackbird known as the ring ouzel, distinguished by a white crescent flared across its breast. Its piercing "whee-whee-whee" called our attention to it.

Now we were getting close to the summit ridge, and it was a great moment to step into the sight of the hidden view, west the twin spires of Ben Cruachan, centre the peaks of Glen Coe, and beyond it the big snowy hump of Ben Nevis and the Mamores, familiar friends wherever we looked, especially Buachaille Etive Mor on which the sheriff looked lovingly.

Seated below the cairn in the warm sun we ate our "piece", sweeping our eyes from the hills of Callander to Ben Macdhui's snow patches. Now we were ready for the next summit, Meall Garbh, sharpest of the Tarmachans and set above snow tongues and a frozen lochan. Over the top and along its delightfully narrow crest it drops suddenly to a col beyond which is Beinn nan Eachan, 3,265ft.

The head of Loch Tay at Killin was right below us. Due north we could have made a nice descent to Bridge of Balgie in Glen Lyon. We struck in the latter direction along a ribbon of snow cornice, easy walking with

112

skylarks singing above us, until we entered a big ravine eastward, enjoying its cavernous snow depths, emerging on the glen floor, whose numerous pools were bubbling with mating frogs.

In one hour from Coire Raidhailt we were back at the car, faces hot with the burning sun and hearts light.

MURRAY'S WAY

". . . in the worst days of the war there shone most often before my eyes the clear vision of that evening on Nevis, when the snow plateau sparkled red at sunset, and of Glencoe, when the frozen towers of Bidian burned in the moon. In the last resort, it is the beauty of the mountain world in the inmost recesses that holds us spellbound, slaves until life ends."

The inmost recesses, those of the soul . . . In the whole corpus of Scottish mountain literature only one mountaineer could have expressed these sentiments so delicately. The quotation comes from *Mountaineering in Scotland,* and I was sitting at the fireside in the home of the man who wrote them in enemy prison camps, W. H. Murray, known to everybody as Bill.

I was in Bournemouth, working as a surveyor, when the book came out in 1947, and I knew I was reading a classic as adventure followed adventure with a dimension of action and powerful description that made you feel that you were one of his companions on the rope, so clearly was each character brought to life. Little did I know then that one day I would be off to the Himalaya with three of the men mentioned in the book, one of them Bill Murray himself.

Down the years we have retained contact, but this was the first time I had visited him at his home perched on the rocky shore of Loch Goil. Since that first book Bill has written nineteen more and won many honours. I suggested to him that it was time he wrote his autobiography since he has so much to say that nobody has heard yet, but the humorous glint in his blue eyes showed me he didn't take me seriously.

Tell me the background to your present life, for I've never really known despite the times we've had together."

For such a tall man, Bill has a small and narrow head, and the thoughtful expression has about the eyes the penetrating gaze of the hawk. He weighs his words carefully, and some people feel uncomfortable at the long pause between question and answer as he searches his mind for the precise choice. In this case the pause was broken by his wife Anne bringing in the morning coffee. Auburn-haired, tall and attractive, Anne is also a climber and writes sensitive poetry. We chatted as a trio about the oddities of the house which used to be a stable, where you go downstairs to the diningroom which used to hold a horse.

But Bill's mind had been working away in the background as we talked,

114

and when were were alone and settled down in armchairs he fired away with fluency.

"Until I was nineteen, mountains never entered my consciousness. Not until I overheard two men talking about a mountain called An Teallach. They were describing a thin, narrow ridge above the clouds with shafts of sunlight striking distant seas and islands. To me it was a positive revelation— a vision of a strange new world, here in Scotland, and not abroad.

"So one April day I went to the Cobbler. I wore my ordinary clothes, shoes, collar and tie. I went to the Cobbler because it was the only mountain I knew by name. There was hard, frozen snow in the corrie, and I kicked steps in it naturally since without an ice-axe it was the only way up. I was frightened by the consequences of a slip, but I got to the top of the centre peak. The rocks of the south peak were bare of snow, so I scrambled up. From the tops I saw a seascape of snowy mountains for the first time. The desire to be a mountaineer was born at that instant, but the idea that any one person could climb them all didn't seem possible.

"I joined the Scottish Youth Hostels Association. In these days of the mid-thirties there were innumerable small hostels, and for a year I climbed by myself, in the Trossachs, the Crianlarich hills, the Cairngorms and on Liathach in Glen Torridon. It was from people in the hostels that I first heard about mountain clubs, and as I wanted to be a rock-climber I joined the Junior Mountaineering Club of Scotland in 1935."

Bill was a trainee banker at this time, which was interesting enough to him, but he spent a lot of time writing short stories, mainly about people in ordinary human situations. "Even at school I wanted to be a writer, but such a career seemed impossible for a boy, because you need experience of life to be a writer."

He was to gain it in the next four years with the men who took him to the Crowberry Ridge and shocked him with its exposure, but exhilarated his mind with the totality of the experience. "I would say I was a naturally good mover on rock and soon came to enjoy the exposure, but what really drew me to winter climbing on the great routes was the nervous tension and suspense which kept building up until you reached the top. Then the relaxation and exhilaration."

Listen to this, after climbing the Crowberry Gully in January 1941 before going off to join the Middle East forces in Egypt. It was Bill's 80th ascent of the Buachaille Etive Mor, and at 7.15p.m. he and his companion R. G. Donaldson reached the summit after being stretched to the limit of their resources on ice-covered rock.

". . . The ring of low crags under the summit, the ground beneath our feet, and all the rocks around were buried in ice crystals. Although night had fallen, yet up there so close to the sky there was not true darkness. A mysterious twilight like that of an old chapel at vespers, pervaded these highest slopes of Buachaille.

"We stood at the everlasting gates, and as so often happens at the close of a great climb, a profound silence came upon my mind, and paradoxically the silence was song and the diversity of things vanished. The mountains and the world and I were one. But that was not all: a strange and powerful feeling that something unknown was almost within my grasp, was trembling into vision, stayed with me until we reached the cairn, where it passed away.

"We went down to Glen Etive for the last time, and I fear we went sadly. The moon shone fitfully through ragged brown clouds."

Bill has no doubt at all in his mind that these pre-war years on the Scottish hills were his best, and that nothing that has come to him since in the Alps or on Everest has brought the ecstasy of climbing hard routes with well-tried companions when he was physically fittest and enthusiasm was highest. For him the men and the mountains came together at the right time. This is what he wrote in reflection as a prisoner of war.

"In three years of squalor in over-crowded prison camps, where misery gnawed at men's fortitude, these stored memories heartened me like 'a light for memory to turn to when it wants a beam on its face'; and youth, some-what crushed in warfare, revived hope for the future from inexhaustible mountain springs. That through mountains I have been given not only vivid memories but lasting joys and friendships more priceless than accumulations of gold, is no idle theory invented in credulous days of comfort and security, but a sure knowledge won in adversity."

"I was lucky to begin climbing when I did, in the same year as the new Glencoe road was opened, when you could buy second-hand cars for a song and pack in climbs with a frequency never before possible at week-ends."

I asked him what had brought him from Glasgow to such an out-of-the-way spot as Lochgoilhead, remembering the icy and twisting single-track I had descended from the summit of the Rest-and-be-Thankful by Glen Mor." After being demobbed, and having given up the bank to try to earn a living as a writer, I was determined to find an environment among growing and living things. I came to see this house on an April day when the cherry blossom was out and the sea loch Mediterranean blue. The view of the rocky hills through the window was enchanting. The rates were only £8 a year—they are £100 now. I bought it and moved here with my mother. I soon found, however, I had less time for writing in the country than in a Glasgow flat, for I now had 2½ acres of land and a house 100 years old that needed a lot of things done to it."

Lochgoilhead was a place to work, nor was its isolation irksome, for he was more often away than in it during the exploration years in Garhwal, in North-west Nepal, and on the Everest reconnaissance with Shipton,

116

finding the route up the Western Cwm by which the mountain was successfully climbed in 1953. Since 1969 he has led four trekking trips to Nepal, taking people to 18,000 feet, so he can hardly be said to be a stay-at-home even now.

He believes that it is important for a writer to get about. While a working writer certainly has the advantage over others of being relatively unaware of high rainfall and restricted views, he nevertheless requires the stimulus of change if he is to keep writing.

What of writing as a way of life after twenty books since 1947? "I'd never advise anyone to take it up as a career. You can earn a lot more with very much less mental stress if you work for an employer. Personally, I never worried until inflation started, but full-time writing is no longer economically viable by itself. You have to keep your mind in a money-earning groove, so one cannot write what one likes. To me the most enjoyable form of writing is fiction, using one's creative imagination, but unless you hit the jackpot the return from it in Britain doesn't justify it. You must have American sales. Of my six thrillers, two were not worth writing from the financial aspect.

"The chief pleasure for me of being a writer is the sharing of experience with a wider public, of events from which I have derived great enjoyment. A non-fiction book takes me two years to write, and I find the hardest aspect the planning of it. Once you have got this out of the way it's the library work that takes the time. The county library service is very good, but you have to spend days in Glasgow and Edinburgh filling loose-leaf notebooks with notes.

"For books like *The Islands of Western Scotland, The Companion Guide to the West Highlands of Scotland, The Hebrides,* and my most recent one, *The Scottish Highlands,* I get advice from experts on what to read about their subject, be it geology, archaeology or whatever. Then when I have written the stuff I send it to them for vetting.

"Looking back, I have no regrets. I think I have had a good life doing what I have done since I have no talent for any other occupation. Medicine is something I *might* have gone in for . . ." He left that statement unfinished, and I remembered how in the Himalaya he had devoted a lot of time to doctoring the sick who came to our camps. His two best-selling books to date are *The Story of Everest,* published in the year of the first ascent—a tale of the mountain from its first sighting to its eventual conquest. It sold 30,000 copies, and went into eight foreign translations, His *Companion Guide* is running second now at over 20,000 and still selling.

One of the more abstract jobs he undertook was to make a survey of the North for the National Trust for Scotland, resulting in a book called *Highland Landscape,* identifying the regions of supreme landscape value. It meant walking over the ground and assessing it against his personal experience of the territories over a period of thirty years.

In his conclusion he writes:

"The outstanding beauty of the Highland scene, which is one of the nation's great natural assets has been haphazardly expended and no account kept. The wasting away of this asset is bound to continue and to accelerate unless discrimination and control are brought to bear by some body created for the purpose and granted powers by the Government, so that checks and safeguards may be instituted. If action to that good end be not taken now, the Scottish people will lose by neglect what remains of their natural heritage."

Well, a body was formed, the Countryside Commission and Bill Murray has been a member of it for ten years. Alas, however, it is not an organisation of real power. Its work is mainly inspirational, and in the end it is the local authorities which call the tune. But Bill has made his voice heard, which is the reason why he became Chairman of the Scottish Countryside Activities Council, representing thirty organisations and 400,000 countryside users.

Until recently, he was Chairman of the Mountaineering Council for Scotland, which is the voice of all mountaineers to Government, and to all others having responsibility for mountain land. It works in partnership with the British Mountaineering Council of which Bill was vice-president. In addition to that he was President of the Scottish Mountaineering Club from 1962-64.

"I had to give up some of these posts because I wasn't getting enough time for writing or climbing. They've been very good for me. I've learned a lot and know the value of the work that has to be done if right decisions affecting the Scottish countryside are to be made. There are whole areas of Argyll where no conservation principles are being put into effect, and that includes Lochgoilhead."

Buachaille Etive Mor remains his most loved mountain. He also has, in his garden, a steep face of rock which even by the easiest way gives a severe problem that a few good climbers have failed to solve. Bill can still do it, "Because I know the holds," he confesses. Nowadays he seeks out more moderate climbs when he goes to the Buachaille, and winter ascents are by the easier gullies cutting steps in the old way. Not for him the modern style.

"If I were starting again I would be all for the special tools and techniques which enable you to climb steep ice as if you were on rock. To do it you need a lot of practice. But I have my reservations. Hamish MacInnes says it has taken a lot of fun out of winter climbing. My own view is that earlier climbers probably got a bigger kick with nothing more than nailed boots and axes than the modern generation get with advanced aids. And when you think of it, the pioneers who did the classic winter climbs on Nevis, Glencoe and other places published astonishingly little

118

detail about the routes. They minimised the difficulties which must have been considerable."

On mountains the need for constant vigilance on steep places is the hardest lesson to remember, and the one which even the best climbers forget at the cost of their lives. The danger is part of the fun. It breeds self-reliance, though Bill is sure the mountains cannot be used for character-building, for something goes astray the moment you try to organise.

Bill Murray is extremely glad that he started off alone, finding his own way. "I am sure I would have lost half my enthusiasm if I had been led by a qualified instructor." He joined a club when he was ready for it, and there he met the team-mates who formed the strongest climbing partnership of the '30's. He regards the clubs as being "Mountaineering's essential backbone—a framework on which tradition and development naturally hang and grow."

Bill's full title is Dr W. H. Murray, O.B.E., and he is the holder of the Mungo Park Medal of the Royal Scottish Geographical Society. For his book, *The Story of Everest,* he received the United States of America Educational Award. His topographical books are amongst the best that have been written in Scotland. Amongst his novels, I rate *Five Frontiers* the highest.

Ospreys Return in Force

All Fool's Day this year brought me one of the nicest surprises ever, the sight of an osprey perched upright on the rim of the tree-top eyrie in Perthshire where it reared two young last year. Pat picked it up at a mile range through binoculars and even at that distance we could see the white on its head and breast as it moved around.

We were on a green crest of meadow above a great spread of Forestry Commission spruces so dense as to be impenetrable. But Pat knew a cunning line round the perimeter of the wood and by devious windings across marsh and scrub we had just got the bird in close view when it took to the air beating high on broad chocolate coloured wings to come cork-screwing down on a carrion crow which cheekily landed on the eyrie.

I expected some fireworks at this invasion of privacy, but no. The osprey merely flew around, beating and gliding, dangling its long shanks occasionally, the sunlight flashing on its contrasting brown and white, the most unmistakable of all predatory birds.

In fact that was just one day after one of the famous pair at Loch Garten had arrived at the historic eyrie with a new mate, while across the country we knew of another pair in South Argyll which had arrived even earlier on 29 March, the day on which I heard my first summer migrant the chiff-chaff.

1980 was the best year for ospreys in Scotland with forty-one young reared from twenty successful eyries which is good news in bad times.

1 April gave us another bird which I hadn't seen for a long time and it's finding led us to a strange encounter. The bird was the orange finch with the white rump, known as the brambling, spotted by me high in a clump of ancient Spanish chestnut trees. And it was there we encountered a burly man whom we wished a good afternoon.

We passed a word or two about the fine weather when he said to me: "I've met you before you know. You probably won't remember me, but I've never forgotten your angry words. You told me I was fifty years behind the times in my outlook. I was a gamekeeper then and I met you on a path on my beat." He named the place and the encounter came back to my mind immediately.

"You've a good memory," I said. The circumstances were this. I was on a path where I had walked for a quarter of a century without interference when suddenly I was shouted at to get back the way I had come as this was private ground. Instead of turning back I walked on, compelling my challenger to run after me. I didn't like his belligerent manner and, in telling him so, must have used the phrase he remembered.

"I owe you an explanation," he said. "I wanted to turn you back because I had used a gin trap, which is illegal, to trap a fox and you were walking right towards it. I was frightened you would see it. I was always very sorry we had words for there are a lot of things I would like to have spoken to you about."

In fact I had learned more about him after our angry words than he supposed for he was very kind to two lonely old ladies who lived in a remote house which got few visitors. I kept in touch with them until their deaths and they told me how sorry he was to have made an enemy when he could have had a friend—which is the way of life, I suppose, caused in this case by the death of a fox.

THE LAND OF KNAPDALE

The trouble about driving to North Knapdale in brilliant weather is that before you can break into that complicated country of narrow lochs and headlands you have to pass through so many places where you want to stop. My wife certainly couldn't pass through cheery Inveraray when there was a display of arts and crafts in the kirk. And I could not turn away from Loch Fyne without calling at Ardrishaig to find out how the dry summer was doing with that most rural of waterways, the Crinan Canal.

"No bother," smiled Brian Adam who takes the cash and hands out lock-operating instructions to yachtsmen. Apart from the sea-lochs and swing bridges at top and bottom of the nine-mile canal, passengers do their own locking, sharing them with other craft where possible in order to conserve water, since it costs 65,000 gallons to make each opening.

Following the canal north, I turned east off the road a mile short of Cairnbaan at a sign to Achnabrek Farm, for there was something I very much wanted to see—the largest area of cup-and-ring marked stones in the British Isles. The farmer pointed out the place, about a quarter of a mile uphill and slightly left of the farm on a ridge of Forestry Commission spruces. We were there in ten minutes.

I have seen a few of the 300 listed cup-and-ring marked sites in Scotland, but nothing to equal the scribblings and indentations on these brown and grey slabs of inclined schist. Professor Alexander Thom of Oxford University has posed the questions. "Do they contain a message, or are they the beginning of a form of writing?" Here on this natural gallery of rock under my feet the artists of the past had really gone to work, inscribing not only concentric circles of various sizes, but overlapping them, dotting some with deep cups for centres, or scooping out whole series of cups. And from some of the circles vertical incisions were off-set like exclamation marks.

For over a hundred years petroglyphs of this cup-and-ring variety have been a puzzle, since they are not confined to Scotland but have a near world-wide distribution according to Ronald W. B. Morris, who, in the past thirteen years, has made them his special study and whose recent book, *The Prehistoric Rock Art of Argyll*, led me to this site.

Mercifully, the Forestry Commission did not surround this first of three collections with trees, so I could look out from the carvings on a sweep of Loch Fyne. Open views are characteristic where cup-and-ring markings occur, says Morris, and usually there is a view of the sea or estuary. Also, they are usually within six miles of places where copper or gold has been

121

worked. There was certainly plenty of copper around Kilmartin just round the corner, where I would have loitered to look at some of my favourite ancient momuments had it not been for the necessity of pressing off west if we were to reach Tayvallich before mid-evening.

I love the drive up from Cairnbaan following the canal and looking north over the strange sea-level flat of the Moine Mhor under rocky Dunadd, where the history of Scotland as a nation began with that Antrim tribe who made it their kingdom. And what a change of scene when you swing on to the B8025 at Bellanoch through a trench of dense conifers, continuing all the way along the narrow salt-water slit of Caol Scotnish!

Suddenly all is change again as from out of the conifers you swing into Loch a' Bhealaich and find yourself looking down on islets white with the wings of hovering terns, and across a horseshoe bay bright with the sails of boats, with the neat houses of Tayvallich ranged round an amphitheatre of rocky hills.

Everything conspired to make the moment of arrival a magic one: the richness of the early evening sunshine on the boats and the rocks and the water, the movement of three yachts curving in gracefully from the main artery of Loch Sween through the tern islets of this loveliest of the five heads of the long sea loch; the cool breeze which we were feeling for the first time that exceptionally hot day.

Tayvallich is derived from the Gaelic, *tigh*, house, and *bealach*, pass, and it's a perfect description, for in less than a mile through the hills you come to the Sound of Jura and the curve of a perfect bay called Carsaig. This was the place to camp, and there was plenty of room amidst spacious greenery with no more than the odd caravan or two on private sites. Nor were there more than twenty people on the beach.

Fine to get the tent down near the farm, cook a meal and eat it while watching the sun sink towards Jura, then set off through natural oaks to the ridge-top to watch the red ball make a path of crimson on the placid sea where eider ducks floated and terns fished. I enjoyed some good rock scrambling, too, before turning in at what passed for darkness on a cloudless night.

The heat of the sun woke us, and I had a stroll to enjoy the singing of the redpolls and sedge warblers flighting over the burial ground of the Campbells, where twites added a Hebridean touch to the scene. Tayvallich was hardly awake as we crossed the pass and turned right, continuing on the B8025 down the Linne Mhuirich, which could be called the thumb of Loch Sween, lying as it does at an angle to its other probing fingers.

Apart from a distant figure turning hay with a fork, we had the world and the narrow road to ourselves, and I was thinking of the once busy traffic of agile cattle that flowed up this way a hundred years ago, walking themselves to Crieff and Falkirk by way of Tayvallich, Kilmichael Glassary, then by Loch Awe and Loch Fyne.

The drovers had loaded the cattle at Lagg in Jura, sailing them six miles

122

across to land them at the end of our road, at Keills, where I was looking forward to seeing the old jetties. It came up to expectations, especially the north landing, built with long slabs of grey stone laid in such a way that you could climb by a rough staircase from the water to its now collapsing top. But the south jetty was intact and angled to allow the cattle to scramble up by an inclined ramp.

The boats were wherries of wide beam lined with heather on which the cattle stood, their heads secured to rings on the gunwhales. Road engineer John Mitchell, who got a lift in one of these boats, left us an account of his passage in his *Reminiscences:*

"At last we cleared the land. How the wind did roar, and how the cattle struggled to get their heads free! The extent of sail we carried was forcing the bow of the boat too deep into the sea, and there was fear of being swamped."

But the beasts could smell the grass, and as they neared Keills they were thrown overboard and swam the last bit to the jetty to scramble ashore. I found it easy to envisage the scene, and hear the shouts of the drovers and the barking of dogs as the cattle were formed for the march which might take nine or ten days.

South of the jetty the slim head-land of a peninsula was set weirdly with what looks like a long line of Druid standing stones. But they owe nothing to man. They are natural pinnacles of slate facing out to an island called Eilean Mor MacCormag, which local folk believe to be haunted. The haunting is said to stem from the murder of a holy man by looters whose black galley still sails round this island of St Abban who died in the 7th century. There are remnants of an early church and beehive cells, and a cross-shaft nearby is thought to mark his grave.

Eilean Mor was Abban's refuge, but Keills on this peninsula was where he taught the Christian faith. All that remains to show its former importance is a medieval chapel used as a museum for worn carved stones, and above it a 9th century Celtic cross. The Solway pirate Paul Jones is said to have been hereabouts in 1779, no doubt waging war on British vessels and taking prizes between Eilean Mor and Ireland.

To explore further it was necessary to go back to Tayvallich and drive northward through the Knapdale Forest to turn the five heads of Loch Sween in order to come down its eastern side. At the road junction I took a look inside the forestry centre. Its maps and diagrams showed five marked walks in something like thirteen square miles of Sitka and Norway spruce plantings. I learned, too, that the staff is thirty-three, and the annual output of timber is 20,000 tonnes, enough to build 500 houses.

We had not gone very far before I met one of the buyers of local timber, Mr L. Moir, who was bending over some green painted wooden trays on the shore. I went over for a chat. "I'm laying down seed oysters. We rear them, and we have about quarter of a million coming to maturity in this bit of water. We hope to raise the figure to ten million if the starfish will let us. An oyster takes about three seasons to complete its growth, and as we started only four years ago, we are just beginning to harvest the crop. Walk across to the island and you'll see our second consignment just about to go off to the South."

He handed me over to sales director Mr A. Hopegood, who took me across the tidal strip to the operation base at Seaween Farms. "The name is a mixture of sea and sween after the loch. This is the product." In a box in front of me was an unappetising-looking mess of warty brown objects. Mr Hopegood took one up, put in the point of a penknife, prised it open and inside were two leaves of pearly flesh.

"Like to try it?" he invited, pouring off the surplus moisture, I shook my head, at which he swallowed with an appreciative look on his bespectacled face. "Lovely, but too expensive! The price at Billingsgate is £220 per 1,000. I'd like to see it come down for oysters deserve to be more popular. But it's the law of supply and demand. I'll take this lot to Colchester where they will sell for twenty pence apiece on the stalls. In 1962-63 the Portuguese oyster was wiped out in the Colchester area. These are Japanese oysters, equal if not superior to the native oyster. We buy the seed from a farm near Connel, and the great advantage of rearing them here is the purity of the water. Experts who know oysters say they have never tasted better. Loch Sween is dead right for us because of its great length, and the way the temperature builds up in a narrow head like this. It makes it rich in phyto-plankton.

"But it's a high risk game because of the time the oysters take to grow, and all the time they are subject to predation by starfish which we are learning to control. We have to, or they would clean us out. Both of us were planters in the Far East before turning to oysters. We were in the oil palm industry, so we are accustomed to overcoming natural problems by trial and error.

"We do everything ourselves, with the help of one employee. We buy in the wood, make the trays, put in the seed oysters, cover them with nylon netting, and sink them in racks fifteen to twenty feet below water. We inspect each tray five times a year by hauling them up, using a boom on a raft. The fresh seed you see there will be harvested two to three years from now."

I left him packing his oysters in bags topped with seaweed, ready to motor South, deliver the goods and do a bit of commercial travelling to open up new outlets. Present productivity is 1,000 a week, and the oysters will keep from seven to ten days out of water.

Twisting down the narrow road, we swung west at a sign pointing to Castle Sween. There was no sight of it until we turned a corner, and then there it was rising squarely behind a large camp and caravan site above a bay alive with what looked like sailing dinghies gone mad. In the keen breeze the coloured craft would shoot forward at high speed, then go about in a swift turn and come racing back with a manoeuvrability I had never seen before.

In fact, they were not boats but surfing boards with a keel and a sail, balanced by bodies in wet-suits who seemed to be able to make the craft do anything. I went down to find out about it and found that the sport had been introduced here for the first time this year, and that for £7.50 you could get a five-hour course of instruction or hire a wind-surfer for £4 for four hours.

One of the instructors described the technique. "It's mainly balance, though you do need a certain amount of strength in your fingers to manipulate the sail-bar."

I left him and made my way over to Castle Sween, the oldest castle in the West. I had not expected anything so impressive considering it was built between 1125 and 1135 by Somerled to help drive the Norsemen from Kintyre and Knapdale. Sween is derived from Suidhean, meaning warrior. The Vikings were defeated, and that success led to 300 years of rule by the kings and lords of Somerled's Clan Donald, whose base was Islay. Perched grandly on a sea-cliff with a floor space of seventy feet by fifty feet inside, the enormously thick-walled tower of Castle Sween was added to in the 13th century. It looks impregnable, but Robert the Bruce captured it twice in the 14th century and Alasdair MacDonald, fighting for Montrose against the Covenanters and the Campbells, burned and destroyed it in 1644.

I was sorry to find the inside of the castle being used for a football game by youngsters who could just as easily have played outside, which shows what comes when planners allow a camp and caravan park on both sides of a historic castle. Surely the bay used by surfers and dinghies would have sufficed without encroaching northward.

Back on the main road we drove to its end at Balimore, stopping en route to look at the 13th century chapel of Kilmory Knap, another of the sites of this name which honours St Maelrubha of Applecross. Restored as a museum, you open the thick oaken door with a huge iron key and find inside a collection of carved grave slabs and rare Celtic stones. In contrast, however, to the fine work done by the Department of the Environment, the junk lying about the steadings beside the chapel is a disgrace. The splendid MacMillan's Cross is a 15th century work of art, but it looks down on 20th century ugliness.

From the chapel a track runs down to the sands of Kilmory Bay, a blissful spot where we paddled our feet and later on as the evening cooled, watched another perfect sunset from the top of a hill. Now I could identify the silver slits of sea dividing the parallel headlands containing Loch Sween, while by contrast the eastern ridges inland shone pale white with quartzite.

What a strange country, with all the linear features flowing north-east

125

to south-west, the hard grits protruding from the grey schist like ribs. The very word Knapdale is derived from the Norse *Knapperdál,* meaning knobbly dale, a perfect description of its pointed hillocks.

Journey to Cape Wrath

The weather forecast said the morning would start misty but clear away to early sunshine, but little did we know what a superlative drive we were in for up the side of a Loch Lomond solidifying out of greyness into a series of enchanting visions.

All was intangible to begin with in the diffusing screen of mist, then the colour came burning through, lighting white cottages, gardens yellow with daffodils, feathery edges of green larches and silver birch, bracken browns and bays limpid with reflections.

We were actually keeping pace with the lifting of the mist, and the best visions held themselves to the last, where the crags and peaks of the Craigroyston shore were just emerging from great wedges of shimmering mist hung in space like steam from a kettle.

In Glen Falloch all was clear to Crianlarich, Glen Coe and Ben Nevis. We seemed to be still ahead of the traffic threading the lochs of the Great Glen, a suntrap of yellow whins and frothing blackthorn taking us to Drumnadrochit for the swing north to the Cromarty Firth and the climb across the Struie for the Kyle of Sutherland for Lairg.

Now we were on the single-track roads which span the chain of lochs running north-west to Laxford Bridge. No problems today along the eighteen miles of Loch Shin, fourth biggest loch in Scotland since hydro-electrification, and made more beautiful than it used to be by forestry. Then past snow patches gleaming on distant Ben More Assynt we came to Loch a' Griama leading to Loch Merkland, Loch More and Loch Stack.

No mistaking that we were getting close to some of the barest rock country in Scotland, with Arkle and Foinaven leaping up in pale quartzite screes, some of the roughest hill walking in Scotland, and on the other side the sharp point of Ben Stack—all classic deer forest and salmon fishing country. Loch Laxford where we met the sea is derived from the Norse word for salmon—lax.

This is where the most dramatic of the rock changes take place, with the ground erupting crests of Lewisian gneiss like waves of the sea, each little group of outcrops encircling dark lochans forcing me out for wee rock scrambles and looking out for red throated divers which are common here.

The warmth of the afternoon sun forced me to strip off, and it was this which set me thinking of leaving my wife with her friends in Rhiconich Hotel while I pushed off on foot into the hills to a place where I'd never been, to Sandwood Bay in the roadless hinterland between Loch Inchard and Cape Wrath.

126

There was no hope of reaching it and getting back before dark of course, not if I wanted to really enjoy it, but I had the kit for a bivouac, food, a sleeping bag and a portable stove.

No evening could have been better for seeing the wee crofting villages which perch so enchantingly all the way along Loch Inchard and beyond to the very end of the road. Ahead there is nothing but wild coast stretching to Cape Wrath a full sixteen difficult miles distant. For me the easiest way was to cut across a peat moor to begin with, then strike west for a pinnacle called Am Buachaille.

The bliss of reaching the edge of the great cliff as the sun was dropping into the Atlantic is something I won't forget in a hurry. But for the fulmar petrels, kittiwakes, razorbills, and some "birling" golden plover the darkening world was all mine. Darkening yes, but at the opposite side of the sky the big easter moon was silvering.

Snipe were drumming as I lit my stove and unrolled my sleeping bag for what was to be a chilly night, but one I would not have missed. The rest of the tale will have to keep, exploring perhaps the finest piece of coast in all Britain.

ORKNEY AND LAND OF HOPE

The biggest surprise I got in my three weeks on Mainland Orkney this summer was discovering its popularity with young outdoor folk. Kirkwall and Stromness seemed to be full of them. Where were they all staying? I found that most were in hostels, official and private, and some in organised camp sites. Many were foreign — French, Germans, Americans, Canadians, Scandinavians, and there was even a cycling family from the Faroes.

What was it they liked about Orkney? "It's a different world," a Californian law student told me. "You don't have to look for quiet here — it's all around you. And everybody's so friendly, Kirkwall and Stromness are like villages — there's hardly any traffic. And there's so much to see — the cathedral, pre-historic burial cairns and the stone-circles, and the way the farms are built. There's no poverty at all. This is how civilisation should be. They've got their values right in Orkney." A perceptive young man.

Another young lad took me into Brown's Hostel in Stromness, situated across the road from dairy, bakery and supermarket on the busiest part of the old-world street. We stepped straight into the small common-room-cum-kitchen. Tight-set with small tables it was an animated scene, with folk cooking, eating, reading, talking.

"I think you'd like it here," said my new-found friend who was from Glasgow. "There are no rules — you can come and go as you like. But anybody who is a nuisance is asked to leave — not by Mrs Brown but by the rest of us."

I had a look at the dormitories and the showers. It was all good value at a price comparable with the official Youth Hostels. The Stromness one had fifty-four beds and the one in Kirkwall has 100. There are other private hostels offering accommodation in Sandwick, Evie, Eday, South Ronaldsay and Hoy. In Birsay there is one that accommodates group parties only.

On this visit I chose to stay on farms mostly, as a way of getting to know how the folk were faring on the most agricultural of all the island groups in Scotland. The striking feature was the quality of the houses and the steadings. Modern machinery was everywhere and the whole land was greener than I remembered it. Nor was it imagination. New grass mixtures and clovers in conjunction with artificial manures, are enabling the land to carry more stock. The demand for beef cattle is brisk, and the present stock could be as high as 110,000 for all the Orkneys, I was told by an island vet.

In the Kirkwall Creamery I was delighted to find that my old friend Alastair Whyte was still manager having completed twenty-seven years in the post. "We have fewer farms supplying us, but they're bigger, so we are producing even more cheese and butter than ever before and still winning prizes for quality," he told me.

The statistics are that sixty-five farms supply about 14,000 gallons of milk a day in the summer, of which 10,000 are made into the famous Claymore butter, and 3000 into Orkney cheese. It's still not enough to meet the demand though.

Unlike Shetland the impact of oil on Orkney has been minimal since it's virtually confined to the terminal at Flotta at the end of the North Sea pipe-line where the oil is stored for loading on to tankers. The scale is small, and the economy has not been disrupted. The present fear of the Orkney folk centres on something else which could have a very damaging effect on their agriculture and way of life — uranium mining.

When the Islands Council banned exploration and the objection was upheld by the Secretary of State for Scotland, they thought they were safe from the threat. Not so. An attempt to bring in legislation against uranium exploration in Orkney failed in 1978, with the South and North of Scotland Electricity Boards objecting to the Council's policy. Orcadians number less than 18,000, and since almost every island has quantities of uranium, they fear their interests and way of life would be sacrificed if justifiable amounts of the nuclear fuel were found.

No right-minded person would deny the validity of their argument, but they represent a small interest when the E.E.C. finances half the cost of exploration for uranium. The Orkney Heritage Society has published "Shout About It" leaflets, and a "No Uranium" delegation lobbied MP's in Westminster during the summer. What a tragedy it would be if the economic balance of this happy and prosperous community were to be destroyed in this hideous way.

Sad thoughts to take away from islands that were looking their loveliest as I left the Bay of Skail and drove for a last look at Kirkwall with its cathedral and Bishop's Palace where Haco, last of the Viking sea kings, died after his defeat by the Scots on the Clyde.

No more than forty-eight hours later I stood overlooking the spot in Sutherland where King Haco anchored his fleet on Loch Eriboll and received an omen of ill before turning Cape Wrath on his fateful sail south. The place is where the Hope River enters the sea and the omen which affected Haco with misgivings was an October eclipse of the sun which turned the world dark.

The short course of the river from this narrow fresh-water loch shows that it was once an arm of the sea with proof of it in the 50 ft. and 100 ft. terraces of former beaches. The single track down its eastern shore was even narrower and more twisting than I expected, with few passing places, but it posed no problems for I had it to myself.

It was a strange day, overcast and grey, but with the tops only lightly veiled with shifting mist. Ben Hope looked good, its first 1,000ft. rising as a rocky step hung with birches, then levelling off to rise another 2,000ft. in a series of soaring rock ribs.

The roadside woods relieved the stark bleakness of the opposite shore which lacked character compared to the steepness of the escarpments running for miles on the Ben Hope side. I was looking out for the broch known as Dun Dornadilla above the brown swirl of the Strathmore River, and suddenly there it was.

It was hereabouts that the Sutherland bard Rob Donn Mackay was born in 1777. His famous song *In Praise of Glen Golly* came to my mind when I came to the rough track leading off to Gobernuisgach Lodge close to the foot of the glen of the song.

The first time I came here it was not along the road but across country from Ben Loyal. That was during the war, and I was on embarkation leave before being posted abroad.

Beginning at the base of Loch Loyal where I had left the Tongue mail bus, I'd shouldered my pack across country to an empty house on the edge of Loch an Dithreibh, a wild oval of water between Ben Hope and Ben Loyal. Three days later, having climbed them both, I struck south-west for Gobernuisgach, steering by compass over the peaty trackless country deep in mist. I remember the relief when I hit the track and saw the meeting of the glens where the lodge is sited.

In my hand now was the stained and tattered Ordnance Survey map I used that day, on paper, price 1/6. Yes, there was the footpath climbing away westward over the jumbled hills of the Reay Forest, disappearing out of sight. I remembered vividly the moment of getting over the other side for the ferocity of the rainstorm which blew up. Crouched under my army gas cape I "cooried doon" expecting such a wild drumming to ease off before long. The world was surely as black as the eclipse which presaged ill for King Haco but then came a sight I have never forgotten. Out of the murk stood the point of Ben Stack, shadow rather than substance, mighty as the Matterhorn, and below it dozens of rocky mounds encradling saucer gleams of lochans. It was a vision of Sutherland I have never had before or since. It didn't seem to belong to this world and I had a sense of loss in the suddenness of its passing as the vapours dispersed and the mystery vanished.

I was thoroughly soaked as I bounded down the pass towards a house marked "Lone" on the map. The name suggested my mood. I was in need of company and decided to go on to Airdchuillan in the hope of a dry comfortable doss for I had no tent. It was an inspirational move, for the Scobbie family, father, mother, son and daughter gave me the kind of welcome you can never forget, not just good food and lodgings but laughter and fun.

In my few days with them I forgot I was a soldier as I climbed everything in sight, played ping-pong at night and heard a wheen of good stories from a sharp-shooter of the First World War. Then came the time to catch the mail car to take me to the train at Lairg. In Glasgow I got a shock when I found I was a wanted man. My unit had been trying to recall me, and had put the police on my trail! My mother was worried stiff but I spoke on the telephone to my adjutant and came home smiling. The alarm had been called off and I was awarded two extra days to add to my fourteen spent in the hills.

You can appreciate why I was in no hurry now to leave the Cobernuisgach track as I mused on these memories, and another one. The time when I came back after the war with my pal Matt and returned to the Reay by walking through Glen Golly and over a pass into Strath Dionard. We found the glen was all that Rob Donn had described, a place of enchantment. Later, with another companion, we were to make the first important routes to be done on the great cliffs of that lonely strath of greenshank and black-throated divers.

Regretfully now I got back into the car and swung away south for Altnaharra on Loch Naver where the sun was shining and Ben Klibreck shining olive-green above the spruce plantations. After the track I had been on, the road to Lairg and Invershin felt almost a highway, but the new experience awaiting me was the crossing over the Cromarty Firth bridge.

It was more than just curiosity to see the new bridge and the broad connecting road linking it that took me this way. It was by way of being a pilgrimage to see again the barn that the writer, Jane Duncan, converted into a home in her beloved Jemimaville, and to go to the nearby cemetery where she lies buried.

It had been my good fortune to meet the author and work as a photographer with her on an article about the village. The piece was entitled "Postmark Poyntzfield" and she began it:

"In the Highlands there is a district called the Black Isle which is neither black nor an island, and in the Black Isle there is a village Post Office called Poyntzfield which is not the name of a village."

The article appeared in October 1965, and until my meeting with the writer, I had never looked at the Black Isle very carefully. Now here I was again outside the double-storied house with the name "Old Store" on the wrought iron gate. In her autobiographical book *Letter from Reachfar* she turned the pages back to her early days in Dumbarton and abroad and then told how she came back here as a widow when she was beginning to make her mark as a writer.

The Black Isle could scarcely have looked better than it did on this recent visit, living up to Jane Duncan's description of it as "an ordered land of comely farms which contain some of the best agricultural land in Scotland". I didn't know how lucky I was with the weather until I crossed the Kessock Ferry and headed south, driving into heavy rain as I sped down the refurbished and fast A9 for Perth. Fatigue was setting in by Kincraig so I put in for the night.

The Spey valley is normally more bracing than the west, but it had a soporific quality following the rain as the morning sun dispersed the mist and brought out scents of heather and pines, putting a burnish on the grey rocks and a touch of blue on the gently winding Spey. Loch Insh, reflecting gay coloured fibre-glass canoes and the bright sails of dinghies, was just coming to recreational life as I took the back road which winds through the birches by Insh and Tromie Bridge to Ruthven Barracks.

A day is a long time in a motor car. I can't stand it, so at Pitlochry I was glad to turn off and make a cross-country dash across to Newtyle and simmer down with friends in a farmhouse on the sunny slopes of the Sidlaws.

For farming this is a country that has everything — good hills for sheep and easy enough to shepherd them from a Land-Rover, big fields of barley, lush fields for cattle and orchards for fruit. In an easy walk I could look across to the blue point of Schiehallion and sweep from Ben Lawers round to the Fife Lomonds, or across to Kirriemuir and the glens rising behind to the Grampians.

I chose to leave late and drive home to Gartocharn on Loch Lomondside in the light of a full moon. The roads were quiet and the huge bulk of Ben Lomond was hard black against the luminescent sky as I turned the key in the door. It was good to be away but I was glad to be back. For me it had been a good summer. To be truthful, I can't really remember a bad one, not in a country like ours that has so many places that are so different.

The Sandwood Shepherd

I do not know anything about transcendental meditation but I do know the absolute peace of mind you get from being alone on the edge of a great sea-cliff looking out on a headland with nothing but sea between it and the North Pole.

In my last short piece I wrote about being there at the time when a red sun was dropping into the Atlantic and the Easter moon rising and silvering in the sky.

Sandwood Bay became lit by the last embers of the declining sun on a curve of softly lit sand two miles across, laced with the white edges of breaking waves, and behind it the succession of cliffy headlands extending in rock ribs to Cape Wrath.

Just to be there at such a time was as near bliss as anything I am likely to find on this earth. I can't say I slept soundly, which was just as well, for I saw the sun light my world first as a yellow point of light like a lantern becoming an edge hoisted into a great ball whose warmth was a great comfort for it was very cold. Then I lit the stove, fried a couple of bits of bacon, put them on a sandwich and brewed some tea.

Unlike my awakening at home, there was no dawn chorus of birds. In fact, the all-night-long drumming of snipe and the birling of golden plover stopped at dawn. The only sounds were of the waves breaking far below me.

By craning my neck I could see the pinnacle of Am Buachaille which has a special significance for me. My friend Tom Patey had climbed it three years before his death when he fell from a formidable sea stack east of Cape Wrath at Whiten Head, Loch Eriboll.

Tom had done his last big rock climb with me just before he was killed. That was on the Cioch of Applecross when he tried to persuade me to come with him to Loch Eriboll and attempt another virgin rock stack. It was then he had told me of the tremendous adventure of climbing Am Buachaille. This has been called one of the finest discoveries of an outstanding climber.

In my mind's eye I could see Tom and his two companions manhandling an odd piece of equipment four miles over the hills, two long alloy ladders not to reach up to the pinnacle, but to lay across a dangerous channel between seashore and pinnacle, for Tom had more fear of the sea than the rocks.

A meticulous planner. Tom had timed things for low tide which would give the party four hours to cross the sea channel, climb the pinnacle, and get down before the ladders were awash.

It must have been a tremendous adventure, and I can almost see the grin on Tom's face crossing the ladders and thrusting himself into the attack for he loved a good grapple on crags and overhangs.

The proof of success was before me. I could see bits of mouldering rope anchored as belay points, loops of yellow nylon tape indicating the extraordinary route from overhanging base to the slender point of the sandstone rock needle.

Following the pink sandstone cliff edge, I had the company of gliding fulmar petrels all the way, these masters of air currents who can maintain a parallel and eye-level course without as much as a flap of a straight wing.

I knew I was getting close to Sandwood Bay by the roaring of the breaking seas on the vast curve of its sands. It was the perfect way to arrive, from a vantage point high enough to command its vast sweep, so charmingly gentle after the cliffy wilds, perhaps the kind of place where it would not be so surprising to meet a mermaid, as a local shepherd is reported to have done in the very corner I was approaching.

REMEMBERING TOM PATEY

On the jacket of the book in front of me there is a colour photograph of a climber swathed in awkward bundles of climbing rope, one hand on an ice-axe plunged into dangerous-looking powder snow, the other clutching a short second axe. From the body rope hang ice-screws and pitons, and the straps on the boots show he is wearing crampons. The strong face beneath the shock of snow-rimed hair is not smiling. The mouth is open in an interrogatory glance, elongating the lines on the cheeks almost to lantern jaws.

The man is Tom Patey, who crashed to his death on 25 May, 1970. *One Man's Mountains* is a collection of his best essays and verses, and they catch the spirit of the '50's and '60's as surely as Alastair Borthwick caught the '30's in his classic *Always a Little Further*.

I discussed this book with Tom when we climbed the Cioch Nose in Applecross together only a few days before he parted from his rope while abseiling from a sea stack called The Maiden at Whiten Head, on the remote north coast.

The day Tom died he was due to meet Olivia Gollancz, publisher of his book. They were going to discuss his work and he intended to resist any rewriting of it. "Because I've worked damn hard on these pieces, and I need the money now." Tom, the unashamed television climber, willing to take part in any B.B.C. circus for the fun as much as the reward, wrote the best of his work for sheer pleasure. And when he did write for money if was often to satirise "The Professionals."

The book shows the evolution of a climber from days of innocence when he was a shy and retiring schoolboy, to his extrovert singing and piano accordion playing on Aberdeen Climbing Club meets, when the bar-room jollity was as important as the climbing. His chapter "Cairngorm Commentary" catches the spirit of these times, and is, I think, one of the best pieces ever written on young men and mountains.

It was on Lochnagar that I first climbed with Tom Patey and his able partner Mike Taylor. Bill Brooker led a separate rope, and we all went to Eagle Ridge, narrowest and steepest of the ridges. As an introduction to rock climbing on Lochnagar it was a test of adhesion for me on holdless slippery granite, hands half frozen in the falling sleet. But Tom was exhuberant as he scraped, lunged, grunted, drawing breath only to extol some feature of the elegant route that I might be missing. By contrast Taylor looked meticulously controlled and demanded his right to lead some of the choicer pitches.

Tom put our ascent to good use by doing the climb again the following week-end when it was submerged in eight inches of powder snow. His companion was Tom Bourdillon, who happened to be giving a lecture on Everest in Aberdeen and found that a by-product of it was to be doing the hardest climb of his life with the reigning Tiger.

I remember on the Bealach nam Bo, as we sat in the car listening to the rain, asking Tom if he had regrets about being a doctor when he might have become a professional climber. His reply was vehement.

"I'd rather be a good doctor any day. Climbing is not a reason for living. Providing a good medical service to a remote region like Ullapool and the North-West is as important to me as any climbing. I've worked hard to build up that practice, and I've enjoyed it, though I'd like more time for climbing."

Then he confided to me his remarkable intention to solo the North Face of the Eiger that August. He reckoned from his past attempts with others that he needed only one good day to top the "greatest mixed route in Europe"—his words. His intention was to prepare the way so as to be able to go up in the dark when conditions were right, using his exceptional speed to forge up the dangerous upper part at break of day, before the stonefall barrage could begin.

Why did he want to do a route that had been done over a hundred times before, when he was such a pioneer of new ways? "Because it has every problem in climbing heaped on top of each other. The big objection to it is the time it takes—so you are liable to be caught out by the weather. Get up it before the stuff starts to fall and you have only gravity to contend with. Every day you are up there lessens your chance of staying alive. And I want to live." Six days later, Tom was dead and Ullapool had lost a good doctor. Winner of the Gold Medal for Physiology in his second year at university, he could have gone very far in medicine had he given free reign to his academic abilities.

Good G.P. though he was, Patey had in him a tough, almost a callous streak, a demand that his friends be as hard as he was. Before he graduated I was due to give a lecture in Aberdeen, but collapsed with flu on the eve of departure from Glasgow. The doctor was called and pronounced me unfit to travel. "Under no circumstances must you go," he warned.

I phoned Adam Watson with the bad news. He was sympathetic. Somebody else would have to be found to take my place. An hour later the ebullient Patey was on the line, assuring me that most doctors were fools, that a man like myself shouldn't be stopped by anything so trivial as flu . . .

So I arrived in Aberdeen. Gave my talk, was whisked about from one house to another afterwards, and finally driven to Ellon in a snowstorm to arrive in the early hours of the morning at a stone-cold house. What Patey did not tell me was that his parents were away and that the house had been lying empty for the last three weeks. The bed was like an ice-box.

135

Yet I enjoyed myself, watching him sit down at the piano the moment we came into the house and, between songs, hearing him enthuse about climbs he had done and was going to do. The fact is that Patey had a way of expanding you with his presence. Our eighteen years of age difference disappeared.

The University Lairig Club flourished then as never before or since with upwards of seventy members attending climbing meets. Many came for the jollity, though nearly all enjoyed a little fresh air prior to the evening's entertainment. I have never been a lover of big parties, so I was rather shaken when Tom joined us one New Year, with what looked like one of these meets of lads and lasses. And they brought with them a potent concoction of spirits, and as Tom took liberal swigs between dance numbers, his agile fingers became livelier and livelier on the accordion. He was still playing when most of the dancers had collapsed.

I don't know when he went to bed. But he was with us in the morning for a climb which he declared to be a new route. True, he looked terrible, pale as a ghost and racked by a cough. But this was not abnormal. The cough came from smoking, the face belied a man with so much stamina that when alone in the Cairngorms, he frequently ran to the crags, punched a few hard routes and jogged back again.

There is a question-and-answer song about Tom.

How does he climb, solo and so briskly?
On twenty fags a day, and Scotland's good malt whisky?

Tom's own satirical songs published in the book are subtly delightful, especially his *Alpine Club Song.*

> Our climbing leaders are no fools,
> They went to the very best Public Schools
> You'll never go wrong with Everest Men,
> So we select them again and again,
> Again and again and again and again.
> You won't go wrong with Everest Men,
> They went to the very best Public Schools,
> They play the game, they know the rules.

Listen to the *Hamish MacInnes's Mountain Patrol* song.

> Gillies and shepherds are shouting Bravo,
> For Hamish MacInnes, the Pride of Glencoe.
> There'll be no mercy mission no marathon slog
> Just lift your receiver and ask them for DOG.
>
> They come from their Kennels to answer the call,
> Cool, calm and courageous the Canine Patrol.
> Sniffing the boulders and scratching the snow,
> They've left their mark on each crag in the Coe &c.

All sorts of characters are mirrored in the verses with an economy that any writer would envy: Bill Murray of the '30's. Chris Bonnington and Joe Brown of the '60's, the stuffier members of the Cairngorm Club; none with wickedness, for Tom was essentially a kindly man, however hard his exterior. For example, I offended him once by writing an ill-chosen phrase which made it look as if I numbered him among the vain-glorious whom I was criticising. He could have satirised me and made me look a fool. He merely told me I was, but accepted my explanation and we remained friends.

He was a son of the manse. But I never heard him talk about God until our last day in Applecross. He opened his heart on many things as we talked in the car. Tom had no conventional religion, but he believed that the good in man lived on after he was dead, therefore there must be an all-seeing God. We talked about the Himalaya, the Mustagh Tower, Rakaposhi, and the Norwegian routes he had been making with Joe Brown. None of them shone for him so much as his early days with his Aberdeen friends.

He did not think it was sentiment. In these early years all of them were true mountain explorers, opening up new corners of Scotland for the very first time. With the rapid sophistication of climbing and its organisation in the '60's something simple and joyous had vanished. There was too much emphasis on reputation, too much talk about character-building.

Freddy Malcolm and his friend "Sticker" are recalled in the book. They were the leaders of a tiny group of working lads who called themselves the Kincorth Club. As Tom says, they came to regard Beinn a' Bhuird as club property and built a subterranean "Howff" on its flank. I was proud to be asked to be their hon. president.

These boys had a quiet style, so quiet that "night after night their torchlit safaris trod stealthily past the Laird's very door, shouldering mighty beams of timber, sections of stove-piping and sheets of corrugated iron. The Howff records the opening ceremony: 'This howff was constructed in the Year of Our Lord 1954, by the Kincorth Club, for the Kincorth Club. All climbers please leave names, and location of intended climbs; female climbers please leave names, addresses and telephone numbers.' "

No outdoor centre could turn out lads like these. They developed their own characters and became first-class performers in any Cairngorm climbing situation, and most of their winter pioneering of hard routes was done in the remotest corries. They knew what they were doing.

This is how Patey sums up his companions of his Cairngorm days:

"The North-East climbers of the early '50's were all individualists, but never rock fanatics. There are no crags in the Cairngorms with easy reach of a motorable road and a typical climbing week-end savoured more of an expedition than of acrobatics. If the weather turned unfavourable, then a long hill walk took the place of the planned climb. All the bothies were well patronised—Luibeg, Lochend, Gelder Shiel, Bynack, the Geldie bothies, Altanour, Corrour and, of course, the Shelter Stone. At one and all you would be assured of friendly company round the fire in the evenings. Everybody knew everybody."

But even the more halycon days had their shadows as Tom recounts, "when in August 1953 Bill Stewart fell to his death on Parallel Gully 'B.' Although his initial slip was a mere six feet, the rope sliced through on a sharp flake of rock and he fell all the way to the corrie floor. It was a cruel twist of fate to overtake such a brilliant young climber, and for many of the 'faithful' it soured the love of the hills they had shared with him.

"The majority of the old brigade took to hill walking and ski-ing, where they could forget unhappy memories and still enjoy the camaraderie of the hills."

But the impetus to make new routes, though by a smaller number of climbers, went on, and rich harvests were reaped by the "faithful." The Aberdeen boys were no stay-at-homes. Patey's men broke new ground in Applecross and Skye, laying siege to Alpine peaks of increasing difficulty season by season. Serving in the Royal Navy from 1957 to 1961, Tom was attached to Royal Marine Commando, thus had plenty of scope in a unit practising mountain warfare at home and abroad. Marriage could not have been very easy for his wife Betty, for a climbing genius is not the most restful man to live with.

Just look at his record over his last half-dozen years, with his assaults on Atlantic rock stacks and forays into every corner of the North-West, including the first winter traverse of the Cuillin of Skye, with a night out on the ridge. Then in 1970 he did what I think is probably the boldest piece of solo climbing in the history of Scottish mountaineering by crossing the great wall of Creag Meaghaidh, in 8,500ft. of traversing in bold situations "unrivalled in Scottish winter climbing."

I know of no one who thought it could be done in a single day, yet Tom, starting around a normal lunch time, finished it in five hours in conditions which were ". . . far from ideal—an unusual amount of black ice and heavy aprons of unstable wind-slab."

But as he says in the book, it was one of these days when a climber is caught up in his own impetus. One description made my stomach turn over in the sheer horror of the situation. He had made a false move and was trying to rectify it when the wind-slab ledge "suddenly heeled off into space and I was left in the position of a praying mantis, crampon points digging into verglassed slabs. It was a moment of high drama—and horror— best contemplated in retrospect. Hanging on by one gloved fist jammed behind some frozen heather roots, I had to extract a small ring spike from my pocket and batter it into the only visible crack. It went in hesitantly for an inch and seemed to bite. Then the crack went blind. Time was running out, as my supporting hand was rapidly losing sensation."

That piton simply had to hold him, and it did, as he used his teeth and free hand to thread the rope through it, then tested it by hanging free on it to try to pendulum on to a lower ledge from where he might continue the traverse.

What a situation! Suspended on an inch of iron which might or might not hold and certain death below if it failed. Even if it held he still had a problem of achieving a landing on the ledge. "If I missed it or swung off backwards I would be spinning in space with little prospect of regaining the cliff face. I arrived in a rush, sinking hands, knees and toes simultaneously into a mound of powder snow." He admits to "teeth-chattering." The way now lay open.

Perhaps you have dismissed Tom in your mind as a fool for exposing himself to such extremes of danger and difficulty when he had a wife, three children and the responsibilities of a scattered medical practice. Yet as Christopher Brasher so well expressed it in his Foreword to the book:

". . . What is a man if he does not explore himself; if he does not challenge the impossible?"

Handa is Strictly for the Birds

To be in the north-west of Sutherland with the sun shining and the famous bird island of Handa close-by gave me the notion of going there—if I could get a boatman to take me over.

So from the limit of the Cape Wrath road I motored south for Scourie, turning right along the tarred road winding down to Tarbet, perfectly described by its place name, on a peninsula between two stretches of water.

I'd been here before, twenty-three years ago, and I had a vision in my mind of this magical little crofting township of seven families perched among the rocks, overlooking a scatter of islets. In particular I remembered the old lady sitting by the roadside with her knitting who stood up to talk to us. "I'm watching my two cows keep on the grass and not go into the corn and the potatoes." And she pointed out the house of crofter-fisherman Donald MacLeod who would surely take me over to Handa.

Handa's special feature is its Great Stack, set sensationally between projecting arms of projecting cliff, every ledge of its sheer sided 350ft. so crammed with seabirds that even St Kilda cannot outshine its concentration, puffins whirling about like bees in a hive, kittiwakes squealing in thousands, guillemots like penguins crammed on every dizzy ledge, not to mention razorbills and fulmars. We had spent a magical two days on the island with the old bothy to ourselves.

The rock is pink Torridonian sandstone, vividly splashed with whitewash above blue sea and backed by the ever changing greys of Sutherland's quartzite hills.

I felt there could be an anti-climax in trying to repeat that magical experience for modernity has struck the crofting townships here as in other places. Tarbet has a car park and the former lobster fisherman's house is a restaurant. Handa itself is a Royal Society for the Protection of Birds Reserve. Thousands go to it. You pay a landing charge, and you must keep to a marked trail, laid with wooden boards over large stretches. The old house has been renovated, with a booking and paying system for RSPB guests. And the island is wardened in the interests of the birds.

No problem of getting over. A boat was on its way, and within an hour I was stepping on to a shell-sand bay and climbing past the old village to a height of 400ft. where suddenly the island ends on a cliff plunging to the sea. There in front is the Great Stack with narrow seas between enclosing headlands like a gorge.

This was the scene of one of the boldest pieces of cragsmanship in the history of birdfowling, when Donald MacDonald of Ness in Lewis went out on a rope suspended between the headlands swinging through space like an over-balanced tight-rope walker.

Donald was chosen for his strength and ability on the gannet cliff Sula Sgeir. He needed it here, and he was almost spent in the final landing struggle. Now he pulled across two stakes to make a block and tackle for a breeches-buoy so that the others could cross easily, bringing with them baskets and spare rope to raid the nearest ledges for guillemots and razorbills which are good eating.

The two stakes were driven into the grassy top of the stack in 1876 and remained a mute challenge, but no climber tried to repeat the rope-trick until Dr Tom Patey came along. He found he had to go out in space for 150ft. above a 350ft. drop into the sea. And, fit as he was, it took him forty-five minutes to make the crossing, all of it hard work despite modern engineering aids.

Patey described the crossing by Donald MacDonald as having no parallel in the history of cliff climbing, done as it was "without modern cheating devices"—Patey's words. Tom certainly got the bird on the Great Stack, from a fulmar petrel which sprayed him with foul smelling oil. There were no fulmars to worry MacDonald. In these far off days it was found only on St Kilda where it was a main item of diet.

IN THE GRAMPIANS ON SKIS

The snow was so shiningly crisp after a night of exceptionally sharp frost that we drove over the drifts rather than through them. "Not much wrong with that," said Iain as we stepped out at 1,800ft. into a world of sparkle and sunlight that had us screwing up our eyes. Far below us was Loch Tay, softly gleaming and edged with green in contrast to our arctic world where the peaks pricked the blue sky like icebergs. Even from here we could see the texture of the summit snows, and gleefully we forecast wind-packed powder as we strapped on sealskins to the soles of our skis, packed an ice-axe in case we had to cut steps, and set off up the glen for Beinn Ghlas, shouldering our skis at first until deepening powder made it easier to slide than sink in at every step.

Voices hailing us drew our eyes to holes in the snow. They were made by men of the 42nd Co. RASC, who had been sleeping out in them as part of an exercise in arctic warfare. They were able to tell us that the temperature was thirteen degrees below freezing point, so they were glad to be outside in the sun rather than inside in the cold.

The great basin opening up before us was like a glacier with all the moraine bumps smoothed and moulded by shadow. As we gained height we left this for a world of frothy snow, soft on top but ice-hard below. A mountain hare we disturbed was so weak that it hobbled rather than ran from us. My belief was that it was near starvation owing to the iron conditions binding the ground. Apart from a raven ragged as a vulture, the only other signs of life up here were snow buntings— not feeding, but just passing over on buoyant white wings; they were true snow sparrows, which would no doubt spend their day down at the stackyards on the lochside. What an encirclement of mountains lay round us, the cornice edges picked out by shadow from Glencoe to the Cairngorms, the remarkable evenness of the vast horizon testifying to its origin when all was a single piece of plateau. But we were in the wind now, and Iain was worried by some fast-moving clouds that had already submerged the peak of Ben Lawers, which was our destination after Beinn Ghlas.

Having arrived on the first top, he paused only long enough to strip off his sealskins, and before I had finished taking a photograph or two he was down at the col between the two peaks. What a delight it was to follow, swinging over the cornices of a switchback, then down an icy chute where the skis rasped on the turns before hitting again ball-bearing smooth powder for the final run-out to the flat beneath Ben Lawers. The rise from this col is steep, and our eyes were watering as we staggered up against the wind in a world of cloud and blowing spindrift. The temperature here must have been around zero, I reckoned, as the hands holding our skis on our shoulders froze in our gloves. Nor was it easy on the summit to fasten the bindings, and find the precise direction of take-off to avoid the cornice plunging over the dangerous slope immediately north.

Our height was 3,984ft. above sea-level as we slid off on a westward bearing. With our clothes flapping, bemused and bewildered by the wind, we skied blind for the first 300ft. or so, then suddenly we were out of the flying spindrift on a tilting quilt of downy powder, rippled by waves so smooth that ski-ing was like flying in a frictionless world which went on for all of 600ft.

We were facing a craggy little peak now, Creag an Fhithich, which had to be climbed if we were to find a safe way down into the corrie below. This was a sheer delight, following a snowy edge with a large drop on each side to a point where a gully fell away in the direction where we wanted to go. The gully was in fact a series of sugar bowls, so narrow that you felt you were on a never-ending spiral as one steep turn led to another, with huge fringes of icicles coming at you from each side. The magic ended in a perplexing place, on a tight col whose only exit was frighteningly steep. Well, we had the ice axe to deal with it if it was too dangerous for ski-ing.

Turning my skis at right-angles to the slope, I let myself side-slip to begin with. The control was adequate, and it enabled me to reach a rock drop debarring further descent from that point. So I went to the right finding myself on the edge of a great curtain of smooth powder whose only danger was possible avalanche. There was only one way to test it, and that was to push off. It was a particularly breathless moment, for Iain had not yet joined me, and as I hung out on the steep face, leaning my body well away from the slope, I could feel the surface snow avalanching from my downhill ski. A kick-turn at the end of the traverse and I came back the other way, swinging this time at the end of it to face a slope of pure silk which went down to the frozen lochan hundreds of feet beneath.

I waited for Iain before embarking on the flight into the corrie, for ski-ing is always more enjoyable in company than alone. It is hard to describe sheer perfection, but this steep headwall provided it, launching us out far over the ice of the loch, from a world of shadow back into the warmth of sunlight. A slight uphill climb and we were at the Lawers burn, ready to follow its trench down to Loch Tay, but hardly expecting exciting ski-ing for the few miles remaining. To our surprise, there was not only a ribbon of cornice twisting along the course of the burn, but the shadowed south wall of the hill was evenly covered, and already it was frostily crisp.

So we coasted easily down, enjoying the sunlit snow, which was soft and slowish, ideal for taking in the view as we serpentined down the burn. Then, as we felt in the mood for something more exciting, we traversed into shadow, accelerating across the hill, diving into drainage troughs, taking the air over sharp bumps, twisting and turning until bent knee muscles ached with the strain of holding. The snow cover was thinning out as the slope flattened, but just when we thought we were going to have to walk, we found the line of an old sledge-track, of the kind used long ago for transporting peat down from the roadless hillsides. This one, deeply counter-sunk, had filled up with a ribbon of snow, which carried us right down to the lochside and the Lawers hotel, where my car was lying.

"I wish we were just setting out," said Iain with feeling as we drove into the sunset to collect his car, the silhouettes of the peaks before us ebony-black against a crimson which had spilled its colour into the loch and into every burn.

"Supposing we had gone to Glencoe today," I said, "we could have had about 30,000ft. of downhill running using the chair-lift and ski-tows. Do you think you would have enjoyed it as much?"

He shook his head. "With the social set and all the mob; queueing and noise. Even the thought of it puts me off. Besides, a *piste* is a *piste*, a slide with hundreds of other people, and when you have done it a few times it has lost its surprise. "Today we have crossed mountains on every kind of snow and ice, and we could have been the only two people in the world for most of the time. The variety of the ski-ing and its surprise—you keep thinking back to it. And even if you forget it, you will never forget the views."

Of course he is right. For him as for me, ski-ing is a dimension of travel rather than a sport. Like mountaineering it is a way of exploring vertically rather than horizontally.

Red Footed Falcon on Loch Lomond

Yes that birdwatch programme on the BBC last Sunday night was superb, not only in capturing the excitement of Minsmere's avocets and a marsh alive and in full cry with nesting activity, but in managing to film the unexpected. Suddenly there was a wheeling osprey turning into a power-dive, splashing into the water and struggling into the air with a fish hanging from a talon. But before it was properly airborne a powerful neighbour came into the attack, a marsh harrier. A re-run in slow motion caught the glory of these two powerful fliers in action, and you felt for the struggling osprey as its fat catch splashed back into the water.

I saw the final showing of the film and was glad I hadn't stayed in to watch the serial happenings of the day, preferring to have a morning and afternoon walk on my home ground to enjoy the real thing. For this place is no different from Minsmere in terms of variety. May this year has been very good, for flowers, early leaf on the trees, a fine rush of summer migrants taking nesting territories in woods, marsh and shore so that by

7 May we had a great overlapping of singing sounds from trilling waders to the chattering of sedge warblers and "reeling" grasshopper warblers against a background of honking Canada geese and cackling shelduck. You just never know what will turn up.

I was enjoying all this on Sunday morning seated on a tree-stump, sandpipers probing and bobbing just in front of me, cuckoos melodiously calling, swifts like fighter planes doing acrobatics over my head making the swallows and sandmartins darting and criss-crossing over the water look sluggish by comparison. Herons flying to and from their nests were being harried constantly as criminals intent on murder.

Peewits were more concerned chasing off carrion crows, and I found a few punctured eggs of three wader species that morning sucked clean of their contents. Walking to look at the newly opened yellow flowers of the water lilies I climbed away towards Balmaha, to a place where I had met three fallow deer a few days ago, antlered bucks, and our surprise had been mutual.

Glassy eyes staring, as if unbelieving, they stood at the alert, but I had no camera to capture their striking differences, two of them a normal brown, the third a pure white animal with the noblest head of the three. Then over the fence sprang a doe and off went the bucks their broad palmated antlers tossing.

Last Sunday I carried my camera at the alert just in case I might find the animals at the same place, no luck. So I left my camera at home when I was joined after lunch with my friend Len who wanted to hear the songs of blackcap and garden warbler. He got them too, but we got something even more exciting which we couldn't identify, a kestrel-like bird, but smaller and infinitely richer in colour, with an unusual feeding habit of dashing to ground and returning immediately to its perch.

It let us creep so close we noted every detail, chestnut head, grey barred mantle, tail like a sparrow hawk, but with pointed wings overlapping it. But the most striking feature was the pale necklace and warm buff chest and belly. The tiny hooked bill was yellowish with a black tip. The feet gripping the fence were fleshy-orange we thought.

What was it? A painting on page sixty-three of "*The Field Guide to the Birds of Britain and Europe*' showed our bird, a female red-footed falcon, a rare vagrant to Britain which summers in Eastern Europe and Asia Minor, whose winter quarters are in tropical and southern Africa.

We phoned the local bird recorder who lives nearby who swallowed his tea hastily and set off but was defeated by thundery rain from searching likely spots where the bird might be sheltering. Nor could I show him the photograph I could easily have taken. Such a chance is unlikely to occur again, but the record is beyond doubt.

Below Buachaille Etive Mor the West Highland Way climbs northwards across the Devil's Staircase.

The "Three Brethern Cairns" look out to the Eildon Hills. This is the highest point reached in the Selkirk Border Riding.

Border Hills near Portmore, Peebles.

The Solway at Caerlaverock, Jimmy Baird's home country.

Jimmy Baird when he was head deer-stalker in Glen Lyon.

Harvesting history. Tom Weir recalls earlier days and the Glasgow Buchts.

Bob Grieve, an unemployed walker of the 30's who aimed at being a successful tramp, but became Sir Robert Grieve and Professor of Town and Country Planning as well as the first Chairman of the H.I.D.B.

Buachaille Etive Mor. W. H. Murray's favourite mountain.

In the Himalayas in 1950. L. to R. Tom Weir, Douglas Scott, W. H. Murray and Tom McKinnon.

A view from Hirta on St. Kilda, looking across to the Island of Soay, from which the most primitive breed of sheep takes its name.

Like creatures from a cave painting, Soay sheep dance across the sheer face of Conachair.

A "weirdie" of the winged isle. The Old Man of Storr, one of a strange family of basalt pinnacles in the north of Skye.

Looking over to the Arrochar Alps from near the summit of Ben Lomond in February.

Remote Sandwood Bay near Cape Wrath.

Magic slippers, high in the Angus hills, on a traverse of Dreish and Mayar.

Laughing dogs, a Border collie and half-beardie working partners.

The River Lyon looking westward up its varied windings, which makes this one of the most scenic glens in Scotland.

Mike Tomkies with the wildcat he reared from a kitten.

Knockan Cliff Nature Trail overlooks the Inverpolly wilderness.

The southern approach to Rannoch Moor from frozen Loch Tulla. It was near here that the great bard Duncan Ban Macintyre was born.

My first meeting with Stan Bradshaw (R), high on the Cuillin Ridge. He has no equal in the veteran class of fell runners.

The most notorious road in Scotland, the infamous Lecht at Cook Bridge in January. It was already blocked when this photo was taken.

Village Bay, St. Kilda, showing the old village and the military camp. Note the hill-top Radar Station for tracking rockets fired from South Uist.

Loch Shiel at Glenfinnan where the clans rallied in 1745 to follow Bonnie Prince Charlie marching on London.

In the wilds of Glen Pean, where the Prince began his foot-slogging adventures after Culloden.

Rory's Refuge high in Corriegoe, hideout of the Seven Men of Glen Moriston who aided the Prince when he most needed help.

The entrance to Rory's Refuge by a tunnel leading under the stones.

Tom Weir looks out from the rocks of Cluny's Cage above Loch Ericht in the wild Ben Alder region. It was here that the Prince received news that French ships were waiting for him on the west coast.

Looking over the silver trench of Loch Laggan to the wild hills of Ben Alder which was the last refuge of Bonnie Prince Charlie. It is uninhabited today as it was in his time.

HAPPY GLEN PROSEN

"I'll meet you at Prosen Bridge at 11 a.m.," I had said to Iain on the phone on Friday. Now I wasn't so sure, as the pleasure of a fine October Saturday morning was dimmed by layers of mist thickening to fog, making the ten miles on each side of Perth slow going. It was delight, therefore, to drive suddenly into sunshine, and above the drifting skiffs of mist see skeins of geese swinging against blue sky, and peewits by the hundreds gleaming on newly-ploughed brown furrows.

Spirits rose in Kirriemuir at the sight of the wee town under the autumn colours of the hills, and in no time I was bearing down on Iain standing by the bridge. The time was within a minute or two of 11 a.m.

It was our first meeting since the Shiants trip described earlier. Now we were off to enjoy a walk in a glen that was new to Iain. A jaunt up to the Airlie Memorial Tower, perched 1,245ft. above the division between Clova and Prosen, seemed a good place to begin. "Great," Iain was exclaiming as we pulled past the Scott Monument, where the first impression of Prosen bursts upon you, rounded hills, heathery-slopes, green meadows each side of a river hung with birch, oak and rowan.

I always think of Prosen as being more like one of the splendid glens of North Yorkshire than most of the glens in Scotland, with its gentleness and the feeling of a man-made landscape of woods and fields. Iain walked across to the monument which commemorates Scott and Wilson of the Antarctic, who spent a holiday here before setting off on the journey to the South Pole from which they did not return.

Climbing through the steep pine wood, I was thinking of Scott and Wilson who probably came up here talking over their plans for the forthcoming polar trip.

Suddenly we were out of the trees, and looking at a junction of two worlds. Southward the wooded ridge below us fell away to the agricultural quilt of Strathmore, a patchwork of pale yellows and browns. Northward the low roll of hills rose ever higher to the 3,000ft. crests of Mayar and Dreish and Broad Cairn over which Iain and I have skied.

It looked innocent enough today, and we have been lucky enough to have had perfect conditions of deep powder snow and sunshine for our traverses. But we knew just what a killer the wild country stretching from here to Braemar could be. A friend of Iain's, who had explored with him in Greenland, died of exposure with his girl friend up there on Jock's Road last winter.

In impossible conditions mountain rescue teams and dog handlers searched for a week before the bodies were found. The victims had been caught out by a turn-round of wind on the twelve miles of hill separating Glen Doll road end from Callater. I recalled, too, the New Year of 1959 when five members of a Glasgow hiking club died on that same crossing on a day of blinding wet snowfall when we had to abandon ski-ing in the intolerable conditions.

Burly Archie White of Spott Farm blocked our way with a flock of rams as we resumed our journey up the glen. I mentioned blizzards to him. He cast his mind back to a January storm of the sixties which suddenly struck a shepherd of his bringing a flock of sheep off the hill. It was getting dark, and the conditions were so blinding that the sheep went into a gully and wouldn't shift.

There was no alternative but to leave them. The worst happened. It snowed steadily for days on end and hard frost set in. Out of 110 which went in, only one came out alive, the others had died of suffocation. "I think the survivor had got under a bank, maybe, and managed to get some air. We called it 'Seventeen' after that, for it had been buried for seventeen days. It was a three-year-old ewe, and it must have been hardy."

Archie had 900 ewes on 2,500 acres, and 40 Aberdeen Angus cattle. His grandfather, William, was one of the pioneers of the breed in this area, and he took me over to the park to see the sleek, shiny black beasts. We also had a look inside the steading where big rams were getting beauty treatment as horns were filed and fettled up to bring out their whiteness. I didn't know that by applying heat to the horns the double-curl can be improved, and this may help to lift the price to £120-£150 each. Getting the rams away was a family affair, and his daughter Patsy and wee grandson were helping.

"The rams are a sideline, a kind of hobby. My neighbour, Stewart McIntosh, does much better. He got £2,200 for one last year, and one of his made £2,000 this year. You'll find him at Glentairie Guest House with his wife, or up at the farm working."

Stewart was away in Dalmally at a sheep sale, we discovered, so we took the hill track that goes up behind Glentairie, following the west side of the attractive wooded gorge made by the Burn of Inchmill. Our target was the top of Balnaboth Craig which is mostly grassy sward on this side. It was delightfully warm up there in the sun, looking across to the "Minister's Track" which links Glen Prosen village to Glen Clova, or tilting our eyes steeply downward to the ruined chapel, parklands and home farm of Balnaboth.

Descent was steep to get down there, by a ride of long heather breaching the pines. A green woodpecker was "yapping," and redwings and fieldfares were flighting from the ivy of the 17th century chapel as we enjoyed the grassy alps and natural birches of this delightful spot. Nor had I any feeling that I was trespassing, for Captain Alastair Ogilvie McLean had given me permission (on a previous visit) to go where I liked.

146

On the former occasion a few weeks before, he had taken me along a narrow stone corridor to his office. "This is the old bit of the house. It's about 400 years old. It may even have been an ancient keep. It looks a good place for a ghost, and we have one, 'Green Jean.' My wife has seen her—an old body dressed in old-fashioned clothes, with a shawl or plaid crossing in front. She saw her just after the birth of our son in August 1950. We have three of a family, the other two are daughters."

Captain McLean explained to me that he was really a West Coaster, tracing back to McLean of Coll whose line has produced so many soldiers and sailors. His father, in the Black Watch, was killed at Gallipoli, as was mine. McLean himself served in the Black Watch and prefers a kilt of Ogilvie tartan to any other dress. A homely man, easy to talk to and without pretence, he told me of the pleasure he finds in Glen Prosen.

"My wife from Wiltshire is in hospital just now, but she feels the same affinity to the place as I do. She overworks, because we have to manage with so few staff. My grandfather used to pay over a dozen people to run this place. We have to manage with a gamekeeper and an overseer. We sold the upper glen to the Forestry Commission and passed the home farm over to a tenant. I enjoy trees. I've planted about 400 acres."

As we talked I was shown the ramifications of the old house, which was added to in 1830, and contains a fascinating mixture of styles and furnishings, each with its bit of history. I was shown the room where Barrie worked on *The Little Minister*, and allowed to read some of his letters under a glass cover.

"Yes, the older one gets the more one thinks back to the past. This house is virtually a museum built up by those who have gone before us. These are difficult times, but we hope the owner's loss is the tenant's gain." I am modernising old houses, and I'll let them to pensioners, perhaps in return for some work. There is pleasure in that."

At Cormuir across the glen I met Stewart McIntosh newly back from Dalmally where the sale had been a surprise. "The sheep made far mair than they should hae done. An' the same wi' beef. The cattle are fetching ower guid a price. No farmer should be complaining this year. Come inside and meet Mither. She'll gie us some coffee." She did, and she also put down on a tray some of the most delicious rock cakes I have ever eaten.

We were in the parlour, and I couldn't help noticing the silver cups and rows of medals behind glass. I got up to look at them and the photograph on the wall of a cheery-faced man in a tammie talking to the Queen Mother. "Yes that's ma father. He's aboot seventy there, and it was taken at Birkhall after he had walked across Jock's Road wi' the Black Watch from Dundee.

"Father had been a sniper at Ypres. He was buried last February on a day sae cauld that the Black Watch piper couldna work his fingers properly. He had never been a regular soldier, but he loved everything to

147

do wi' the Black Watch." The parlour still held his personality. I noticed one medal had eight bars on it. "That's the Donegal Medal. Father is the only marksman in the small bore rifle club to have won it eight times."

We were getting on so well that Stewart decided to come with us up the glen and point out some landmarks. We stopped two miles up at the big white shooting lodge. "I love the grouse season. It's great sport, and I'm a keen shot myself. It wis bonnie in the auld days of a fine mornin' when you took a string o' ponies wi' the lunch baskets on panniers to the butts. It's mechanisation now. There's only three families livin' between Cormuir and the heid o' the glen."

Up the deteriorating track we went to the rocky headwall of the glen whose corrie is now planted with Forestry Commission trees. Formerly part of Balnaboth, the Commission had sold the unwanted part of the high ground, so that from the bare tops nothing but deer forest stretches ahead all the way to Deeside in high, heather country where the ptarmigan reaches its highest density in Scotland.

"They say it takes forty years tae be a glenner," chuckled Stewart. "I still feel I belong to Cormuir, though it's five years since we gave up living there to take the wee guest-house of Glentairie. Frances, my wife, enjoys catering and cooking and running the shop. It's a funny thing, but most of the people who come to stay wi' us are English fowk. It disnae seem to appeal sae much to oor ain fowk, maybe because the scenery's too tame."

Next door, however, was Fifer Iain Nelson from Saline, who is a real enthusiast for Glen Prosen. Iain is one of Scotlands most accomplished master potters, and he enjoys it here because he can get on with his work with few interruptions. For recreation he has half an acre of alpine garden and vegetable plot.

"I got this cottage when I came back from America in 1970 and built a kiln. I had been thinking of setting up a pottery here while in the U.S.A. I knew the glen well from coming here as a grouse-beating student. I thought of it as a full-time job, but took a job in Edinburgh Art College which I find stimulating. It means that at week-ends and holidays I can do my own thing here. The work I do is mainly for exhibitions. I don't go in for souvenirs.

"I like to think of the pots I make as well-designed pieces that can be put to use and not just ornamental. Right now I'm working under a certain amount of pressure for three group exhibitions in December, at the Open Eye Gallery and the 57 Gallery in Edinburgh, and in a Stirling gallery."

Iain is thirty-five, black-bearded, lithe and a bachelor, who could be described as eligible. A local man had described him to me as a man who is "not easy gotten to ken," adding, "He maks great muckle pots wi' little mannies on them keekin' oot frae the side. Ken, ye'd think they were livin'. And he sits for oors in the gairden pickin' weeds, grapin' awa at naething. The gairden looks a richt mess, then it blooms all of a sudden, and it's the bonniest thing you ever saw wi' a' kinds o' coloured flooers among the rocks."

I saw what the speaker meant when Iain took me across his garden to his massive kiln of firebricks and brought out some of his "pieces," wonderful things turned on the wheel first of all, then modelled with human heads and animals. There were tiny things, too, one an exquisitely-made little box for a dressing-table.

And just round the corner from Iain in Glen Prosen village, opposite the church, is another artist, Norah Cotogno, who was busy painting in oils for an exhibition in the spring. She also designs and makes jewellery, using gem stones as centre-pieces. Despite the foreign-sounding name Miss Cotogno hails from Alyth.

Originally she came only at week-ends, but the price of petrol decided her to move in and try to make a living working full-time as an artist. Her home is the old schoolhouse, containing the original fireplace and old swey. She has had visitors who remember when the lunch-time soup used to be cooked on that fire for the children.

A lonely life? "No. The summer is busy. I have so many friends calling. I find life completely satisfying here. I used to work at Invergowrie, and I may have to take on a wee job if I get too poor. Meantime, with three cats and a garden and a place like Glen Prosen to live. I'm rich!"

Her sentiments were general in this glen of happy people.

Greetings From a Golden Eagle

Now that the white flourish is on the rowans, mingling its scent with the white May of the hawthorn and the sweetness of bluebells we should make most of the fleeting splendour. My old friend John has his birthday then, and he always likes to celebrate it with a special outing that is new to him. Last year it was a traverse of the three peaks of the Cobbler by the delightful Buttermilk Burn with its waterfalls and tree-clad banks leading to spruces, then into the joys of a wild corrie of noble rocks. Pat, the long-shanked kiltie was there too, so I was the baby of the party, for Pat is two years my senior and John last year was seventy-three.

Where was it to be this year? With dark clouds threatening the 3,000ft. tops we chose an outing to lesser summits that would be new to us all, beginning with a climb up the spectacular waterfall of the Ben Glas Burn at the lower end of Glen Falloch. There is no way you can avoid its steepness, and if you keep to the edge as we did you have to watch your step on the broken ground.

After the recent rain the waterfall was in noisy white spurt, but even it couldn't drown out the bird song coming out of the tree-hung ravine, as we edged up a staircased rock garden of gem-like little plants, pink lousewort, blue milkwort, yellow tormentil, and pimpernel with stars of flowering butterwort in the wetter places.

The plunge below us on the steeper places was quite sensational, then suddenly we were over a lip and on easy ground rising in heather towards the reedy wee loch that feeds the burn a good two miles on.

Before we got there we struck north along the flanks of Meall Mor nan Eag rising craggily to 2,037ft. Up there we had a ring ouzel stridently calling and a raven soaring so grandly that we thought at first it was an eagle.

We were now congratulating ourselves on our choice of outing for the clouds were lowering on the highest tops while our own splendid little rock peaks were clear. We reckoned we had better have the special birthday feast before the rain got to us, so on a made-to-measure slab we opened the bottle of wine and celebrated with slices of John's birthday cake. And up there he opened the cards which had been sent to him.

Fortified, we thought of climbing something else, Stob Creag and Fhitich, the sharp rock of the raven, and on the way found a punctured egg sucked clean of meat, perhaps by the bird of ill omen. Below us was Lochan a' Casteil—the small loch of the castle. Our peak certainly had battlements of rock guarding it. To John we gave the honour of being first to stand on top.

Now we could look across Glen Falloch to the passes which Rob Roy knew so well by the Dubh Eas for Loch Shira, or the Lairg Arnain for Glen Fyne, routes used by Cattle drovers between the west and the Falkirk Trysts.

We could have descended due north-west to the Falls of Falloch, but preferred to detour into more unknown ground among rock escarpments and huge boulders. It was here we picked up the silhouette of a fast flying falcon beating towards a large soaring bird which we thought was a raven until it put on an avoiding spurt with great sweeping strokes and wheeled to show us the broad straight wings and shortish square-cut tail of the king of all hill birds—the golden eagle itself the most perfect of all birthday presents.

ON THE BRAES OF ANGUS

"Eight o'clock," said the voice from the door, and with a start I realised I was in Iain's house in Dundee. What will you have for breakfast—ham and fried eggs, or would you rather have them boiled?" I gave my order, "Soft, four minutes," while Iain apologised for the absence of geese. "They usually come flying across the Tay at dawn, against the sunrise like a Peter Scott painting, four or five hundred of them."

The house overlooks the airfield. You can watch seals on the sandbars of the estuary from the window. Right now it was a thrush which was attracting my attention, repeating a simple phrase from a tree-top, and my first for 1967. South over the firth the sky was clear green, tinged pink in the east. Iain was packing as I swallowed my eggs, and we were away by nine, skis lashed to the roof of the car, heading north on the Glamis road.

To a Westerner like myself, the quality of light in the east is brittle, as if all vapoury softness has been removed from it, to sharpen the shine on the bark of birch and beech, make ploughed fields glow more warmly brown and white-washed cottages whiter than white.

Yet for all that I was unprepared for the clarity of Strathmore and the Grampians from the high road, with fields of yellow, brown and green peppered with shining villages, with roofs of snow across the whole horizon.

Iain's joy was tempered by a comparison he was making in his mind of the same scene a week before, when the snow stretched right down to the glens. Mild weather and a drastic thaw had now produced spring conditions in January, and as we swung into Glen Clova we were beginning to dismiss from our minds the possibilities of ski-touring in favour of climbing one of the long gullies of Corrie Fee.

But as we got past the Milton of Clova we began to have misgivings even about this, for the rock face was mainly black, the snow cornices hardly penetrating the gullies, so any route up the face would hardly merit the description of a winter climb. However, we took the rope and axes, enjoying ourselves just to be walking through bluffs of larch and pine into the wild rock cirque of Mayar.

Following the Fee Burn, we were soon under the Roman nose of Craig Rennet and looking out for a cleft called Slanting Gully, said to be 400ft. and technically hard. We found it, and were interested enough in its very steep finish to be on the point of climbing up to it, when a bit broke off from the cornice in the sun, spattering bouncing fragments of ice over the

151

route. It was a warning to clear off.

In view of present danger and past experience, we opted to scramble up the ice of the waterfall to enter the exhilarating world of the snowfields. The suddenness of the change was extraordinary, for although the thaw had smudged the tablecloth, the feeling was of a predominantly white world except where grey clouds touched.

The moment of stepping on to the top of Mayar was thrilling for another change of landscape mood. Instead of upland snow, we now looked on a Lowland world of steel-blues and greys, receding wave upon wave to the mouth of the Tay, with Fife signposted by the twin islands of the Lomonds thrusting out of a low cloud sea. We would have lingered awhile to identify the surrounding peaks but for the strong wind, so we pushed on to Dreish, arriving just as the low sun began to gild the western clouds.

Reluctant to go down if a fine sunset was going to develop, we strolled back the way we had come, over Little Dreish to Mayar, as parallel bars of gold became bright pink, staining the snows with alpen-glow and transforming the tenuous mists to crimson. The wind had dropped, so we could sit comfortably watching the new moon turn silver, and far far away we could see the twinkling lights of towns from the darkness, 3,000ft. down in the Lowlands.

It was high time we were moving, since there was a lot of icy ground between us and Glen Doll. We managed without the torch, until we got amongst the trees, when we had to get out the map and plot a course to find a bridge over the river, and we got to Milton of Clova just in time for dinner.

Our plans for the morning now hinged on the frosty night which seemed certain to develop out of a clear sky of stars, for, given crisp snow, we had seen the line of a grand ski-tour over ground mostly covered in snow. To our delight the conditions were exactly what we hoped for, the frosted fields and trees sparkling like cut crystals as we tied skis on the pack-frame and climbed once again up to the snow world—this time by the path called Jock's Road.

What a grand walk it was. "Makes you feel good to be alive," said two Dundonians we met on the way. "You'll get plenty of ski-ing today." Meantime it was all walking, up to the summit of "the road"—now mostly buried beneath the snow, then northward over the Knaps of Fafernie where we threw down our loads just to enjoy the fantastic glitter of the plateau.

Beautiful in itself, it was, nevertheless, a mere foreground for the most impressive view I have seen of the Cairngorms, rising from the void of Glen Callater, giving both depth and height. Compact and flawlessly white, they had shape and form, etched sharply by shadow in the deep recesses where the sun cannot penetrate.

"That's where we should be," said Iain. It was a traitorous thought, but I had to agree that Braeriach or Ben Macdhui would have given the finest

152

ski running in Scotland that day, over countless miles of smoothed plateau. I dismissed the thought, remembering Tom Longstaff's formula for happiness. "To live in the present and soak in the great moments so that they will never come out. Enjoy—and for always, as you can through concentration."

And there was plenty of the special to enjoy about this place, the wild life for one thing, with ptarmigan strutting about on every other snow patch, tails cocked up like barnyard fowls, until they took the air with the grace of doves, ermine white except for the black edgings of the tail. But what really surprised me was the distribution of red grouse among the ptarmigan.

No doubt the grouse had been attracted up to the sunshine of the tops when the glens were in frosty shadow, the advantage being shared by a herd of deer about twenty strong, standing like statues on the snow near the top of our next mountain, two miles off.

That peak was Fafernie, and when we got to it we began to think in terms of continuing to Lochnagar, another four miles on, but with relatively little climbing involved. The only thing that put us off was the weather, the fear of a shut-down, since many of the tops were already lost under clouds.

We compromised by dumping our skis on Fafernie and continuing on foot to Cairn Bannoch, hoping to see down to the Dubh Loch or Loch Muick, but both glacier-trenched lochs lay too deep to be visible, so we hurried back to our skis as wisps of mist came scurrying across to threaten our run.

"No pleasure without pain," said Iain. "We've been going since 9.15, and it's now two o'clock, so I'm going to take this descent nice and gently."

That was what he said he was going to do. In fact, I couldn't keep up with him, perhaps because his skis are of wood while mine are metal, and wood skis, being stiffer, tend to run fast on icy snow, whereas mine do best on powder, due to their greater flexibility. It mattered not. I know that the exhilaration of swinging back and fore across that slope had me singing as the lip of Glen Callater seemed to swing up all too suddenly, warning us to shoulder skis and climb again to the Tolmount col.

Through a fine little gully we found ourselves facing a spacious punchbowl, allowing a spin round and back again to swoop into its bottom and coast for a mile on the covered-in burn, only visible where three-feet thick snowbridges had collapsed. Gravity was just pulling us along, until the enclosing walls and a drop into sugar basins gave us a grand finish, below the bothy built by Davie Glen following the Glen Doll tragedy.

There is a plaque on a stone at this windy spot, commemorating the five members of the Universal Hiking Club who died near here in a New Year blizzard after walking Jock's Road from Braemar Youth Hostel.

Looking at my watch, I found it hard to believe that it had not stopped, for it said only ten-past three. We had time to dawdle, and it was fine

153

strolling down the rocky glen of the Doll, trying to visualise what it will be like here in thirty years, when the hillsides of tiny trees in the state forest are well grown. The forest edges the botanically rich corries which are second only to Ben Lawers for mountain flowers.

On these hillsides a Lomond Mountaineering Club friend of mine, Mr Alf Slack, rediscovered the alpine coltsfoot, last seen in Scotland by Forfar's George Don 150 years before, an ice-age relic like the alpine milk vetch, yellow oxytropis, blue sow thistle and alpine catchfly, which are special to the Clova region.

Nor are the rarities confined to the high ground. The twin flower and the dwarf cornel occupy low ground here, if you know where to look in this environment of fertile schists and acid rocks, each having plant communities of outstanding interest. Look at the richness of the Caenlochan Nature Reserve, stretching from here to the Elbow. The amazing total of 291 vascular plants, 230 mosses, 87 liverworts and 210 lichens has been recorded.

Talking of this and that, we were soon back at the car, hardly noticing the weight of the skis, but feeling in good fettle for tea, though Iain settled for a glass of ale, since he was due to make a speech that evening at the Queen's College Rucksack Club's annual dinner. Later I was reflecting what a wonderfully varied and small place Scotland is, for I left Clova at 6.50 p.m., and was home on Loch Lomond, at 9.20 p.m., sniffing air very much milder than that which I had left.

Winning in the Rain

No doubt about it. There's a lot of goodwill about, and good nature too, from all ages and sizes, as you would have seen had you been at Rowardennan last Sunday morning waiting in the rain and mist to collect your card for a sponsored climb of Ben Lomond to raise money for the Royal Commonwealth Society for the Blind. Last year 590 climbers averaged £17 per head, bringing in just under £10,000.

Nobody seemed to be downhearted, least of all the campers emerging from a wet night and a midge-biting morning in the tents. By 9.15 there was a queue at the marquee to book-in and collect check-cards, despite the dismal news that it was cold up there with strong wind and thick mist. The Loch Lomond Mountain Rescue Team were weighing the safety angle. You could go in for three sections of varying difficulty, have the pleasure of going up at your own speed, of racing to go faster up and down than anyone else, or of walking a section of the Forestry Commission track contouring the ups and downs of the Craigroyston shore.

My wife and I chose the last, and even the low mist could not diminish the glory of rhododendron bloom, purple above rioting yellow broom in a fragrance of bluebell scent. Birds were in good voice, too, especially wood warblers and garden warblers. As for fellow walkers we seemed to have the track to ourselves once the last tents had been left behind, until we were overtaken by two strong-looking backpackers shouldering 40lb. apiece as if they were day-sacks.

Yes, they were on their way to Fort William, doing the whole ninety-five miles of the West Highland Way. They had started out from Milngavie on Friday afternoon, camping that night near Drymen and on Saturday traversing the Garadhban Forest trail which leads to the Mar Burn, then the Way is over the top of Conic Hill in a lovely descent on the very spine of the Highland Boundary Fault to Balmaha.

That was the magical bit for them, seeing Loch Lomond suddenly spread below them with all the Highland hills colourfully clear above a chain of islands.

They had camped that fine night two miles from Rowardennan and got a shock on the wet Sunday morning to walk into a jamboree of which they knew nothing, for they had travelled from Manchester and Cheltenham to have their first walking holiday in Scotland. They had done plenty in England and Wales, but nothing as ambitious as this. Their plan was to arrive in Fort William on Thursday night, climb Ben Nevis on Friday, then home.

You learn quite a bit about folk as you walk and talk and share a common bond. First they were just Mark and Eric, then we found out they were brothers, Mark, the elder, a department store manager, Eric an accountant. Also that they had decided, since they were doing the walk anyway, that they should try to turn it to good account by trying to raise money for some charity, at 1p or 2p per mile. Given success they expected to be able to raise £300, which they now proposed to donate to swell the funds of the Ben Lomond climb.

We walked with them to within a mile and a half from Inversnaid, and they even got a picture of the wild goats, white hairy nannies with noble horns and black kids at foot. In heavy rain we waved our farewells and were gey drookit by the time we got back to Rowardennan and heard how fierce conditions had been on the top, but there was only one minor case of exposure.

They were shuffling the cards to account for every person registered when I left. Organisation and safety precautions were superb.

Perhaps the most important piece of advice given to all participants on the Ben Lomond climb was about weather. Wear suitable clothing and stout footwear for what may be a cold, wet, windy day. You have been warned! Arctic conditions can prevail as late as June. The fathers of Scottish mountaineering who said it can be winter any day on the high hills have still to be proved wrong.

In an unsettled week I'm still wondering how Mark and Eric are getting on, and if they made it. One thing at least, the rain went off early on Sunday evening as the Ben Lomond climbers went home.

They did the big walk but were beaten by Ben Nevis. How did they find the West Highland Way? Harder than they expected, especially crossing the swollen burns near the top of Loch Lomond.

LIFE IN THE WILDERNESS

Just now and then you read a book by an adventurous man which is so superbly written that you feel you must talk to the author. Not since Gavin Maxwell's *Ring of Bright Water*, with its incredibly rich vision of the Western Highlands, had I been so powerfully moved. What otters were to Maxwell—a source of inspiration giving meaning to his life when he most needed it—so, I felt, were wildcats to Mike Tomkies. Where Tomkies differed from Maxwell was that he had no wish to make pets of his wildcats. Having rescued them when they were abandoned by the mother, he felt it his duty to rear them and let them loose. But strange events conspired to turn the whole affair into an extraordinary story.

I reviewed the book *My Wilderness Wildcats* enthusiastically but I had no clue to where the wilderness was, for no place-names were given. The author obviously wanted to keep the location secret and, respecting his privacy, I didn't even consider trying to find out. Then the unexpected happened: he wrote to thank me for the review. I replied suggesting we meet and so we did, at the remote post office where he collects his mail once a week in summer.

It was a blind date. What would he be like? I had to wait longer than I expected before a tall and lithe figure, wearing a camouflage jacket, held out his hand and said, "Mike Tomkies. Sorry I'm late." His manner was matter of fact, not effusive. The voice was English. The determined face had a fringe of whiskers and a chin beard, with a few grey hairs among the dark.

I thought we would be off immediately to the remote road-end where he keeps his boat. Instead, he gazed at me thoughtfully, then came out with it:

"I should really visit a golden eagle eyrie. It's important I look at it to see if it's in use. But it's a twenty-mile drive back the way you've come, then a steep climb to the foot of the cliff, and I expect you've had enough for one day." The time was 4.30 p.m.

I rather liked the idea, even although mist was smirring as I put on my boots and transferred to his Land-Rover, while Mike ordered Moobli the Alsation into the back seat. So back round the sea-loch we went and over a 1000ft. pass while he talked of eagles and the exhausting work of visiting every eyrie in one of the wildest stretches of Scotland. "I did thirty-three treks last season checking over a score of eyries. I'll tell you this—writing about wildlife is a lot easier than taking photographs of it. I spent five nights out in a small hide at one eyrie. The longest continuous spell was

157

thirty-one hours. I felt terrible at the end of it. Even with a sleeping-bag it was freezing cold and uncomfortable. But I found out what I wanted to know— that the eagle hunts and brings in prey at night. The problem of flying into a cliff ledge under an overhang with trees and landing on it must be really difficult. I also discovered that it sleeps with its head under its wing like a duck brooding its chick all the while.

"The big thrill was to be awake while the eagle was asleep , then see it push its head out, open its eyes, close them again and nuzzle down for another forty winks. I was waiting for the sunrise, and I'll never forget the moment when the eyrie was touched with gold and I pressed the camera shutter to get my best picture of an eagle with its chick.

"My most terrifying moment was one day when the male rocketed straight at the hide as if to destroy it. But all it wanted was a sprig of heather from above my face, stuff I had used to camouflage my hide, to add to the nest material. There were four days when prey must have been scarce, so little was being brought in. I offered the eaglet steak that I carried up to supplement its diet, but it wouldn't eat it until the mother tore it up.

"I'm frightened of heights, and it slightly worries me that I have to take so many chances. I've had my pack blown off a ledge, such was the force of the wind. Eagles really test you. You can be exhausted, despondent, and in a state of exultation all in a day."

We were over the pass now and contouring a fresh-water loch enclosed by spruce and larch forest. "This is the place," said Mike, pulling the vehicle in close and leaving Moobli as guard while the pair of us took a steep ride through the trees. An hour of steady plugging, and I happened to be looking up the face, when the broad, out-stretched wings of an eagle came over the ridge and dipped into the rocks. "You've brought me luck. The eyrie must be in use," said Mike, excitement in his voice.

Closer to the rocks we could see the big stick-pile of the eyrie on a precarious ledge. Soon I was up there, looking obliquely into the nest cup containing two pale eggs, while Mike traversed across by a different route.

Now we turned for home, driving into heavier rain as we went west to the road-end where the fibre-glass boat lay anchored. A few carries of heavy gear down the steep bank, a pull at the outboard engine, and we were away into an out-of-focus world of grey water and creeping mist.

"Yes, it's a dangerous loch," said Mike in answer to my query. "I've had two narrow escapes from drowning— once when the boat was swamped in a squall and I had to swim for it. The boat sank, but I got some buoyancy from a box with a wildcat kitten in it and from a watertight attache case containing my valuables. I got some help from the dog, too, by grabbing his tail. Training it from being a pup to stay close to me paid off. The other bad moment was due to engine failure in stormy conditions."

"Welcome to Wilderness!" were his next words as we pulled sharply into what was little more than a slit of inlet below a white crofthouse flanked and backed by noble trees. Even in the dim light it had welcoming charm. It was good to get in, light the Tilley lamps and have a dram while the steak was cooking on the Calor gas stove. I was too ready for my bunk to take much in. Eiderdown bag unrolled, I was asleep in minutes, and woke up to the steady drumming of rain on the tin roof.

Mike was already up and at breakfast of cereal and fruit in his own quarters, which combine his bedroom, office and living-room. "Help yourself," he nodded to the kitchen table, and I took the hint, for I, too, am not by nature talkative in the morning. However, once the fire was lit and Mike's pipe of tobacco was drawing, he was ready to expand.

"I'm not quite a Sassenach," he said. "My mother was a McKinlay Stewart from Islay, but she died when I was four and I didn't know of my Highland connections until I was forty-two. At that time I was living in a log cabin which I'd built myself on a piece of virgin coast in British Columbia. No neighbours except deer, racoons, mink, bald eagles, skunk, pack rats, salmon and the odd cougar and black bear. I had cut myself off from my old way of life to try to write a great novel. In that wilderness, with a boat and sea full of fish, I could live easily on five dollars a week.

"But the loneliness of living in the wilderness nearly broke me especially the first long winter when nature seemed to be conspiring against me. I worked ten hours a day on the novel, trying to banish the pangs of solitude, but they kept gnawing at me. In three and a half years of patience-testing discipline I wrote and rewrote that novel. And the manuscripts are across the room from you in that wooden chest, still unsold.

"It was a purging experience. There were depths, but a change was taking place in me as I became attuned to the wilderness and drew more and more joy from its wildlife. Then I did a solo trek into the mountainous grizzly bear country, going back there later with a wise old Indian, a marvellous backwoodsman who really opened my eyes." Mike has written about the experience in a book called *Alone In The Wilderness*, which I have read and enjoyed since I saw him.

Two questions came to my mind. What made him leave Britain for the wilds of Canada? The other was— why did he leave British Columbia for Scotland when he was getting so much from the wilderness experience out there? He referred me to his Canadian book, and its opening chapter, "The Immigrant," where he writes:

"Before my move from Britain I had found myself becoming bored and depressed. The reasons perhaps reached back to my youth. During the early years as a cub reporter in country villages, I had dreamed only of making it to London. The British capital then seemed to me in my painful naïvety a magic journalistic mecca where I'd be accepted into an exciting world of earls, politicians, glamorous women, movie stars and athletes.

"After more than a decade in London I indeed dallied with the illustrious, the beautiful and the swift. I was flying between Paris, Rome, Athens, Madrid, Vienna, New York and Hollywood, mixing drinks, talk, life and copy with vaunted famous names whose images I'd once worshipped as a village youth. Meeting whom I chose, writing about whom I liked, my name at the head of columns in widely read magazines, money simply flooded in. I became the complete hedonist. I went through sports cars like a frustrated racing driver, and reacted against my shy and awkward countrybred youth by squiring some of the world's most beautiful women.

"It was around my 34th birthday that this fast life began to go sour. Quite suddenly nothing seemed to lie ahead but boring repetition. A self-contempt grew as I realised that I ought to be doing something more intelligent with my life. Material success was no longer enough."

Having changed horses in mid-stream around that age myself, I could understand his state of discontent. "But why come back to Britain after being in a big country that you were enjoying?" He answers this question in the end chapter of *Alone In The Wilderness* titled "Time To Move On."

"Canada had been good to me, good for me. It had taken me from a city rut and had shown me a finer and fuller life here on this lonely cliff, five thousand miles from all I had previously known, my mind had been freed. I felt as if a new self had been formed . . . I had lived close to nature, seen both its beauty and its callousness, and had been shown a path, a way that led beyond hope or fear, success or failure.

"I knew now the time had come to move on. I did not know when or where I would go, only that my life, minor and of little account though it was, would be bound up somehow in the future between man and the last wild places . . ."

Astonishingly, it was the chance find of a paperback which he picked off a rubbish heap in Canada which brought him to Scotland. The book was *A Ring Of Bright Water,* by Gavin Maxwell. "As I read about Camusfearna and Maxwell's magical description of the Western Highlands, it set me wondering if I could find a place like that in Scotland. The idea was reinforced by an article I'd read about the Adventure School which the Atlantic rower John Ridgeway had set up in Sutherland.

"Uncertainties were resolved when the land next to mine was sold to city folk who began building log cabins on it. I sold up, came eventually to Scotland and visited the beautiful bay where Camusfearna used to stand. Then I drove north to Ardmore. I admired Ridgeway, but I wanted not an Adventure School, but a wild place of my own to study. I started looking around and tried fourteen different landowners without success.

"I visited Scotland again in March 1970, and it was on that trip I first saw Arisaig, and beyond its white sands, these strange islands—Rum,

Eigg and the Cuillin peaks of Skye. I was so powerfully moved by the sudden impact of it all that I got out the car and kissed the ground. And it was from that moment onwards my difficulties were smoothed as I was passed from one helpful person to another, and got the offer of a dilapitated wooden croft on a small Atlantic island if I cared to make it habitable.

"I knew it was the place for me the moment I saw it, and I soon learned that the tides and currents of this coast were more dangerous than the Pacific Coast where I'd come from. There was a lot of boating to do, towing timber and cement and building materials to the house to make it weather tight. I needed cash to buy the stuff, and got it, thanks to an advance of £500 from a publisher for a biography of John Wayne which I later wrote on the island.

"And it was there, too, that I began writing about the wilderness experience in Canada. It happened because an editor friend of mine thought it would be a good magazine article. Strangely enough, as I sat down to write, I realised that it was exactly four years to the very day that I had arrived in Canada. Something unusual happened as I started to put down the log cabin experience. The typewriter carriage ran away with me. I typed right through the night and produced 30,000 words in three days. All the doubts and uncertainties and the hard treks came back to me. The result was more than a series of articles. It became my best book: *Alone In the Wilderness*.

"So much was happening every day there. I felt I had become a part of the natural life of the island. Seals would follow my boat for a hand-out of mackerel. I could call a kestrel down from the sky. I was adopted by a crow and I trained a young sparrow-hawk. Crabs and plaice would ride on the waves right up to the very edge of my beach to snatch insects blown from the trees, Then when the tide fell, along would come the oystercatchers to pick up what had been left. Next would come the fox looking for bigger spoils cast up by the tide."

While we talked the mist was lifting and the rain had eased. We put on our boots and Mike led me to the waterfall spouting white through the oaks and birches. Moss, grey rocks, fragrant scents of the new leaf, the little garden he had created amidst his three acres and the native trees he had planted were so much as he had described in his *Wildcats* book that I felt I had been here before as we strolled, with a background of woodland birdsong and sandpipers calling from the shore.

This is how Mike has written of the area:

It was a lovely kingdom, one that really extended for fifteen miles, for mine was the only home along that length of roadless shore, and it stretched back to the north for a good six miles of glens and mountains before striking a road. It was, in fact, one of the largest uninhabited areas left in the British Isles—a kingdom of red deer stags that roared in the autumn as they rounded up their harems of hinds, of golden eagles, ravens, buzzards, kestrels and sparrowhawks, of foxes, badgers and otters, who had their holts along the rocky shores, of roe deer who sheltered in and shared my woods with a pair of red squirrels.

He explained how he had come here: "I heard of this lonely house situated on a freshwater loch with no road to it when I was living on the island. I had to see it, so I borrowed a boat and came on a February night to take a look. I had no tent, only a plastic sheet and sleeping-bag and the weather was bad. I spent two nights out, and something told me this was the place I was looking for—true wilderness, with twenty-six varieties of trees on a loch shore surrounded by rocky mountains. I remember standing below the trees and addressing an unknown presence, saying, 'If you want me to stay, tell me to stay.' The answer was 'Yes.'"

Our stroll took us to the wildcat's den. "She hunts at night," said Mike as he crept out of sight and reappeared with the tiger-striped animal held close to his face. "Who says you can't tame a wildcat?" he smiled. "But be quick if you want a picture, for if she decides to go I've no chance of holding her. This is Liane, and I've just written a book about her. She's the offspring of one of the wildcat kittens I reared, and I actually saw her being born. I don't believe in taming wild animals, but this one was such a runt she would have died without my help. I've reared her from birth but she's free to come and go as she chooses."

The cat showed how fast she could move when Mike lowered her to the ground and Moobli went forward as if to pounce. It was play, and the Alsation had no chance of catching her in the twenty-yard spurt to the den where she sleeps by day. Peering down the narrow entrance tunnel, I could just make out the whiskery face and round eyes staring out.

I asked Mike about the winters. How does he find them—long, lonely, tedious? The answer was no; the winter is too short when you have a lot of writing to do. You have to use these hours if you want to be free in the summer for wildlife studies as well as writing. "I wrote one book and drafted another which has got to be finished." One is the story of the rearing of the wildcat Liane, the other is about life on his Atlantic island, called *Between Earth and Paradise*.

We talked about the future. "I want to continue this way of life in the Highlands. I have two more books planned, then I'd like to go into animal biographies, books that are definitive about wildlife and land use in the Highlands. My sole purpose is to enhance awareness of this unique and magnificent country and all its wildlife in the hope that the natural, unspoiled, places will be conserved.

"But I must have peace to work, for I don't find writing and photography throughout the year easy." Too many interruptions would wreck his work programme.

"Once, in a mood of recall, I wrote of the pitiless rain day after day on my log cabin in Canada when I was trying to write that novel. I said, 'Rain does more than wet you. It rains on your heart, your spirits, dampening every process of thought.' But your spirit soars when the rain goes off and the sun shines. When we destroy nature we are left with nothing. Even the grandeur of the Highlands would pall for many visitors if the wildlife had gone. That is what I want to get across to the people who love this land and who are responsible for it."

Getting the Bird

Enjoying the scented air and the sight of graceful sea-swallows buoyantly diving and splashing for small fish on the sparkling river where it entered the sea, I was joined by a wee gamekeeper, spry for the weight of his years.

He greeted me as if he knew me. "Aye we net the salmon there. It's good to have the arctic terns nesting in the shingle. I'm away up to the house for a cup of tea if you'd like one."

Before long he was showing me two pairs of spotted flycatchers nesting in his garden and talking amusingly of the changes in sporting attitudes he had seen in his long lifetime.

"There was no such thing as grouse driving here when I started keepering over seventy years ago. We had over a hundred setters in the kennels and the gentlemen walked and shot over them. It's the same with the deer stalking, the young toffs don't want to climb and crawl over the high tops when they can go salmon or trout fishing.

"I'll tell you about a young gentleman who wouldn't walk a step unless he had to. I kept carrier pigeons in these days, and he had me take them to the hill and send him back a message when I'd found a stag worth shooting. Then he would come galloping along on a horse to a meeting place. His one idea was to get it over as quickly as possible, leaving us to get the beast home on the ponies. Many a time he was at his dinner while we were out on the hill. But we got fly for that fellow by not letting the pigeons go unless it was going to suit us." Old Ronnie was chuckling at the memory.

"Some of the old toffs were very unreasonable. 'Why don't you go out McNicol, and get me a snipe,' said her Ladyship, thinking she had only to take the notion and it would be on her plate. I went off to try, but with the marsh hard frozen I didn't expect anything.

"I kept the gun at the ready of course, and just as I came round the corner of the wood I saw a sparrow-hawk and had a blaze at him, and as the shot went off I saw something drop from its claws. And before it got to the ground in came another sparrow-hawk and caught it, and as he was turning I let fly at him. I missed, but he let go the prey like the first one and the dog brought it to me.

163

"What was it but a snipe, still warm, with the bloodmark on its head; otherwise it was perfect. I handed it into the larder but I didn't see her Ladyship until next day. 'That was a delicious snipe you got me,' she said. 'I'm glad to hear it,' I said, 'but you didn't get it from me, but from a sparrow-hawk.' "

In return for that strange tale I was able to tell him one of my own in the same unlikely vein, of the finest red grouse which I had ever eaten, plucked of its feathers as if by the finest poultryman. Alas I was the only one who got any good out of the ending of a sad story. That grouse was the freshest of three lying side by side on the rim of a golden eagle's eyrie whose deep cup contained a downy white chick which had died of starvation.

It didn't take much detective work to deduce the sequence of events. Somebody had lain in wait for a parent bird to arrive and shoot it as it came carrying food. The cartridge cases were below the cliff, feathers were scattered around. The surviving parent had continued to hunt, but with no mate to tear up the prey and feed morsels to the chick it had died in the midst of plenty.

I took the chick for analysis. Its gizzard was empty but its carcase held no trace of poison. At the same time I notified the police that a protected bird had been killed, the law had been broken, and that inquiries should be made if only to frighten the person nearby whom I suspected.

As for the plump grouse, a butcher gave me advice how to cook it, stuffed with sausage meat, covered in fatty bacon, and placed in a hot oven for half an hour. It made a real royal repast, and the old keeper nodded his approval as I told him of the eating of it, then in measured tones told me he had never yet shot a bird off a nest, nor a bird on the ground. Yes he had raised his gun at sparrow-hawks but they were not protected then as they are now. The merry look in his eye was enough to tell me that he had kissed the blarney stone in his time.

THE FUTURE OF RANNOCH MOOR

I do not accept that Rannoch Moor is desolate. Its liveliness is its most astonishing feature, from the moment you leave the Glen Coe road at Loch Ba and strike eastward along the trail of water that leads all the way to the railway line. It is a route without a road, in a brown waste of moraines and erratic blocks. Here is no ordinary moor, but a granite plateau, a museum of history, from the spillage of glacial rubble to the stumps of the forest whose roots trail like skeletons from the peat. Walk it in the dry east winds of spring, when the great peaks of Glen Coe are wreathed in snow, and you realise that you are trapped by mountains. The Ben Dorain group to the south, the Black Mount to the west and Perthshire's Schiehallion away out front. Follow your nose for eleven miles, keeping to the drier ground above the marshy edges of the lochs, and you will taste delight.

To me desolation means lack of life, Rannoch of the bobbing wheatears and purring dunlin is the negation of that word. My mind goes back to it last May, when over my head three short-eared owls were indulging in a communal courtship display, wheeling a thousand feet up, rubbing their wings to make a castanet rattle as they dived. I was enjoying myself, watching a black-throated diver submerging with eerie precision round some whooper swans, while from behind me came the flute-like calls of golden plover and the ringing staccato of greenshank.

Moors of mere heather become depressing. Here there was bog-bean in the lochs, waving white heads of cotton grass and aromatic scents of bog myrtle, and the little islands in the loch were green with rowan and birch. When I went over to them, teal sprang up from under my feet, though the nest I found was that of a mallard. Walking easily among the moraines and scored rocks, I tried to imagine this triangular expanse of fifty-six square miles when it was an ice-cap, fed from the surrounding peaks, squeezing its overflow eastward into what is now Loch Rannoch and Loch Tummel.

The granite mass has somehow withstood erosion, resisting ice and water, for the unusual feature of this shallow, high-altitude bog is its even height. The peat blanket is no more than a mattress, formed as waves of vegetation succeeded the melting of the ice, gaining and waning with fluctuations of climate. I sat down on a stump of Caledonian pine to try to puzzle out how much time had passed since this grey stump was a tall tree growing from a floor of pine needles.

How old? Rannoch Moor, it is said, was a forest in Roman times, and there is evidence that as recently as 300 years ago trees were being burned to exterminate wolves and outlaws who preyed upon travellers. I have been testing the truth of this by reading some of the accounts of early writers, and conclude that any burning that was done must have been to the east of the moor, for this is what Thomas Pennant says about his journey down the west edge in 1770: "Most of this long day's journey from the Black Mountain was truly melancholy, almost one continued scene of dusky moors, without arable land, trees, houses, or living creatures, for numbers of miles. The names of the wild tracts I passed through were Buachilety, Corricha-Ba, and Bendoran."

Pennant was too good an observer to have missed any trees, and he is supported by another writer in 1792, the Rev. John Lettice, of Sussex, who described the moor as: "An immense vacuity, with nothing in it to contemplate, unless numberless mis-shapen blocks of stone rising hideously above the surface of the earth."

That was a view of Rannoch Moor that persisted until the middle of the 19th century, when Principal Shairp, Professor of poetry at Oxford, wrote the vigorous poem:

Buachaille Etive's furrowed visage
To Schiehallion looked sublime,
O'er a wide and wasted desert
Old and unreclaimed as time.

Yea! a desert wide and wasted,
Washed by rainfloods to the bones
League on league of heather blasted
Storm-gashed moss, grey boulder-stones.

With the passage of the years the view of Principal Shairp has gained ground, and at the moment of writing there is concern lest the wild beauty of Rannoch Moor be concealed under a mat of sitka spruce or *Pinus contorta*; or the character of its lochs be lost by flooding if a dam is built at the west end of Loch Laidon to act as an additional reservoir for the Gaur Power Station. Two fears arise from this. The first is that the scenery of Glen Coe would be lessened if its complement of wild moor and loch were to be lost beneath a blanket of trees. And that threat becomes more imminent, because of the success of an experimental plot of conifers planted in an exposed position on the moor near Loch Ba at over 1,000ft. The second fear is that a dam would raise the water level and inundate the little islands and charming bays that remove these stretches of water from the ordinary.

Personally, I hope for a compromise. I think that many of the drier parts of the moor, such as the moraines, should be planted with trees to diversify the landscape without obscuring the views or altering the wild nature of the place. And I would hope that those watch-dogs, the Nature Conservancy, who bought 3,700 acres of high-altitude bog very close to the proposed site of the dam, will ensure that hydro-electric developments do minimum damage to shore lines.

The water of Rannoch Moor has been used for many years in the generation of electricity, and is the first link in eight power stations, with a total catchment area of 212 square miles, in which sixty miles are tunnels and aqueducts. The bog is in fact a reservoir of water, and although it could be deep-drained for trees by modern machinery, in my opinion this would be a criminal act since Rannoch is one of the last great bogs left to us.

And this brings me to the events that transformed the almost level granite plateau from forest to moor. I believe the destruction of the pine forest occurred between the 13th and the 15th century, and I base this calculation on the fact that there was a deterioration of climate in this period, which caused the Norse settlers in Greenland to fail. Study of weather in recent times shows clearly that what happens in Greenland vitally affects us here in Scotland. I believe, therefore, that the Rannoch described by Pennant had been that way for 200 to 300 years before his visit.

You have to travel a good way east of the railway line before you can see an expanse of Caledonian Forest akin to that which once covered the moor. You meet it in the celebrated Black Wood that fringes Loch Rannoch and climbs high on the hillsides, spreading wine-red boughs and needles of soft bottle green. Walk there, and you are among birch, alders, rowan and juniper, with great anthills dotted here and there among the blaeberry and heather.

This is where the pines were burned to exterminate caterans and wolves over 300 years ago. And thousands of trees were cut, to be floated eastward by the Tummel and Tay to Perth. Now, just 200 years later, the Forestry Commission are trying to redress the balance by planting 670 acres of Caledonian pines grown from local seed, while in other parts of the wood they are mixing native trees with commercial conifers of faster growth. It has taken a long time, but at last the value of our own native pines is being appreciated, for it is true that Scots pines of native origin grow a good deal better in Scotland than any imported Scots pine.

Thousands of men were billeted on Rannoch Moor to build the West Highland Railway. The next invasion was when the new Glen Coe road was built in the '30s and a great camp sprang up near Bridge of Orchy, to drive a £6 million road east of Loch Tulla, swinging up in a great bend over Black Mount, then threading a neat way between Loch na A'Claise and Loch Ba, so that you have the thrust of Clachlet towering over you on one side, and the great moor sweeping eastward, as an amazing gateway to the narrow defile of Glen Coe. Probably the easiest crossing of the moor in a west to east direction is from Kingshouse, on a good track to Black Corries, then a further nine miles of walking following telegraph poles to Rannoch.

167

Wherever you go you are likely to see red deer, and if you look closely at the ground vegetation you may find the only plant that is unique to Rannoch, *Scheuchzeria palustris,* the Rannoch rush, which is less than a foot high with six-petalled yellow-green flowers. It grows in the bog pools, and it is also found in Ireland.

I have spent much time in the remnants of the Caledonian Forest, and have been delighted of recent years at the steady build-up of capercaillie and the recolonisation by jays and crossbills of some parts of it. I know a badgers' sett above the trees, where for an hour before dark you can see them playing round the stones of a former summer shieling. And it was in a Rannoch eyrie that I found a golden eagle's varied collection of prey containing two fox cubs, a leg of lamb and a grouse.

Rannoch Moor is one of the last great wild places in Britain. Man hastened the decline of the forest, but I believe that most of what we see is a natural creation, and that it has existed for 500 years. We can only conjecture what the plateau of trailing lochs and granite boulders was like before that time, when wild boar foraged in the bogs, and caribou were stalked by wolves, and elk and lynx shared the same woods with brown bears. That page in our history is, alas, gone. But we can ensure that we preserve what is left, if we make room for the preservation of wilderness in our planning.

Go North for Good Weather in Skye

Crossing to Skye in the rain, I suggested we get as far away as possible from the Cuillins and head for the lower country of Trotternish, the most northern wing of the island where the clouds do not hang about the way they do in the south.

Faith indeed, and well rewarded too, for in Uig we had the first burst of sunshine and the sight of white crofts sparkling in an amphitheatre of greenery stopped us in our tracks.

Yes, this was the place to stay in a natural corrie verdant with flowers and gullies white with blossom. Moreover there was a sound I love coming from the fields, the "rasp-rasp" of corncrakes which I hadn't heard for a long time. Booking into the hotel we found we shared it with a happy bus party from a' the airts of Scotland, Borderers, Paisley buddies, Glaswegians, and they were enraptured with the scene, especially as their first two days had been dreich.

No doubt about it the finest visibility always comes after rain. We certainly had it in good measure next day in sunshine that lasted from dawn till sunset. Distance was banished. Even the high hills of Harris revealed fine detail of grey rock and ridge, especially from the buttress ruins of Duntulm Castle perched on a cliff hazed with bluebells. Skylarks poured down their songs. Looking down on a field yellow with buttercups

I actually "saw" a concrake.

Normally you don't get so much as a glimpse of this rasper, maybe a merest mouse-glimpse in long grass. This one was actually showing off from a stance, and we could see its head turning and its bill opening and closing as it "crake-craked". It elongated its neck, too, as if to throw the voice better, and the impression I had was of a slim longish bird with rich red-brown feathering— a summer migrant which seems to be disappearing from all areas— even in the croftlands where it was once common.

It certainly is not scarce in Trotternish, not around this north-western part once known as the granary of Skye—"laughing with corn"— and thereby hangs a very interesting tale of how the best land was won from a loch that covered it— moreover a loch with an island on it called after St. Columba. From a small chapel on it his missionaries spread Christianity through Skye. Later it became a monastery, to be taken over by invading Norsemen.

Today the flat cornland is reverting to marsh, and finding a dry enough route to the ruins of the chapel made a fascinating bog-hop along the edges of silted-up ditches yellow with marsh marigolds and iris where sedge warbler and reed bunting songs mingled with the chuckles of wheatears and twites, barking ravens, curlews, redshanks, and peewits.

The ruins, mostly flattened by time, were much more extensive than we expected with remains of bee-hive dwellings in what we took to be the chapel foundation. Perched on the former island-top we could look across to the gaunt ruins of Monkstadt— the monks steading— the home of the MacDonald chief in the time of the 1745 Rising.

A big detour over very wet ground took us to the substantial house and steadings, from where we descended to a historic spot, Prince Charlie's Point. This was where Flora MacDonald brought him dressed as her maid Betty Burke, leaving him on the shore while she called at Monkstadt and held an enemy officer in conversation while arrangements were being made to spirit Charlie away.

Charlie must have been a bonny walker by the big swatches of rough ground he covered, especially his night march from Portree to Elgol via a pass across the Red Cuillin to be confronted across another pass by the bulk of Blaven. No wonder he exclaimed that even the Devil wouldn't be able to find him now.

THE HILLS OF DEE

There we were, Adam Watson and myself, watching the sunset gold on the winding Dee from the top of a heathery hill above Glen Dye. Through a gap in the hills we could see skyscraper blocks in Aberdeen, fairy towers tinged with pink in the soft light, and westward of them the hard blue edge of Bennachie soaring up as if to announce the beginning of the Highlands. Fields of yellow and green sloped to Banchory and the sweep of the Hill of Fare. Against the red ball of the sun, ridge after ridge stood silhouetted against each other.

"It's not often you get such clarity in summer," observed Adam. "From the top of Glas Maol today you could see hills away down the Forth." The forecast had been gloomier than the weather turned out to be — only a few showers of hail instead of the snow we had been told to expect on the tops.

We had met up that morning at 9.30 a.m., but had gone our different ways because Adam had scientific work to do with his pointer dogs. He uses them in his study areas to put up grouse and ptarmigan so that he can count the numbers of adults to young and thus get an accurate picture of breeding success. It is slow, demanding work, calling for concentration, and as tedious for a companion as watching a man angling.

So instead of joining Adam I invited his father to come with me and my wife to Bennachie, which might be old hat to him but would be new to us. I've meant to climb it often enough, knowing how beloved it is by Aberdonians. Indeed, we were nearly run down by some of the six bus-loads of children aged from six to twelve who were running, leaping and sliding down the path as we got on to the steeps of the Mither Tap.

The 250 or so kids were from various parts of Aberdeen, and it was fortuitous, I learned, that they had all opted for the same outing on the same day. Spread out along half the mountain, they were enjoying themselves on a peak that is just the right height for good fun without too much fatigue. I was enchanted by the route from Maiden Castle, past the early Christian Maiden Stone, a 10ft-high plinth of pinkish granite embossed with strange Pictish symbols. Weird legends surround the 1000-year-old stone. Forestry Commission spruces grow above it high on the hill now, which makes the revelation all the greater when you emerge from the trees into the open and get the view over an agricultural quilt, of fields and farms rolling in waves below you. Adam senior swept his hand to indicate the Garioch district extending to Buchan in the east, complemented the other way by the River Don winding to Monymusk:

Ae mile o Don's worth twa o Dee,
Except it be for fish an tree.

You could see the truth of the couplet in the well-populated countryside with its wealth of farms, compared to the wilder Dee enclosed by hills and woods.

The higher we climbed the more interesting the peak above us looked, a point above a rocky girdle of cliffs with a path winding steeply through them. A portion of enormously thick wall is the remains of an ancient fortification inside which Iron Age men no doubt sought safety. We chose to scramble up the rocks, stepping on to the summit as a cold shower passed and rainbows stood over the brilliant fields stretching to the sea. Tap o' Noth, the cone of Ben Rinnes, Lochnagar, the Cairngorms, they were all visible at different times as the showers passed and a superb afternoon developed.

Now we went west to take in the highest "tap", Oxen Craig, 1,733ft., and its neighbour, Watch Craig, below which the Gadie runs. Forestry Commission woods ring all the lower slopes of the three-mile-long ridge, but it used to be common land where folk cut their peats and grazed their stock. Then in the early 19th century, when there was genuine land-hunger, the needier folk built shacks on the hill and tried to farm the land. This is when the lairds took action. With the help of Parliament, they divided Bennachie between them, charged rents, and evicted those who could not pay. In time even those who stayed had to emigrate, for the land was too poor to support them. Perhaps it was the exiles who sang the song:

> Oh, gin I were far Gadie rins,
> Far Gadie rins, far Gadie rins,
> Oh, gin I were far Gadie rins
> At the back o Bennachie.

That day, before climbing the hill, we had done a circuit of the Hill of Fare, for I'd just been hearing the words of a new ballad sung to the tune of "Bonny Banchory Oh," by Scott Skinner. The words, by Mrs Betty Allan, go like this:

> It's uranium they're after, and they're bent
>   on howkin't oot.
> And they think we've got it here at Bonny
>   Banchory oh!
> Weel, we nivver felt the wont o't, and we'd
>   raither dae withoot.
> We're the guardians o this bonny Deeside
>   country oh!

171

No, we canna let them connach Bonny
    Banchory oh!
No, we canna let them connach Bonny
    Banchory oh!
They wid spoil the Hill o Fare—
Leave it desolate and bare—
No, we canna let them connach Bonny
    Banchory oh!

The future sad Deesiders, if there's any
    livin here
A hundred years fae noo in Bonny
    Banchory oh!
Wi their carcinogenic water, and their
    radioactive air
Will be lookin roon in vain for ony sanctuary
    oh!

Then fit will they think o us in Bonny
    Banchory oh?
When they're chokin in the dust at Bonny
    Banchory oh!
No, we canna let them doon!
We maun aa defend oor toon!
Will the con men talk us roon?
No! Bonny Banchory, NO!

The Hill of Fare is just two miles north of Banchory, a 1,400ft. wooded bump surrounded by charming farmland, cut up by tiny roads which are rural backwaters. Local people became alert to the dangers of uranium mining after the Orcadians had rejected totally any prospecting for it, on the grounds that if quantities were found an evil they do not want would be inflicted on them.

Deeside folk are worried because the prospectors, the South of Scotland Electricity Board, aim to prospect in two areas north and south of Banchory. What the local folk would like is a clear statement about what is going on. They want to know what a mine would be like. And they want to know the policy of the planning authorities on uranium extraction.

Since visiting the Hill of Fare, I have been reading a report by Friends of the Earth (Aberdeen) called *A Promise to Move Mountains,* which is about the search for uranium on Deeside. Other areas where a search may be made to find fuel for future nuclear power stations are Caithness, Sutherland and Skye. Residents in these regions should read this report which is published by Aberdeen People's Press, 167 King Street, Aberdeen, price 50p.

The dangers are uglier than anything I envisaged, not only because of

172

the mammoth size of the mine-workings, but in terms of radioactive waste or gas which could be released. Uranium is safe in the ground, but when concentrated to produce fuel for nuclear energy it carries grave risks to man and animals. It makes a mockery of any of our pleas for conservation.

Adam and I talked about some of these things as we sat on top of the hill watching the sunset and hatching a plan for the next day. His father would drive us to the Spittal of Muick, leave us there and take the car round to Invercauld, so we would be in position to climb Lochnagar by the north-eastern corrie, traverse the tops and descend northwards through the ancient pines of Ballochbuie, the finest fragment of primeval forest remaining in Scotland.

Nor did that sunset belie its promises for the next day was full of colour, the heather tints nearly as pink as the granite in the Pass of Ballater.

Glen Muick has become more popular since I was last there, thanks to the creation of an information centre for visitors to the Scottish Wildlife Trust Reserve arranged in conjunction with Balmoral Estate. We didn't take the path, but struck directly across the north shoulder of the pointed Meikle Pap among blaeberries soon purpling our lips with their juice. Above us floated St Mark's flies, little hang-gliders with dangling legs. A grouse rose and pitched down a dozen yards away on top of a heather knoll, her red wattle, speckled throat and reddish breast towards us. "It's a hen with young chicks in the heather," said Adam.

At which the crafty grouse researcher made a sharp staccato whistle in imitation of the anxiety call of chicks. This had an instant effect on the mother. She rose and dropped within a few yards of us. At the same moment three chicks rose, followed a moment or two later by a fourth bird rising to a repeat of Adam's whistle.

Dr Adam Watson D.Sc., to give him his full title, directs the grouse-research team from the Institute of Terrestrial Ecology H.Q. at Blackhall, Banchory, and much of his work is on the hills and moors studying the behaviour of grouse and ptarmigan. He told me this had been an unusual year, with grouse on the lower moors doing poorly because of the cold spring and poor heather growth, while the high nesting birds did well because they lay their eggs later and thus missed the killing combination of cold and lack of food at a critical time.

On the other hand, the high-living ptarmigan of the Cairngorms did poorly because so much snow covered their feeding grounds at 3,500ft., while birds on the lower hills did reasonably around 3,000ft. As for dotterel, I was astonished to hear that in late July a cock was still on eggs and that some young were still very small. "I wish you could have been with us on Ben Macdhui in May; the amount of snow was quite incredible, every bump covered and the sun shining day after day."

However, you can't be in two places at once, so I could only marvel at the tales of mid-summer ski-ing while I was out in the Hebrides. "This is snow-bed vegetation we are on now," said Adam, pointing to patches of

173

Arctic blaeberry which has bigger leaves and is a darker green than the common plant. Soon we were boulder-hopping, progressing literally by leaps and bounds on gigantic granite blocks spilling down towards the hidden loch at the foot of the Muckle corrie.

What a spot! A dark oval of loch beneath a perfect horseshoe of savage cliffs rising dramatically from hanging screes in a total rise of 1,200ft. Halfway up the cliffs, like flies on a wall, were three climbers on Eagle Ridge. We watched them through the glasses, remembering the grim November ascent we had done with Tom Patey in rain, sleet and eventually snow.

Today, however, we agreed we would rather be doing what we were doing, enjoying the edge of the horseshoe, scrambling on the boulders in the sunshine and cool breeze. Swifts wheeled over us, and we could hear their wings cleaving the air as they hunted down insects.

"Look!" said Adam as we came over the top. "There's Ben Nevis and the Tower Ridge. That's Morven in Caithness, and there's your own hills, Ben More and Stobinian, away to the south." At the cairn the only sign of the Jubilee bonfire was a black circle on the ground and big granite blocks split with the heat. Snow and bad weather made it dangerous to go up Lochnagar on Jubilee night, and no one knows who put a match to the ten tons of combustible material which was being kept for mid-summer night.

Lochnagar is Adam's favourite mountain, with eleven tops over 3,000ft. sixty-three square miles over 1,250ft., three corrie lochans, plenty of alpine grassland, shady places where rare alpine plants grow, and, distributed over it from woodlands to summit the whole range of Cairngorm birds.

We tramped across to the Stuic, past the silky white seed-hairs of the least willow which would 'soon be blowing on the wind. Deer, rich red in the sunlight of a perfect late afternoon, were lying down or feeding like cattle on the shoulder we were descending. Right in front of us we could see the slabs of Devil's Point gleaming redly under Cairntoul. Immediately opposite rose Beinn a' Bhuird and Ben Avon, looking deceptively near.

Now and again we stopped to enjoy the richness of the light on the heather and granite boulders at our backs, where last winter's snow still gleamed. Then we were into the first pines of that most marvellous forest, Ballochbuie, enjoying the comfortable descent all the way to the glittering River Dee where the car was waiting for us, and so was a flask of tea which was nectar.

Weirdies of the Winged Isle

You can't exhaust Trotternish of Skye in a week, especially if you are a hill man interested in such bizarre rock formations as the Quirang and the Storr where eroding pinnacles reach their craziest form.

In the mist we took the track that runs from Loch Langaig, climbing and traversing into one of the most dramatic changes of scene to be found in Scotland, mysterious that morning by reason of the drizzling cloud.

With no real point of focus we had the feeling of entering a hanging valley, of weird knolls imprisoning black pools of water under the loom of towering crags. Upward movement seemed unlikely, yet I knew that is where we must go, for I'd been here before in clear weather. The dim shadow of a pinnacle over our heads suggested we were getting close.

Could this spire be the Needle? If it were, then I knew the route must be up the very steep screes above us, unlikely as they looked. The word Quirang is from the Gaelic Cuith-raing, meaning Pillared Stronghold, and the Needle is part of the upper cliff which has collapsed, eroding to a slim overhanging spire 120ft. high, guarding the entrance to a weird tumble of material intersected by gullies and backed by unclimbably loose cliff.

Up we went, feeling our way, nosing into unlikely places by blind gullies until we hit two tight rock portals, the magic entry to the very Everest of natural rock gardens hanging in alpine flowers, sprays of mossy and starry saxifrages, clumps of golden roseroot, ledges of purple orchis, bunches of red and bladder campion, tall stems of water avens and many another. The voice of the misty place was appropriate too, the shrill calls of the mountain blackbird, the ring ouzel.

The flowers thrive on the disintegrating volcanic rock and up we scrambled to perhaps the most extraordinary feature of this collapsed cliff—"The Table," a close cropped flat of green where in former times shinty matches were played to celebrate mid-summer day, a table, though, whose legs are sheer cliffs in places.

We had the inner sanctuary of the Quirang to ourselves that misty day, and had the weather been clear we would have traversed round past the Needle and wended our way to the 1,779ft. summit for the mighty view of north-west Scotland stretching from the 130-mile chain of the Outer Hebrides to the peaks of Torridon and Sutherland. Indeed you can walk from that summit for nineteen miles, following a switch-back of summits involving nearly 8,000ft. of climbing, to descend near Portree.

But whatever you do, try not to miss the highest summit of that group, the Storr by way of the Old Man which stands above the road like a factory chimney 160ft. high, the senior of an extraordinary family of weirdies carved from the lavas of the last volcanic eruption in Tertiary times.

The word storr is derived from the Gaelic and has the double meaning of high cliff and decayed tooth. It could also include eye-sockets through which daylight gleams, carved out by erosion. The Old Man has a drunken lean about him and one day must fall, but meantime you can shelter from the rain under its overhanging base. Astonishingly even for these days of high technology, it has been climbed by two different routes.

Sensible folk will find a nice easy way to the 2,358ft. summit of the Storr

175

by traversing north below the cliff and turning up the grassy slopes at the first opportunity. Scrambling botanists will have fun by going directly up from the Old Man, where flowers festoon the ledges as on the Quirang.

Whichever way you go, the top of Ben Storr is the place to view "The Winged Isle" of the Gael, an excellent topographical description. It was the Norsemen who named it Skye—Isle of Cloud—which even in mist is never dull.

ROB ROY'S COUNTRY

After the marvellous summer of 1976 we did not expect the bonus of an autumn whose lingering colours lasted into winter in an abnormally windless October and November. One frosty morning was specially memorable, the golden ball of the sun rising into a cloudless sky glittering on the foreground rime and setting off the red bracken colours so sharply that I felt as if I was seeing my own backdoor view for the first time.

Back from a walk to enjoy the exceptional visibility I quickly packed my bag with flask and piece, picked up my camera, and took the road to Loch Katrine by Loch Ard and Loch Chon. Having to pass picture after picture round every bend was a photographer's despair. The roadside colours were fantastic enough. It was the reflections on the oil-smooth waters which were compelling: glowing carpets richer than any Persian rug in patterns of reds and yellows and coppery colours from golden birches, smoky larches, green spruces, reds of bracken and crimson deer grass.

A little grebe was diving smoothly, creating rippling concentric rings. Fieldfares were bursting from roadside trees in soft greys and rich browns. A big flock of siskins and redpolls flew above the road.

In contrast to all this was the rise to bare Loch Arklet with the rampart of the Arrochar Alps stretched across its western skyline, a knobbly mass of grey schist thrusting up so close that you would never know that Loch Lomond was trenched before them. My destination was the other way, east for half a mile into the wee world of Stronachlachar at the edge of Loch Katrine.

I wanted to walk the two miles of oaks and birches between me and Royal Cottage, but I was brought up short almost at once by an unusual sight, a gleaming white ship not on the water, but on shore. Standing looking at it was a man I knew, Arthur Campbell who is superintendent of the Loch Katrine waterworks for the Strathclyde Regional Council. "No it's not there by accident," he said cheerfully. "The *Sir Walter Scott* is up on her cradle for the Board of Trade Inspectors who are expected shortly. I'm going aboard. Are you coming?"

I didn't need a second invitation. As we went on board, up from below came John Mowat, engineer, the mate, John Fraser, and deckhand Robin Frame.

After he had talked business with the skipper, Arthur Campbell walked down to Royal Cottage with me. "I never expected to be put in charge of the 25,000 acres of this estate when I came here as a plumber," he said. "But it's a very happy place. There's more social life here than in the city.

177

The women have the Rural, the children have a club, and so do the men. There are sixty-four employed, and we have billiards and darts, and a game we play called 'Summer Ice' — a kind of indoor curling. They say it was brought here by the Irishmen who constructed the tunnels, and we have a league with the surrounding villages."

I asked him what all the men did. "Well, there's six in the boat crew, sailing daily from Trossachs Pier to Stronachlachar in summer. Half of them work on the estate in the winter. We have fifty houses so we need a maintenance staff of joiners, plumbers, painters and an electrician. We have 9,000 sheep on the hills so we have twelve shepherds. We have hill cattle, and we do a certain amount of vermin control.

Loch Katrine is eight miles long, one mile wide, and about half of it reaches a depth of 400ft. "We don't allow car access except at Stronachlachar and Trossachs Pier. It's a conservation measure because the water which goes to Glasgow is so pure that it doesn't need treatment. The estate is free for walking or cycling, but we'd risk pollution if we made it a free-for-all and opened the shore as a motor road."

For me the charm of Loch Katrine is that it is such an exciting place for walking and cycling, and there is no better two-mile stretch than down to Royal Cottage, with its fine views across the loch to the spine of knobbly crests that block the way to Balquhidder. On the walk you pass the aqueduct which diverts the water of Loch Arklet into Loch Katrine, without which it would tip westwards into Loch Lomond.

From Royal Cottage, Loch Katrine gushes out by tunnel to be carried through aqueducts by gravity to Glasgow. Archie took me down to the inlet point to read the height-marker. "It's two feet from the brim at the moment, and at this level the 90,000,000 gallons or more we send to Glasgow draws off no more than one inch per day. We could go for four months without rain here, and one of the reasons why the drought didn't affect Glasgow was because we had so much rain during the winter and spring that Loch Katrine was abnormally high when the heatwave set in.

"But we did a historic thing last summer. We actually fed some Loch Lomond water into our system, by pumping water from their pipeline into ours. The two pipelines lie close to each other at Balmore, and about 10,000,000 gallons was pumped from Loch Lomond into our Milngavie aqueduct. We also let out about five million gallons per day to Loch Achray and Loch Venachar as compensation water to feed the River Teith. Lochs Venachar and Drunkie supply the main compensation water for the Teith, totalling about 50,000 gallons a day from the three sources."

Glasgow was ahead of the rest of Britain by acquiring Loch Katrine and building the first modern aqueduct. Queen Victoria performed the opening ceremony in 1859 by sailing in the *Rob Roy* to Royal Cottage and opening the sluice gates to send Loch Katrine water rushing by tunnel and pipelines 25¾ miles to Milngavie without the need for filtration.

Mounting water-demand necessitated a second aqueduct being opened thirty years later, and in all Loch Katrine has been raised three times to enable Glasgow to cream off 17ft. of reservoir. Arthur Campbell's main task is to control the amount of water going to Glasgow.

Driving back along the road, we stopped to look at the Factor's Isle, now embanked against erosion by the artificial level of the loch. This is where Graham of Killearn, Factor to Montrose was marooned by Rob Roy after being relieved of the £3,000 he was carrying in rent. Meanwhile, the bold Rob was awaiting a reply to a letter he had sent to the Duke demanding a ransom of 3,400 merks. No reply came, so Rob kept the cash he had in hand and released the furious Factor after five or six days.

Rob was born at the head of Loch Katrine, at Glengyle, and the modern mansion on the site incorporates a lintel of the original MacGregor homestead. Above the house is the ancient graveyard of the Dugald Ciar Mhor sept of the "nameless clan". Blood-thirsty Dugald was Rob Roy's ancestor, and is remembered in history for a dastardly act at the Battle of Glenfruin. Placed on guard over a party of young students who had come to watch the fight, Dugald murdered them. The year was 1603. Between two and three hundred Colquhouns had been slain in the battle and James VI took action by ordering that all members of the MacGregor clan be hunted down and exterminated.

Rob himself was not a bloodthirsty man. Leader of the infamous "Highland Watch" he used his brains rather than his noted skill with the claymore. He would take your money and guarantee to drive your cattle safely to market. If you didn't pay, the cattle would mysteriously vanish. He was not all rogue. In these wild times of the late 17th century and into the 18th he was a force for keeping law and order.

I was thinking about Rob as I drove back to Loch Arklet and stopped at a farm called Corriearklet halfway along the north side of the moorland shore. It was in a house of the same name on this spot that Rob married Mary of Comer at New Year in 1693. That date is just one year after the massacre of Glencoe, and it is not generally realised that Rob Roy's mother was a sister of Campbell of Glen Lyon who was given the luckless task of master-minding that vile deed. This was the reason that Rob changed his name to Campbell when King William proscribed again the MacGregor clan shortly after the massacre.

Farther west of Corriearklet at the end of the loch are Inversnaid Cottages where Rob had his house when he was master of Craig Royston and had made the whole eastern shore of Loch Lomond his charge. It was here he made his greatest blunder. Fleeing north from the law he should have taken his wife and family with him. He didn't, and Mary and her three children fell victim to constables and bailiffs under the command of Graham of Killearn. Roughly handled and beaten, Mary was turned out into the darkness of a November night in 1712 and Inversnaid House set alight. Montrose was behind the affair. From that day he was Rob's implacable enemy, hence the affair of the Factor's Island which came later.

So the "Glengyle Watch" had a new role, to wage war on Montrose, which they did with such effect that a "Garrison" was built at Inversnaid so that troops could be stationed to contain Rob and his men. I visited the ruins at dusk and had a chuckle to myself when I thought of Rob waiting until the building was nearly completed, when he swooped down, blew it up, set fire to the bunk beds and made off. Today the old walls are used as a sheep fank, and the Loch Katrine children attend the wee school next door.

Just a fortnight later I was back in Rob's country, in Aberfoyle this time, with a surprise of sunshine as I drove out of mist on the low ground into blue skies and the blazing autumn colours still continuing. My port of call was the David Marshall Lodge to report myself ready to do my duty by performing an offical opening ceremony in the Loch Achray Forest. The occasion was the starting of the new "Wayfaring Course" and I had the honour of being the first "Wayfarer".

It was nice to see so many faces known to me, my old friend Pat Sandeman the ornithologist, Bill Murray, with whom I have explored in the Himalaya, Mrs Jean Balfour of the Countryside Commission, Bill McMurtrie of the Border Hillwalkers, and many another. My pleasant task was to plot my way to a control point, and be the first to receive a certificate. Basically, the idea is to test yourself with a map among a maze of paths by finding your own way through the forest. Sponsors of the scheme are the Forestry Commission and the British Orienteering Federation.

"Wayfaring" is a simpler sport than orienteering in that you can make it as easy or as difficult as you like. The starting point is one mile past the David Marshall Lodge, and you need a Wayfaring Pack available at the Lodge for 30p. For this money, you get a map, a control card and instructions on how to use the course.

The starting point is signposted, and there you will find the master map showing all the control points. It is up to you to select an easy, an intermediate, or a difficult course. Having taken your pick, you must copy the control points from the master map on to your own map — the one you got in the Wayfaring Pack. Now you can set off reading your way from one control point to the next.

In my view it is an excellent way to get some excitement from forest trails which in themselves tend to be dull because one path through dense forest tends to be very much like another. With observation and the map you can have a lot of fun sorting out the maze of paths. You also qualify for a certificate even if you only navigate from one point to another.

Actually, the finest way of seeing the Achray Forest is to go to the top of the Duke's Pass. Just over the crest you will find a car park with steps leading uphill from it to a scenic viewpoint. From there you can appreciate how nature and man have managed to mix natural oaks and birches with Sitka spruce and larch. Nature has taught the forester lessons by blowing down geometrical blocks and forcing him to replant with more ragged edges. The result you can see before you in trees of various ages and species giving great richness of colour and variety.

Today, there are something like 170 miles of paths in the Queen Elizabeth Forest Park, and even Rob Roy, whose map was in his head could get lost here. My own feeling is that in my lifetime this side of the Trossachs has been beautified immensely since it became a State Forest forty years ago. It holds an infinitely greater wealth of wild life than in the old days.

As for Loch Katrine, I think we could call it our first real Nature Reserve, thanks to water conservation and the necessity of keeping it free of pollution. Any one can enjoy Loch Katrine, but to explore its shores and glens you must pay a capital price of foot-poundage, or push a bicycle. The balance between access and inaccessibility is nicely held, benefiting us all.

Raasay: Island of the Big Men

Raasay was certainly looking green that morning when I landed with Dr Sorley MacLean who can trace eight generations of his forbears to the island where he was born.

His poetry, to be read in Gaelic for full appreciation, concerns itself with love of its woods, the charm of its inward and outward views, mingled with sad reflections on the past peoples who have gone.

Red Hills and Black Cuillin peaks tower hugely over the crofts of Oscaig which is his township. "Did you know that Raasay used to be called the island of the big men?" he asks, as he tells me of the extraordinary fertility of its fields. A hundred of its population of 600 people marched with Prince Charlie and suffered for it. Over 300 houses were burned and all the livestock killed.

The fourteen-mile-long island has an extraordinary geology, ancient gneiss in the north with Torridonian sandstone, yet on the Glam is rich oolite soil of great depth rising green to 900ft. In gorge walls heather reaches jungle proportions and birches cling in the gullies. Its west coast road rises to 700ft. ending at the ruinous eyrie of Brochel Castle. The superb eastern side is spanned only by a footpath overlooking the deepest water round the coast of Britain.

Just north of Churchtown Bay where most of Raasay's 130 folk live you don't have to look hard to find the ruins of settlements dating to the time when Raasay's expanding population reached 900. Another crumbling relic, but of more recent times, is the iron-ore mine building, on a high road between east and west side, worked during the First World War by German prisoners. The "miner's rows" built to house the miners at Inverarish were bought up by the Raasay folk for £30 each at the end of the last war. It was a bargain period for property seekers which caused the downfall of Raasay house, bought up by the late Dr Green who let it fall into decay. When he bought it, the lovely house was a thirty bedroom hotel with historic connections. Dr Johnson and Boswell had stayed in it in 1773 when it was the elegant home of MacLeod of Raasay, who was able to boast that despite what Raasay had suffered in the Jacobite aftermath not one man had left the island.

Eviction began however when the last of the McLeod lairds sold out to Mr George Rainey who cleared ninety-four families between 1846 and 1849. From 900 the population had dropped to 354 in 1931. Twenty years later it was 280, and is 130 as the island gets a new hotel in 1980. The question then is what has Raasay to offer the summer visitor which Skye has not?

My answer would be the lure of a small island, especially for those who can walk and climb. The highest peak is Dun Caan, a mere 1456ft. but commanding from its little table top an extraordinary complication of peaky mountains and a fret-work of sea and lochs. Even the indolent Boswell felt energetic enough to dance a jig on top of it. The little table mountain has oil shale and iron ore and may yet yield some treasure, for the seams though low grade are extensive.

Meantime the car-ferry operating from Sconsor on a daily schedule had brought some life to the island and made it easy for folk to load cattle or sheep direct on a lorry, drive off to a sale, and be back the same day. Sheep are worked on a club system, 2000 of stock divided into ten shares.

The late Dr John Green of Bexhill-on-Sea is remembered for his most unsympathetic statement: "Raasay is an island of outstanding natural beauty where you can get right away from modern life. In my view the whole idea of a ferry scheme is hopelessly uneconomic and perfectly stupid. If the islanders don't like things as they are they can leave."

At the time of writing it he had visited his mouldering properties only once since their purchase ten years before, and only for a couple of hours at that.

He is certainly right about the natural beauty. Visit it if you can. You will find Raasay House being restored by lads to make an outdoor and adventure centre.

ST. KILDA IN THE ROCKET AGE

What are the most striking changes a St Kildan would find were he to return to his old village, abandoned in 1930 when the population of forty-three removed to make new lives on the Scottish mainland, sad yet glad to leave the remoteness of an island that had become a prison to them? They left when they were better fed and better housed than at any time in the island's long history; but for them the old ways of fishing, wild-fowling, cultivating the small fields and herding sheep and cattle had lost its savour. They sailed away with some sticks of furniture and a few precious belongings, and for twenty-seven years the island lay empty; only the odd exception of visiting naturalists broke the isolation, finding delight in the millions of birds and the unique mice and sheep for which St. Kilda is famous.

Then, in 1957, the Royal Air Force became the new colonists of Village Bay, bringing with them the first wheeled vehicles in the island's history, as beach landing-craft unloaded the materials for constructing a modern radar station, together with stone-crushing machinery, electricity-generating plant and high explosives for blowing a hole in the storm beach to expand the beach-head.

I was there shortly after the RAF landed and was amazed at the drive put into blasting and bulldozing St. Kilda, as men worked round the clock in a shift system, while members of the Ordnance Survey shone beacon lamps from the summit of Conachair to tie St. Kilda to the main triangulation of Britain, so that it would have national-grid status — important for the tracking of rockets fired from South Uist some fifty miles away.

In the bang and clatter of machines, amid a great coming and going of workmen, I was glad that I had known St. Kilda when it had the status of a desert island; when in July the drumming of snipe went on right round the clock, and time seemed to stand still as the sun wheeled day after day from horizon to horizon. Apart from the cottages whose roofs had fallen in, the island looked very much as it must have done for 1,000 years.

A St. Kildan would be amazed were he to return to his old village today. He would see wheeled vehicles running swiftly from the village area to a radar station on the summit of Ruival containing some of the most advanced instruments in the world; and in the NAAFI canteen he could drink beer while watching television. Would his mind quicken with memories of the community who lived along one tiny street, cut off from the outside world for six months of every year? Would he regret that he gave up an old way of life without wages, when goods were obtained by barter and rent was paid by birds and wool? Whichever way his thoughts might run, it was inevitable that the steady rundown of St. Kilda could not be halted. Subsistence was not enough.

Probably the biggest surprise to a visiting St. Kildan would be the Soay sheep. Formerly these aboriginal sheep were confined to neighbouring Soay but after the St. Kildans left, 107 of them were rounded up on their small native island and released on the wider acres of Hirta. That herd at the time of writing is now over 1,600 strong; thus the most important breed of primitive sheep left in the world has reached a balance of population not so very far from the equivalent of the domestic stock kept by the St. Kildans. Behind that figure of 1,600 lies a most interesting story, revealing how nature controls the population density of an animal roaming wild in a closed environment. Study of the Soay sheep has shown that numbers build up for four or five years to reach a peak population, then crash by disease, leaving a population reduced to nearly half.

Who brought the Soay sheep to St. Kilda is not known, but it is certain that the species is very close to the wild moufflon of Asia and the Mediterranean mountains, and it also has an affinity with the peat sheep first domesticated by Neolithic man in Asia. Long-legged and fleet-footed, it is more like a goat than a sheep, and by the happy accident of isolation it remains to us as a link with primitive man, whose ancestors are supposed to have begun their wanderings in Central Asia.

The St. Kildan would find that the house-mouse, which shared his cottage, has now been replaced by the almost rat-like field-mouse. *Mus muralis* did not survive the passing of the people upon whom it depended. It could not compete with its more numerous neighbour, *Apodemus hirtensis,* which is thriving inside and outside the houses nowadays. The last house-mouse seen alive was in 1931, so a uniquely adapted rodent has vanished from the face of the earth.

No one quite knew what the wren population of St. Kilda was, until Kenneth Williamson worked out the population density by listening to singing cocks and plotting their territories. His number of 230 pairs shows how well this largest and loudest singing wren in the world is holding its own, despite its stormy environment. Williamson showed me nests built into the corner of "cleitts" (dome-shaped stone structures), so we were able to examine the greyer plumage and stouter bill that differentiate it from other wrens. I found that, wherever I went on St. Kilda, I would hear the song of these delightful birds, which is shrill enough to compete with the ocean waves.

I slept out several nights on various parts of the cliffs. One memorable expedition was to Carn More, with Dr. Eggeling, of the Nature Conservancy, to try and discover whether or not Leach's petrels return to their burrows in early May, since no one had previously studied the arrival dates of these rare birds on St. Kilda. We took sleeping bags, since the night was cold, and were lucky to find a cleitt for shelter. From our eyrie we looked down a plunge of darkness to the sea like crinkled satin in the veiled moonlight. Immense headlands plunged sheer on every side.

We pricked up our ears when the first shearwaters came in, whizzing over our heads with witch's screams. It was after midnight now, and still no Leach's petrels; and we were resolving to turn into our sleeping bags, when from over our heads came a laughing phrase — short, staccato and unmistakable. Soon we could discern darker streaks flickering on the night sky as they danced over our heads. Dr. Eggeling had never seen a Leach's petrel, and it looked as if he were not going to see one that night He turned in at 2.30 a.m., while I sat outside our stone bedchamber, which had just room enough inside for two. I was taking my last look round outside, when I felt the brush of feathers on my face, and next moment heard a rustle inside the cleitt. Instantly I flashed my torch, and down its beam fluttered a grey shape, with jet-black eyes and legs, trying to hide among our sleeping bags.

"Wake up!" I said to Eggeling. "Here's a Leach's petrel come to see you." So he had the pleasure of examining this musty-smelling bird as it lay quietly in his hand, while he spread its forked tail, looked at its white rump, and felt the delicate tube of its nostrils. I had the thrill of finding a new colony of these birds half way down the face of Conachair, among boulders whose recesses were shared by Manx shearwaters and thousands of puffins.

It was an astonishing sight to watch the orange ball of the sun rise from the Atlantic behind the three greatest rock stacks in the North Atlantic — Stac an Armin (627 ft.), a sharp tooth spiking higher than the more rotund Stac Li, and above them both the wall of Boreray rising in a cliff twice as high again, all three white with gannets.

A St. Kildan would be surprised to find that, since man left the islands, the great Atlantic seal has moved in to the Manse area of the village shore, to Gleann Bay and to the Dun Slabs. These greatest of British mammals breed on St. Kilda from August until November, and about 100 pups are born annually. The RAF watchers have shown that the peak of breeding activity is between the end of October and the beginning of November, when bulls, cows and pups lie on rocks and in caves. It is clear that depopulation of remote islands in various parts of Scotland has opened up new breeding grounds for seals: hence, perhaps, the remarkable increase of these animals in recent years. Atlantic seals were given protection at a time when commercial exploitation had almost ceased, and the world population is now thought to be around 50,000; whereas fifty years ago numbers were perhaps less than 1,000. It is still, however, the rarest seal in the world.

No doubt a St. Kildan coming back to the island would be chiefly interested in the new works of man and his electronic equipment; but the visiting scientist is much more interested in unravelling the mystery of the stone dwellings that tell of successive ages of man there. I mentioned

185

sleeping in one of the stone cleitts. There are hundreds of these curious structures dotted over St. Kilda — dome-shaped, with overlapping slabs so that the wind can whistle through while no rain gets inside. They are, in fact, Stone-Age drying-machines. They were used by the St. Kildans for storing anything that would be affected by damp.

Different from them are two beehive structures with bedchambers probably used by man about 1,000 years ago. Other stone structures of different shape enabled Dr. Iain Whittaker, of the School of Scottish Studies, to find the site of a village built before 1830. This anthropologist also recorded a pre-Viking settlement of beehive houses in Gleann Bay, each group in a cluster of three, untouched and unspoiled. Thanks to the vigilance of the National Trust, nothing is being disturbed or excavated except under expert guidance.

History and natural history pose exciting problems to the student of life and wild life. Man left behind him his primitive sheep, and he has left behind him dwellings whose foundations are disguised or concealed by subsequent structures. St. Kilda is isolated in the North Atlantic in an environment separated from the Arctic only by water, and the pattern of bird migration is complex, yet certain trends are being revealed by their regularity. As surely as spring days lengthen towards summer, a passage of golden plovers, whimbrels, wheatears, white wagtails, red-wings and snipe occurs as these birds pass from Scotland to the Faeroes, Iceland and Greenland. A growing list of accidental visitors shows the effect of down-wind drift as birds are caught up in the weather environment and cast down on St. Kilda.

And what a weather environment! — with winds of over 130 mph, so frightening that, according to one RAF officer, men are sometimes blown over by the strong gusts, quite unable to keep their feet against the sudden buffeting. In these winds the Nature Conservancy find that their barograph falls below the 952-millibar reading on the chart, and the anemometer cannot cope. The fact that Stone-Age structures still stand when sixty-year-old cottages are in total ruin shows how well early man built against hurling spindrift and roaring seas.

IN THE FOOTSTEPS OF PRINCE CHARLIE

I would like to make it clear that these articles are in no way an attempt at a historical reconstruction of the flight of Prince Charlie. Rather are they an attempt to describe the countryside through which he travelled and to give some account of the changes since 1746.

For me the journey has also an inner significance. I am now more than twice the age I was when I first explored this largely deserted magnificence of peaks and glens. Bernard Shaw once said that until he is forty no man acquires a sense of history. The discovery of such a feeling for the past has made this journey doubly rewarding for me. I only hope I will be able to impart some of my pleasure to my readers.

Traversing west to Skye and the Outer Hebrides, north to Glen Cannich and east to Ben Alder, I began to realise that the story I was following was as complex as anything that could have been dreamed up by a novelist.

I have many people to thank for their help, especially Dr. Sorley MacLean the great Gaelic poet and his brother Alasdair; and not least John S. Gibson, whose researches in the French archives have yielded up such great treasure.

*   *   *

In the moonlight, listening to the roar of the rivers coming down from the snow-peaks, I felt a sense of excitement and history, as if two and a half centuries had been banished and that everywhere in these hills were people, watching and waiting for news of battle. I could not have chosen a better April evening to come to the west end of Loch Arkaig, because the winter and spring were so like these seasons in 1745-46, when snow hampered the troops as early as November, and blew in their faces on the fateful day of the battle.

There are days which have a kind of aura about them, days you can never forget. And this was one of them. Clear, sunny, frosty, the lochs blue and the snow-peaks silver. But the main drama had been reserved for sunset, in a glare that was hurtful to the eyes. Then the sun dropped behind a peak and in the strong back-lighting the other mountains appeared as suddenly as if they had been put there by a scene-shifter. Against the gold of the loch, every headland and bay was a black silhouette, until the moon rose and filled the pale world with ghosts.

There, across the loch, were the ruins of Donald Cameron's house. He must have got out of bed with alarm on the night of 17 April 1746, at the sound of horses and voices. His chief had been shot through the legs that day, but carried off by members of the clan. Now Donald was to entertain a king in his thatched cottage. And a hungry king at that, glad to eat curds and butter, drink milk and then to stretch out.

Thinking, wondering at the might-have-beens of history, I found it hard to sleep. I was grateful to the snipe which filled the air with eerie "bleating" when I went out at 10 p.m. to look at Streap and Sgor Thuilm, rising in knife-blade ridges from the narrow saddle between them. Over that pass lay Glen Finnan, only nine miles away; the place where Prince Charles Edward, the Stuart heir, raised his standard in an attempt to restore to his family the Crown of Great Britain and Ireland.

I was thinking of just how insensitive a young man can be, of the Prince and myself. For I was his age, around twenty-five, when I first climbed these peaks in two week-ends from Glasgow, stamping over the tops from Glen Finnan on one trip, and on another, going from Loch Eil-side, over the top of Gulvain, to carry my rucksack into the Caledonian pines of Glen Mallie. I slept out there, then hastened on to Achnacarry, stopping only to look at the Mucomer Falls and running the last two miles to Spean Bridge, or I would have missed the train.

I reckon I had about the same lack of imagination as the Prince, though a greater horror of war, into which I was shortly to be swept. I had climbed more than three-quarters of the peaks in Scotland and traversed most of its glens before I went into the army, yet I was hardly aware that I was walking over a devastated country; that this desert which I loved so much was deliberately created by a dramatic change of land use when sheep became more valuable than people.

"How much did the Prince *accept* when he came to the Highlands?" I pondered, as we left the tent next morning for Glen Pean. My own belief is that, like me, he took everything for granted. I do not think he bothered to understand the Highlands or Highlanders, because he lived in a private world of fantasy. Things went too well for him. True, he had trouble with the chiefs; he knew they were jealous, proud men, but they always stood by him. He had reason to live in the present and not worry about the future; his volunteer army, fighting by instinct rather than leadership, never lost a battle until Culloden.

The easiest person to deceive is yourself. And Charles had been doing it for so long that his world of fantasy was real. The possibility of defeat was not. Nor did he seem to realise the consequences for the Highlands should his army be cut to ribbons. But as he waited in the shieling all next day for news and none came, he was facing a harder world. There was only one way of escape, and that was on his two feet, so off he went at 5 p.m.

Much has been written of the physical toughness of Bonnie Prince Charlie. This was one of the things I wanted to find out by walking down Glen Pean, for it is reported that he was "utterly tired out" by the time he reached its far end. Another reason for traversing it was that I have never met anyone who had walked it.

It is hard to convey in words the nobility of this superb pass which has so many changes of character that it is several glens in one. It begins by being broad and soggy, with stepping-stones leading across the river to a little ruined settlement, with lazybeds still projecting like ribs from dry ground; and there are more of them in other places; relics of Cumberland's butchery and the Clearances which followed.

In three miles or so the mountains begin to close in, until at the Lochan Leum an-t-Sagairt you are in a miniature of Glen Coe, with birchwoods hanging on crags above you and a wild looking ravine beyond.

It was a good place to sit down, have a sandwich, listen to a dipper chuckling and see it joined by another white-bibbed bird, the pair of them splashing in and out the water as they chased each other. A good loch for fish, I imagine, and perhaps the osprey took a trout or two in Charlie's time, since Loch Arkaig was one of its known nesting places.

The route ahead is not obvious from here, but the south slopes looked more promising than the rockier north and we came across a little cairn as we started our climb, a marker leading to a sheep track winding in and out the gullies high above the loch. Back down in the glen we climbed through a water-logged defile, where the shrinking stream wriggled like a snake towards a litter of giant boulders.

This is marked Coir' a' Bheigh on the map and it is the wildest surprise of Glen Pean, with walls of rock rising from tangled blocks, themselves cradling a minute loch. The crest of the corrie is the summit of the pass, the window to the west, and in a step we were there, looking over the slit of a gorge to a fragment of grey Loch Morar.

We had started in sunshine, but the sky was now steely, with the threat of snow on a bitter wind. Wherever we looked there were black rocks and tangled brown ridges, a bitter hard country. Yet there was a path. The walking was actually easier than before and we looked forward eagerly to getting to Oban, at the head of Loch Morar, hoping to meet somebody.

Alas, like the head of Loch Arkaig, Loch Morar had nobody, only an empty house, steel-shuttered, but part of the corrugated roof was hanging off and we could have entered from above. The green sward across the loch at Kinloch Morar was likewise abandoned, so the country is much more inhospitable than in Charlie's day. He stayed that night at Meoble in "a small sheal house near a wood". For us, we had to turn about and tramp back into the wind, and a long way it seemed, with the moon brilliant by the time we got back to the tent.

Examining my physical state I had to admit that I was a bit weary, but far from being "utterly tired out". Nor had I started absolutely fresh, since the previous day I had done ten hours on the hills, including a 3,000ft top. But I could not really judge myself against Charlie on this walk, for he had been ill with fever in March, then on top of that had been the nervous strain of battle, the hard ride from Inverness and the fears and uncertainties of the future.

189

I feel it is time now for me to go back to Culloden and try to visualise the country as it was in 1746 before the Forestry Commission woods obscured the character of the moor. First, I went down to the Nairn Valley to see where Cumberland's troops had camped and where they should have been attacked. Then I went to Balvraid Farm, where there is a tall, slender ash tree from which Prince Charles is supposed to have watched the massacre of his men.

By moving about this high vantage point you can see the Inverness Firth and the slope of the land from flat Drumossie Moor to the Nairn valley. Cumberland was in camp, ready to strike, but the food of the Highland army was in Inverness. The opportunity to take the enemy by surprise was lost and it is no use analysing why, beyond saying that the chance was frittered away. And the blame must lie squarely on the Prince for failure to command when it was most needed.

But all was not lost because the night attack misfired. Charles could have withdrawn. And had he been a calculating man, instead of an emotional one, he would have done so. But his vanity was aroused. He was the son of a king determined to fight another son of a king, William Augustus, Duke of Cumberland. He took no account of the unprepared state of his men. Luck would have to take the place of staff work. His adjutant-general O'Sullivan must be represented as perhaps the worst quartermaster in history. Appropriately, the choice of Culloden Moor as the place to stand and fight was his.

Well, everyone who saw the superb presentation of Culloden on B.B.C. television knows what happened on the field and afterwards, when half-dead men were spiked by bayonets where they lay, and wounded were pulled out of houses and murdered. Worse still was the terrorism, to women and children, as homes were burned and the cattle on which they depended, driven off. It was Cumberland's own troops who gave him the name of "the bloody butcher".

The Prince was the lucky one. He escaped. His army did not. The rape of the Highlands by Cumberland was calculated to ensure that a "fifth column" would never again rise to menace the safety of England. The word "atrocities' had little political meaning until the Massacre of Glencoe, fifty-four years earlier, when a quibble over an oath of allegiance was taken as an excuse for foul murder. The infamous "Massacre" was nothing compared with the outrage of crimes by Cumberland.

He began the carve-up. And it was continued for another hundred years by the more subtle means of inducing emigration through poverty, clearing off people to make way for sheep, and turning the land over to deer when that failed. And a new reservoir of soldiers had been found by the raising of the Highland regiments. I am appalled to think that I lived to the age of thirty or so before I began to understand anything about the mountainlands which had given me so much pleasure.

Not so my friend Bob Grieve. His order of thought is "place, people, work", and before he was Chairman of the Highlands and Islands Development Board he talked to me about the vast areas which have never recovered from Culloden. Well, he has been given the job of rehabilitating the Highlands, and ironically, when he took up his post he removed from Glasgow to the east wing of Culloden House, where Prince Charles had dilly-dallied fishing, shooting and generally amusing himself while Cumberland celebrated his birthday at Nairn.

The house has been rebuilt since then, but it incorporates some of its original structure, including the vaults, where seventeen Jacobite officers lay in hiding after the battle, to be taken out and shot when they were discovered.

Leaving its vast sitting-room overlooking beautiful grounds, with weeping willows drooping over a pond, I went to the H.Q. of the Board, in Inverness, where ITV were busy making a film in the tall office block which overlooks the new bridge across the river. Bob's room is dominated by a huge wall map of the Highlands, and I pointed out to him where I was going next; to the Fords of Faillie over the Nairn, then to the Great Glen, and down the west side of Loch Lochy to Loch Arkaig and the west.

I would have preferred to be on horseback than in a car as we dropped down to the Nairn, looking for the line of the old ford which is no longer known. But I learned from the farmer at Faillie Bridge that it is somewhere not so far up-stream, in the knobbly country which is dotted with cattle and upland farms.

The agriculture gradually gives way to bleaker moor as you mount towards Stratherrick, and I had a thrill when on a telephone wire I saw a perching bird flash down to the heather and rise again, like an outsized wagtail of grey, black and white. It was a great grey shrike, dark hooked bill, piratical black face mask, white chest and grey back, a delight to the eye as it fluttered like a great butterfly, catching something in the heather.

What it was hunting I have no idea, but I was very taken by the cheek of a little meadow pipit which began scolding the thrush-sized Continental bird, alighting alongside it to make its point more forcibly — a dangerous proceeding, since the last shrike I saw in the Highlands killed a wren as I watched.

I was looking out for a house called Gorthleck on Loch Mhor, where the Prince dismounted to break the bad news of Culloden to Lord Lovat. As luck would have it, the man I asked happened to be a Presbyterian minister, and without any prompting from me he gave out, "It would have been a bad day for Scotland had the news been any different". I refrained from giving a contrary opinion, since the fate of Scotland has always been more important to me than denominational religion. And the events of history prove that the Highlands could hardly have had a worse fate than

191

what was in store by deliberate economic destruction.

The old house has a modern annexe built on to it, and the ancient structure is used only as a store. An elderly lady was kind enough to let me see over it, showing me upstairs to a door with the words "Prince's Room" painted on it. "They say the Prince was sleeping here when he heard a noise, and he jumped out of that window on to his horse and went away," she said.

This is a local tradition, but historical accounts do not credit Lovat with giving the Prince a bed. It is written that he could hardly get rid of the loser of the battle quickly enough, since he always liked to be on the winning side. And he was adept at playing with the English hare and hunting with the Jacobite hounds. The tale is that the tired and hungry Prince was offered no more than three glasses of wine, and urged on his way along the monotonous straight of the road spanning the bleak uplands.

He was riding hard for Lochiel's country, and he must have been in the saddle for the best part of sixteen hours before he got to Invergarry Castle, to find it empty. I took a walk round the hulk left by Cumberland when he fired it, and amongst the daffodils looked down on the loch where Ned Burke of North Uist made the providential find of two salmon in a stake net for a savoury breakfast.

The route he followed down the west bank of Loch Lochy is now spanned by a forestry road twisting through a vast plantation quilting the slopes of Sron a' Choire Ghairbh, and the view he saw of "terrible mountains" is mostly hidden by monotonous conifers, until you get to the Dark Mile where the great ridge of peaks stretching from Ben Nevis, along the whole ridge of the Grey Corries, makes one of the most powerful views in Scotland.

The Prince had left Invergarry at 3 p.m., so his timing must have been about the same as our own as we swung into the Dark Mile, disturbing a buzzard from a piece of prey which it had dropped. This I found to be a hedgehog, which it had dismembered, all but the skin and an adhering pin-cushion of spines. I trusted it would not get anything stuck in its throat as it flapped impatiently, waiting for us to go away.

And a few things must have been sticking in the Prince's throat as he rode westward. He had left an army which did not even have a rendezvous arranged for reassembling after the battle. And he must have been trying to convince himself that it was in the interest of the royal cause that he should get back to France as quickly as possible, to raise an army to resume the fight.

Perhaps he was too weary to care, for even with a few hours' rest and the meal of salmon to get back his strength, there were still ten miles to ride to Kinloch Arkaig, and the cottage at the mouth of Glen Pean.

He was so tired when he got there that he had to be helped out of his clothing. And I have already described how he rested until 5p.m. before setting out by Glen Pean, which was described by his party as "the cruelist road yet could be seen", past one of the highest and wildest mountains in the Highlands.

192

Little did Charlie know that he would spend the night out on this mountain, Sgor Thuilm, in the coming months, and that after a narrow escape from falling over a cliff he would be able to take a real mountaineering claim, namely that in the whole of Scottish history, his was the first recorded ascent of A'Chralaig and Sgurr nan Conbhairean, peaks of over 3,600ft. between Glen Clunie and Glen Affric.

But this was all in the future. Before I follow him there I have to go to that wood at Moeble where we left him sleeping above Loch Morar.

What kind of a man was Bonnie Prince Charlie?

From various descriptions, I see him in my mind's eye as a rangy-looking character, tall, red-haired, with a long stride and an agreeable expression which established a quick rapport with ordinary people. I think he was at his best in situations of discomfort, facing danger, hunger, cold, fatigue, and capture. Indeed, I am certain that the happiest days of his life were the five months following Culloden, when he was the fox and Cumberland's forces, with the patrolling Royal Navy, were the pack, picking up an illusory scent to far St Kilda, leaving a clear Arisaig coast when it was most needed by the Culloden refugees.

But it was not only of the Prince I was thinking as we stood on Loch Morarside, among the drystone ruins of Meoble. I was reflecting on the real heroes of the piece — the common clansfolk, who lived amongst this tangle of hills, who had marched to Derby, fought at Falkirk, retreated at Culloden, and, in the last chapter, pitted their wits against an occupying army strung across every glen and sea exit from Loch Shiel to Loch Hourn.

Now he was resting "to recruit more strength" for a moonlight hill crossing to the coast at Borradale — Borradale, where only eight months earlier he had stepped ashore to rally the clans. Now his hopes were set on a French ship to bear him far from Scotland.

In the few westward miles from the head of Loch Morar to Meoble I found a startling change of scene. A green oasis opened to the south, with dots of white houses beneath fine stands of larch and spruce. There was even a gravel road with a Land-Rover standing on it, and on the haughs of the sluggish river grazed dozens of Highland cattle, many with new-born calves. The only blot on the landscape was a fierce-looking bull which we detoured to avoid.

This was better than the emptiness which had been our lot since entering these hills — houses with smoking chimneys and a tiny school with desks and a little vase of primroses, showing it was in use. But when we knocked on the nearest door there was no reply. And no reply from the next one across the river. It was beginning to look as if Cumberland's dragoons had been here!

"Curious," I thought. "Five o'clock of a midweek afternoon; house with fires burning; a school — and not a soul about the place." We contin walking up the drive, and almost any moment I expected to see a "Pr Avenue" notice as we entered into a shelter belt of trees, with green

193

and ornamental shrubs stretching to the river, the whole breathing an air of elegance.

Round the corner was a dream of a house — not large, but ultra-modern, low and streamlined, like the speedboat parked beneath an open wing — the right kind of "Bentley" for this part of the world, whose highway is Loch Morar, the only other access being by footpaths. The gravel road extends for only four miles to the fishing lochs.

."Gracious living, indeed," I was saying. "Complete privacy. A farm of sheep and cattle. A deer forest, and a tracked "Weasel" to take the labour out of walking. A fishing river running past your door. Who owns it, I wonder?" I was given the answer when half a dozen men poured out of an outhouse to resume work on the house, which is a new shooting lodge, replacing one recently burned down.

The workers were mostly tradesmen, lodging at Meoble until the job was done. But the dark-haired keeper had been born in the place, and he told me the resident population was eight, including the schoolteacher, whose pupils came from the next place, about four miles down the loch, as well as from here.

This estate at Meoble marches with Lochiel's at Glen Pean, and, like most sporting estates in the Highlands nowadays, it is also a farm. This is an improvement on the old system of nothing but deer which existed over too much of the north in my early travels in the Highlands.

The keeper told us how to get to Prince Charlie's Cave above Loch Beoraid, the one known as MacEachine's Refuge. This bolthole was never used by the Prince. Weeks later, when the noose had almost closed on the Arisaig coast, it was earmarked for him. But the highly efficient intelligence system of clansmen, always a step ahead of the hunt, warned of the concentration of troops in the area, and left him with no choice but to attempt to break through the cordon.

From Meoble we climbed 1,000ft. from Loch Morar to pick up in part Charlie's moonlight route to the coast. We passed fairly close to the cave at a point where two miles of narrow Loch Beoraid lay below us, and the view was to the wild cirque of peaks which form the north wall of Glen Pean. We had not much time for lingering, for our destination was Loch Eilt, reached in a quick descent from the crest of the ridge.

It was dusk when we came down to the Mallaig road, just a bit tired, for we had set out from Glen Beasdale for the walk to Meoble, which meant we had a long plod ahead of us back to the car unless we could hitch a lift. We were in luck. A fish lorry stopped for us, and at 9 p.m. we were pitching our small tent among the natural oaks of the Beasdale Burn, with woodcock flitting back and fore over our heads.

Now that I had been to Meoble I could follow in my mind's eye Charlie's vements as, strength recruited after lying up for the day, his little party d up the Amhainn Chlachach, a deep glen marked by an unusual r of sparkling white quartz, which penetrates at a steepening angle

194

into a wilderness of peat.

They must have had a good guide to traverse this in darkness, winding among reedy lochans imprisoned among the hags, and hitting off the heathery corrie which encloses the scoop of Glen Beasdale. In walking it in daylight I had been glad to check my direction by compass, so featureless is the highest ground. It was six in the morning when the Prince arrived on Loch nan Uamh, the first time he had been back since the raising of the standard eight months earlier.

And if it looked as beautiful to him as it looked to us next morning he must have had a stab at the heart, the water shimmering in the April sunlight, the birches silver against the gold of last year's bracken, and everywhere the bulge of snowpeaks made more lovely by the willow catkins tossing yellow in the breeze, wafting honey scents. Bees were buzzing in the pollen, and on that shore I saw my first tortoiseshell butterfly of the season.

In this place we could have only one immediate destination — Borradale House, and the glittering curve of bay beneath it which plays such a large part in any story of the 1745 rising. It was here the Prince first set foot on the Scottish mainland; it was here the Highland chiefs tried to dissuade him from his mad fantasy of conquering Britain; and it was here on 20 April he met his staff officers who had survived Culloden.

I had to see the stage before I could visualise the play, so the first call was at Borradale House to obtain permission to walk through the grounds to the shore and locate the Prince's Cave, which was to be his shelter later, after Cumberland had burned down the house. The plain, square building is still spoken of as the house where the Prince stayed, and is part of a farm in a vital setting of brown hills, which suddenly smooth to a tableland of greensward sheltered by oakwoods and ending in a white curve of bay.

I doubt if in all the Highlands there is any corner more beautiful. Nor are there many views so inspiring as that from the mouth of the cave, about 30ft. up on a cliff. You would miss the cave unless you were looking for it, for the entrance is like a hole among boulders, a mere vent descending into darkness. I found it a delightful surprise, squeezing through the manhole into a dark vault with wet sides, gradually becoming bone-dry where it flattened into a narrow chamber, with accommodation for half a dozen or more men.

We were lucky to meet some other visitors with an electric torch, or we would have been unable to examine it properly. Although uneven on the floor, I would call it a comfortable cave, sheltered as it is from every wind, and a party sitting at the entrance could observe without being seen. It can be reached from Drumdarroch as well as from Borradale, and it lies fairly close to the gate where the driveway from the latter house ends in a field. A board with the word marked "Cave" on it will tell you when you are there, but no signposts mark the way.

And round a headland from it, carved out of the rock, was a natural deep water jetty, the one the Prince sailed from, most probably, on the night of 26 April, against the advice of the old boatman, Donald MacLeod of Skye, who forecast a storm and wanted to wait. But the Prince, always a powerful persuader of other men, got his way in the face of wisdom, and he was hardly out of the Sound of Arisaig before he was asking the impossible, to be set ashore again.

Well, he raised the standard against advice; he forced the issue of Culloden against advice; and now, against advice, he was on the sea in an eight-oared boat, heading out into the Atlantic, into the blackness of a night that got worse and worse as waves broke over them, the wind becoming a gale, and rain adding to the misery of seasickness.

Without compass, and with bowsprit broken, they could have been wrecked on Skye or driven far west of the Long Island. But the personal luck which never failed him, held. At dawn they saw land, and were able to pull in at Rossinish in Benbecula, close to a deserted hut which must have seemed like a palace, with wood for a fire and shelter from the raw wind which was still blowing.

The object of their dangerous journey was to try to get a vessel to France. If they had waited only a day or two longer at Borradale a vessel would have come to them — two vessels, in fact, the *Bellona* and the *Mars,* bringing muskets, ammunition, and 36,000 French Louis D'or, from the King of France.

I tried to picture the scene as I sat by the jetty in the sun, looking over the shining loch to Fros-Bheinn, as a chase of oyster-catchers filled the air with shrill pipings. I could see the faces of the war-scarred Jacobite leaders, peering from cover at the two ships under sail, thinking them English naval vessels come to harry them, then with relief realising that the flags were French, and rushing down to them with a cheer.

But a shock was coming when in the early morning the Jacobites waiting on the shore saw three more ships under sail rounding the bay, and they were not French. They were the English frigates *Greyhound, Baltimore,* and *Terror,* down from Fort William, closing in for a gun battle.

You need a flashback from the movies to visualise the scene of recoiling cannon, bursts of smoke, men falling dead, the English ships in full sail trying to blow up the ships at anchor, while all the time the Jacobite shore party struggle to unload casks of money and brandy for the three hours that the battle lasts, until the English frigates hoist sail and break off the engagement, leaving the French victorious.

And into exile on the *Bellona* and *Mars* sailed many Jacobites, harbouring hard thoughts about the Prince who had sailed west only a few days before. Meantime there was loot for those who stayed at Borradale, and before the money had been conveyed to Loch Arkaig robbery had been done. Young Barrisdale and his clansmen, laden with gold and casks of brandy, made off, while Murray of Broughton is reviled for not going with the Jacobites to France, but remaining to turn traitor and loot the treasure.

Yes, a quiet place Borradale, full of the ghosts of history; but so is this whole coast.

The Prince had lost his chance of easy escape to France by being in too big a hurry to get away from Borradale. He was in an even bigger hurry to get back to it on 5 July, after two months of boats and bothies, tramping over the hills of Harris, Uist and Skye as he fled from naval frigates or dodged searching troops. But always, when things seemed most hopeless, some ordinary person, usually non-Jacobite, would risk everything for him, spurning a reward of £30,000.

The day-to-day life of unexpected happenings seemed to suit the Prince's temperament. In an alarm he was cool; in an excursion he was strong; and I like the idea of his sharing the cooking with Ned Burke, mixing meal with brains of cow to make his own special bannock, or cooking fish on the little island in Loch Shell, Lewis, while waiting for supposed enemy ships to clear off and leave their course open to the south. Unluckily for Charlie, his hunch that the ships could be French was correct.

They were the *Bellona* and the *Mars,* limping back to France after their damaging gun battle in Loch nan Uamh. Charlie had pleaded with the boatmen to hail and intercept the ships, but fearing capture should they be British, they refused his request even when Charlie tried to bribe them with money.

Now the party had to endure four stormy days on the island before setting sail for Lochmaddy where they were to be chased by the enemy before making landfall on Benbecula, then to South Uist where they were to have three weeks of happy times before the net began tightening again and they were forced back to Benbecula.

It was from here the Prince sailed to Skye with Flora MacDonald, dressed as her maid, Betty Burke, perhaps the best-known story in the campaign. I find myself wondering if he ever managed to keep track of his topography, or if he just followed blindly wherever he was taken. Was every "wild muir and glen" like the last one, or were some a bit worse than others, as his route through the heart of the Skye mountains to Elgol by Glen Sligachan, and between Glamaig and Marsco to the head of Loch Ainort, where, looking round, he is reputed to have said, "I am sure the Devil cannot find us now!"

How little Lewis and Harris have changed since Charlie's time; probably less than the rest of Europe, because the agricultural pattern is still the same, and even the impact of tourism has had a negligible effect on the landscape. Stornoway has changed most, growing from a large village into a biggish town, where a third of the total population of Lewis and Harris live.

Lowlanders did not give much for the beauty of the Highlands in 1745. Like the Alps in Switzerland, the country was regarded as rude, barbaric, savage, ugly, fearsome, gloomy, or terrible. These detested ingredients are now the most sought after by tourists, and one of the most popular areas of Scotland for the caravanner and camper is the Arisaig coast, as I saw at Easter, with an occupying force in every desirable bay of silver sands, looking out to the islands, a dream of soft blue.

So much for remoteness, when half the campers were from England, making a week-end of it in their cars. Mallaig was advertising evening bingo, and everywhere, it seemed, were young hikers and climbers. But, so far as I could see, nobody went into Knoydart, where we were going.

I wanted to look first at Loch Nevis, where the Prince landed from Skye, still hopeful that he would find a ship to take him to France. He could scarcely have arrived at an unhealthier spot, since the whole region was under occupation. The populace was subdued, and in three nights they could find nobody willing to give them a roof. Challenged by militiamen as they rowed up the coast, they refused the order to come ashore, and, putting on a spurt, outdistanced a pursuing boat.

I asked an old man from Sandaig if he remembered any legends of the Prince. "Och, well, there's Glas Island out there. Charlie is supposed to have landed on it when the English were after him. It's not much of an island." "Do you believe the story?" I asked. "Why should I not? Why would they be calling it the Prince's island to this day if there wasn't something in it?"

It was after this very chase that the Prince was taken to the cave on the shore below Borrodale, the house where he had received so much hospitality in the past having been burned down by searching soldiers. "What was in his mind?" I wondered, as, after staying in MacLeod's Cave, "upon a high precipice in the woods of Borradale", he was being urged back to the Braes of Morar and Meoble by John MacDonald, Borradale's son, who reported to him that "the whole coast was surrounded by ships of war and tenders, as also the country by other military forces".

The springing of the net is one of the great escape stories of history. So I felt a sense of excitement as I went north again into the region where he was to have his narrowest escapes from capture and from death.

For photographic reasons we took the fishing boat *Western Isles* for a sail to the head of the Loch of Heaven which is the English translation of Loch Nevis, perhaps it is so named because the lowness of the hills on its south retaining wall allows the north slopes to get all the sun that's going, unlike dark Loch Hourn to the north which in translation is the Loch of Hell.

Our purpose was to capture on film the wide mouth open to the Point of Sleat where the Old Chief of MacKinnon brought Bonnie Prince Charlie on 5 July 1746 at 4 o'clock in the morning in a rowing boat from Elgol. It was the end of the Prince's varied Hebridean adventures, but the beginning of more difficult trials and strenuous night climbs in Knoydart, where his only hope of escape lay in breaking across the tangle of peaks known as the Rough Bounds stretching between Loch Nevis and Loch Hourn, even to this day unspanned by any road.

From Inverie superb cross-country rights-of-way lead through the hills to Barrisdale on Loch Hourn and Loch Arkaig via the head of Loch Nevis, not to mention lovely circuits nearer at hand to Airor and Inverguseran on the Sound of Sleat. Then from the tip of the peninsula you can return to Inverie by inland glens. After Inverie the loch swings south-east to Tarbert Bay.

Now came the most interesting bit of the sail for me, through the river-like narrows to reach the inner loch, Kyles Knoydart to the north, Kyles Morar to the south, foreground to the great rampart of peaks whose roughness was to be Charlie's saviour. Of these Sgurr na Ciche was the one that compelled the eye, soaring to a point and equal in grace to the best in Scotland.

On the day of our sail, flotillas of eider drakes afloat on the water and sea-swallows flickering over the surface gave the feeling that Loch Nevis is a benign place — an impression proved false shortly afterwards when we heard that two canoeists had drowned in stormforce gusts. In fact it is notoriously windy and we got a chilly reminder of it before we were back into the warmth of Mallaig.

We were heading direct to Kintail because in April the camera team had traversed Loch Arkaig with me and walked through Glen Pean to Loch Morar where I told the story of Prince Charlie's night climbs over the ridges to break the enemy cordon of troops watching for him. Then after a trying day lying close enough to the sentries to hear them talking, he made it under cover of darkness over the next ridge by the Bealach Duibh Leac into Glen Shiel.

In Kintail I wanted to find the boulder which Charlie's party of three MacDonalds with Donald Cameron of Glen Pean reached at three in the morning feeling weak from lack of food and tired with strain. I knew the stone was near the sheep farm of Achnangart, but I wouldn't have found it without the help of the lithe young shepherd who pointed it out on the side of a steep gully a few hundred feet on the far side of the River Shiel on the slope of Sgurr na Ciste Duibhe.

Our first problem was to get across the bouldery and fast descending river, which meant stockings off, then boots back on again for the slippery crossing, for bare feet are lethal when you have to cope with stones of every shape, some of them razor sharp. From the glen you would never have known that the dark-faced stone which the shepherd had pointed out had a hollow under it, not particularly commodious, but with a superb outlook in all directions, so that you couldn't be taken by surprise, except from above.

Seated under the lip, I wondered if the Prince realised the ironic twist of fate that had brought him to Glen Shiel, the very place where his father's hopes of a crown had ended in the Jacobite battle fought here on

10 June 1719, the Old Pretender's 31st birthday. On that occasion, though, the self-styled James VIII of Scotland and III of Britain was nowhere near Scotland. He had gone to his seventeen-year-old bride in Italy, Princess Maria Clementina Sobieska, and Bonnie Prince Charlie was a result, born in 1720 and now, like his father, anxious to escape the consequences of his actions.

Lord George Murray, ablest of Bonnie Prince Charlie's commanders at Culloden and elsewhere, could have told him about the battle of Glen Shiel which took place below the peak of Sgurr nan Spainteach, the peak of the Spaniards. This battle came to life for me when the Achnangart shepherd showed me some bullets which his father had picked up in a leather bag which he had found in a peat hag below the trenches dug by the Spaniards who are commemorated forever in the Gaelic name of one of the "Five Sisters".

"Yes," said Dolin MacMillan the shepherd, "the Spaniards are said to have retreated up the hill. I believe it was the first time that mortars had ever been used in warfare, and they were demoralised. About 200 of them went over the top to come down Glen Lichd making for the ships, which had been captured and so were they."

This battle, like Culloden, should never have been fought. Retreat would have been better, then they could have chosen the time and place for a surprise attack. The circumstances leading to the battle were this. The Marquis of Tullibardine and the fifth Earl of Seaforth had sailed from France with 300 Spanish troops to hold Eilean Donan Castle and spearhead a Scottish Rising against George of Hanover. At the same time 5,000 Spanish troops led by the Duke of Ormonde were to land on the west coast of England to equip an army of 30,000 Jacobites. The Risings in Scotland and England were to coincide, disorganise the government and put James on the throne.

The main body of Jacobites in Kintail, totalling 1,100, including Lochiel, Clanranald, and later Rob Roy were waiting at Eilean Donan or in camp nearby when bad news reached them. Storms had shattered the troopships off Cape Finisterre. The Battle Commanders were advised to embark their Spanish troops for home and disperse the clansmen.

Too late however. Even as the warning despatches were being read, three English frigates sailed into Loch Alsh and bombarded the 13th century castle into ruins after capturing its garrison and stores. The spread of this news stopped further support coming from loyal clans, but the Jacobites already gathered stayed on through the month of May. When they heard that a Hanoverian force was advancing on Kintail from Glen Shiel they moved, taking positions on both sides of the river on 9 June, with Lord George Murray on the south bank, and Tullibardine on the north, with the Spaniards entrenched below to provide covering fire in the expected attack.

Murray took the brunt of the mortar fire first and repelled three charges, without help from the demoralised Spaniards, then the heather caught fire forcing his men to retreat. Now it was the Seaforth Mackenzies who took the exploding mortars, and when their chief fell badly wounded they began climbing uphill and by nightfall the Jacobites were nearly on top of the 3,000ft. hill.

By reason of that battle the great Mackenzie clan's lands and titles were forfeited and never restored, and even when a grandson raised the Seaforth Highlanders and became an Earl for his services to Britain, his title died with him. As for Eilean Donan, built by Alexander II against the Norsemen, it remained a ruin until 1912 when it was restored over a period of twenty years by Lt.-Col. John MacRae Gilstrap at a cost of £¼ million. It was a tribute to his forebears, "The Wild MacRaes" renowned as "Mackenzie's Shirts of Mail", hereditary keepers of Eilean Donan from 1520. Inside the castle you can see a letter summoning the Chieftains to the raising of the clans at Glenfinnan signed, "Charles P/R" (Pro-Rex, on behalf of the King). There is also a lock of the Prince's hair, taken from him when he was sixteen.

Charlie is said to have been depressed and in poor spirits that hot day of 22 July as he lay under the stone in Glen Shiel, while a foraging party went off to find food. They returned with a salty store of cheese and butter and groaten meal which parched them with thirst until at sunset they could descend to the river and drink their fill. Luck was with the party though when they met up with a Glengarry lad who offered to guide them to Glen Moriston where he was seeking safety, since his father had been shot by redcoats the previous day.

It was through that fortunate meeting that the Prince's party were put in touch with the Seven Men of Glen Moriston after a night out near the top of Sgurr nan Conbhairean crouched against a rock while rain and mist soaked them. These "Seven" were honest tacksmen who had sworn never to give up the fight against Whig Highlanders and Hanoverian soldiers, but to pursue a guerilla war so long as they had life and liberty.

Their most secret hide-out was Rory's Cave in Coire Dho where the Prince found himself ". . . as comfortably lodged as in a Royal palace, a roof over this head, with the finest purling steam that could be running by his bedside within the grotto". While he was living well on mutton, beef, butter, cheese and whisky, the Seven Men became his Privy Council, his first since Culloden, dedicated to seeing him through his trials.

Of course, our next move had to be the cave in Coire Meadhoin, reached by following the River Doe and striking off at its middle tributary which would take us to the rocky corrie. Luckily the farmers who run this 25,000 acre estate of Ceahnacroc are old friends, and the problem of logistics was solved when Martin Girvan drove us in his Land-Rover for as far as the private road went, then transferred us to his cross-country Snowtrack for the final two hour climb.

What a wonderful day we had for the trip, a grey morning giving way to brilliant sunshine, with the ground dry enough to allow good progress.

I had promised our cameraman not just a dark cave, but a fine piece of rock architecture, a thrilling jumble of boulders enclosing a natural grotto admitting shafts of light to give a stained-glass feeling to the interior.

He was not disappointed, for the whole wild setting is in keeping with the adventurous story of weather-beaten men raiding and foraging a neighbourhood which was too close for comfort to the Fort Augustus garrison. The good days ended with bad news when they heard that Black Campbell of Kintail was less than four miles away, lifting cattle with his militia of Ross-shire men.

The whole party moved north by climbing over the ridge of Tigh Mor na Seilge to drop down to Loch Affric and thence to a point near Leitre in Glen Cannich, the most northerly of the Prince's travels. That bit of the story we reserved in order to link it to Ben Alder. Meantime we had various bits of photography around Eilean Donan and Strath Cluanie to tie up while the weather was in our favour.

Afterwards, I had the weekend off and I arranged a jaunt with Roger Robb, who lives in Dingwall. He arrived sure enough, with rock-climbing gear and the camping kit, but a drastic change to wind and rain had set in even as he left home. So we abandoned our plan of climbing on the Cuillin and stayed in Kintail going for the long mountain, Ben Attow, which I had never climbed, though its pinnacled north-west end has attracted me for decades.

That wet morning we took the mountain from the east, up the unremitting slope above Glen Lichd, encouraged by only one thing, that our peak was clear of mist despite the downpour which soon soaked me to the skin. The cold was a spur to keep moving, though the wind was rising to gale-force and unbalancing us. Great to reach the main cairn, crouch behind it, and sort out the amazing tangle of gloomy peaks and ridges around us.

From our position at over 3,000ft. we looked east along the great trench of Glen Affric, its elongated lochs pale slits of mercury in a charcoal world, while just behind us, across Glen Lichd rose the sinister bulk of Sgurr nan Spainteach, which I'd climbed years ago, like those of Glen Affric, without giving a thought to the stirring events that once took place in this historic district.

* * *

In anybody's life there are occasions when bad news can turn out to be good news, when changes of direction lead to a desired end-result. Thus when Prince Charlie reached his farthest north in Glen Cannich, it was bad news brought to him which decided his party to retreat back south once again into more dangerous country, this time by Glen Garry to Loch Arkaig.

In the desperate five months after Culloden, this particular bit of the chase intrigues me most, for I've never been able fully to understand how it came about that the French were able to track down such an erratic quarry to a remote lair on Ben Alder when his movements were dictated by day-to-day events.

I know now, thanks to the discovery of the log of the *Prince de Conti*, the ship which took him off, plus the narrative of a French officer on board the *Bien Trouvé*, a rescue ship which failed to find him. These discoveries were made in the Archives Nationales in Paris by Mr John S. Gibson, whose excellent book *Ships of the '45* brought home the vital role played by the British Navy in defeating the Jacobites and paid tribute to the persistence of the French ships which finally achieved the Prince's rescue.

But, to return to Glen Cannich and the bad news, brought to him on the 7 August by two of his devoted party who had done the return march to Poolewe, a hard forty miles each way across the hills. It was that a French ship had called inquiring for the Prince, and, getting no news, had landed two officers who were making for Locheil country with despatches.

This was the bad news which decided the Prince's party to return southward to Loch Arkaig in the hope of making contact with them. It was a vital decision, all the better for being cautiously delayed for a few days, waiting in their safe shelter in the depth of a wood at Cannich, at the place where the power house of the Glen Affric hydro-electric station now stands.

The party moved out on the morning of 12 August by Guisachan and Loch Benevean, getting to Glen Moriston in four hours, pausing on a hilltop until an enemy search party had cleared off. In fact the search for Charlie was cooling off, for on the 13th the main body of Albemarle's Redcoats were marched away from Fort Augustus southward, and Argyll's Campbell militia had set off for Inveraray, leaving Lord Loudon's regiment and seventeen companies of militia to garrison the fort.

On that day of troop movements, three of Charlie's party of ten were out reconnoitring the way ahead, one scout reporting that Glen Garry was clear, while two of the Glen Moriston men went on a longer journey to Loch Arkaigside to make contact with an important man, Cameron of Clunes. Now the party moved by Loch Loyne down to the swollen River Garry, forded it with difficulty, then climbed to spend an uncomfortable night — on the hill in the rain without cover. No wonder Prince Charlie gets an honourable mention in the annals of Scottish Mountaineering, for not only was his undoubted stamina being tested, but so was his stomach, for once again it was empty.

So without breakfast, wet and hungry, they moved on next day to meet up with their Loch Arkaig scouts who had a message from Cameron telling them to go to a certain place where he would meet them on the following day, almost certainly at the cave in the wood above Glen Cia-aig whose

203

notable waterfall is near the end of the Dark Mile. There they were to have a welcome feast of venison, by shooting a big red stag when they most needed it, and that night they were to have the company of other outlaws, MacDonald of Lochgarry and Captain MacRaw, plus one other.

Joined by Cameron of Clunes, they moved to the foot of Loch Arkaig and three days later, on 20 August, were joined by Dr Cameron and the Rev. John Cameron who arrived with Locheil's apology for sending his brother, the doctor, instead of coming in person. Next day, the Prince, disguised as Captain Drummond, was introduced to the two French officers from Poolewe on their way back from meeting a wary Locheil who feared they were spies and didn't trust them, especially as their despatches contained nothing of value.

In fact one of the officers was a former commander of the Prince's bodyguard who knew the Prince very well and was instantly recognised by Charlie. The message which was not entrusted to paper was this: "Keep in touch with the west coast. The King of France will see to your rescue." The officer who passed the message was the Chevalier de Lancize. (How de Lancize found the Prince is another exciting story of hardship, one of his companions dying of exposure, another caught and hanged at Fort Augustus, but the important message was delivered which makes de Lancize an important agent in the miraculous escape. (For the addition of this missing piece of the jig-saw we have to thank John Gibson.)

Any feeling of being safe here in the Dark Mile was shattered when troops of Louden's regiment searching for fugitives forced a retreat northward to the top of the hill called Meall an Tagraidh on a soaking night, to spend the next two nights in remote Glen Kingie. It was time to clear out of here, and on the 27th, Lochgarry and Dr Cameron were ready to guide the Prince to Locheil, which meant saying farewell to the Seven Men of Glen Moriston who were now eight, one Hugh MacMillan having joined them on the march to Glen Cannich.

These devoted men had stayed with the Prince for over three weeks, parting from him only when they were sure he was in good hands. Fare-wells were sad, the Prince making them a token gift of twenty-four guineas and promising fervently never to forget them when he came into his own.

The night of 28 August saw the Prince's party starting their thirty mile journey across the Great Glen for the headwaters of the River Spey, to climb over the shoulder of Creag Meaghaidh and down to Loch Laggan for Ben Alder. They moved briskly, for the significant part of the walk was done in two hard nights, with very little food and cat-naps instead of normal sleep. Praising the Prince, Lochgarry exclaimed, "Show me a King or Prince in Europe who could have borne the like, or the tenth part of it".

Charlie was advancing towards luxury now as he met up with the wounded Lochiel and Cluny MacPherson, who took the tired men to various hideouts before moving on 5 September to the specially prepared "Cluny's Cage", well provisioned with mutton, ham, minced collops and whisky, with a natural hearth for cooking and fireplace openings to let the smoke disperse invisibly round the structure. With servants and sentries and a soft dry couch for a bed, shoes on his feet and a new coat on his back, the Prince felt himself a King, eating well, sleeping and passing his days playing cards and enjoying the excellent company.

They had a news service too, their spies reporting what was happening in the nearest enemy camp at Dalwhinnie.

So far so good, in the extraordinary chain of events which had led the Prince to Ben Alder, the most secret of all his hideouts, where he lay in comfort from 6 to 12 September. Then we have the dramatic statement in the records:

"At one o'clock in the morning, hearing of the arrival of the ships in Loch nan Uamh, the party started for the coast. Simple as that! How do we square that with the French Minister of the Navy writing in despair:

"The Prince is so well concealed from his enemies and those who would help him, that both seek with the same lack of success."

How they found the Prince was the bit of the story I have never been able to unravel, let alone the logistics of getting him from Ben Alder to a waiting ship which would have to run the gauntlet of the British Navy.

The chain of events was even more extraordinary than I ever imagined. On the very day that Charlie arrived at Cluny's Cage, 5 September, two French ships lay anchored at Loch Boisdale in South Uist, and had landed an armed force who were marching the three miles to Kilbride led by Commanders Warren and Sheridon who had been with the Highland army. It was the Laird of Boisdale they were seeking, a delicate mission since, officially, he was on the enemy side, but known to be sympathetic to the Prince. When the ships sailed they took with them a local man to act as pilot, one who had already served the Jacobite cause well.

That pilot was none other than Rory MacDonald, one of the Uist men who had crewed the boat carrying Flora MacDonald and her serving maid Betty Burke to her home in Skye. The "maid" of course, was none other than the Prince in disguise. As for Boisdale himself, his part in the Prince's escape to Skye in June can hardly be rated too highly though he steadfastly preserved his front of non-involvement, an invaluable way of serving a cause with which he was supposed to have no sympathy.

Rory now piloted the ships to Loch nan Uamh, the most likely place to find true Jacobites who would know something of the Prince's recent movements. Now for the incredibly bold part, considering the vigilance of the Royal Navy. The two ships carrying 500 men and 65 guns lay in the loch from 6 to 19 September. Of course, they didn't advertise that they were French. They flew British colours. Contact with the shore Jacobites was made. Credentials from France were carefully scrutinised and away went Major John MacDonald of Glenadale for Glenfinnan and over the hills to Loch Arkaig to locate the Prince.

He drew a blank. Nobody knew anything. Then he met "a poor woman who divulged to the Major where Cameron of Clunes was skulking in a summer shieling. Straight away Clunes's son was sent off to Ben Alder to try to find the Prince in one of the numerous hiding places thereabouts. For the Major it was back across the hills to Loch nan Uamh and report to the French commanders of the ships what was happening and ask them to wait.

Now for another stroke of luck when Clunes's son handed over the search for the Prince to one of Locheil's tenants called John McColvain because he knew the ground, and the likely hideout. But McColvain didn't know that the Prince had been moved, nor did he know anything at all about the secret Cage. In fact he was en route to the wrong place, travelling in the darkness as fast as he could, when figures loomed up close, none other than Dr Cameron and Cluny MacPherson en route to Loch Arkaig, with some followers on a shadowy errand.

Instantly McColvain was redirected and given one of Cluny's men to guide him to the Cage with the glad news that French ships were awaiting in Loch nan Uamh. There was nothing unlucky about the first hour of 13 September as the excited fugitives bundled things together and the whole party set off immediately into the darkness, lying in another hideout when daylight came. By the 17th, travelling always by night, they had met up with Dr Cameron and Cluny MacPherson at the head of Loch Arkaig. There they slept, tramping on next day to arrive at the waiting ships on the 19th.

Yes, six days walking from Ben Alder to the Atlantic Coast, but today only a short helicopter flip over what is still some of the wildest country in Scotland. Our cameraman covered this by air to show the route, and I had the privilege of lifting off from Invermoriston and flying over the Corrieyairack and the head of Glen Roy, slanting over Creag Meaghaidh for Loch Ericht to pin-point the Cage below the rocky flank of the remote mountain. What a thrilling experience it was to hover like a bird, flit through moving banks of cloud and gleams of sun, and look down the slit of the Great Glen as the golden eagle sees it.

The bold officers of the *L'Heureux* and *Prince de Conti* must have been as overjoyed as the Prince that evening when, against all odds, they welcomed the Jacobite party aboard and could hoist sail in the early hours of next morning in a very fresh wind from the north, bending for Barrahead to round Ireland for France.

No doubt the question in your mind is "Where was the British Navy during the long time these French ships lay unmolested at Loch nan Uamh? They were in the Orkneys trying to prevent exceptionally heavy losses of merchant ships by attacking French privateers. But for this diversion the fleet would have been patrolling from Tobermory. True there were naval sloops at Stornoway but nobody from Uist or Skye thought to report the presence of two French ships in their neighbourhood. Never was a "blind eye" more convenient in serving the last move in the mad game".

In *Ships of the '45* Gibson makes the point that it was Franco-Irish shipowners operating out of Dunkirk, Boulogne, St Malo and Nantes who began the '45. They specialised in raiding British merchantmen, benefitting from the fact of British naval power being diverted elsewhere. There was French complicity too, of course; the Rising was politically expedient. It is to the eternal credit of French and Irish officers after Culloden that they did not fail the Prince, but took so many risks to bring him home whatever the difficulty and danger.

After the '45 nothing of Charlie's life was of any consequence. The desire to begin another Jacobite Rising obsessed him. Frustrated in this, he became miserable and unhappy, refusing to leave France and return to Rome. Quarrelling with his mistress, Clementina Walkinshaw, and drinking heavily, he refused to recognise that the Stuart cause was dead. Then in 1772 he thought it his duty to marry, choosing Princess Louise of Stolberg, aged twenty while he was fifty-two and the poorest of company. Not surprisingly she left him for a lover eight years after the marriage. He never lived down the fact that Pope Clement XIII refused the recognition of *de jure* sovereignty granted to his father. How dearly he would have loved to be Charles III. He died on 30 January 1788, not so very long ago.

In making this story into a television series I had no intention to romanticise a Prince who was a disaster for the Highlands. Perhaps for his own sake the best thing that could have happened would have been to stop a bullet early on in a campaign that had no hope of success. Locheil knew it would fail, but allowed his heart to rule his head, as did most of the other clan chiefs. They followed him for a noble reason — loyalty to the house of Stuart.

They, and not the Prince, were the real heroes of the '45. As for the naval patrols in small sailing ships, marvellous things were done by both sides, taking extraordinary risks in uncharted waters among the sea lochs and wild skerries of the Hebrides. Truly the aftermath of Culloden is a remarkable tale — even yet not fully told.